JOURNAL FOR THE STUDY OF THE NEW TESTAMENT
SUPPLEMENT SERIES
111

Executive Editor
Stanley E. Porter

Sheffield Academic Press
Sheffield

Chiasmus in the
Pauline Letters

Ian H. Thomson

Journal for the Study of the New Testament
Supplement Series 111

Copyright © 1995 Sheffield Academic Press

Published by
Sheffield Academic Press Ltd
Mansion House
19 Kingfield Road
Sheffield, S11 9AS
England

Typeset by Sheffield Academic Press
and
Printed on acid-free paper in Great Britain
by Bookcraft
Midsomer Norton, Somerset

British Library Cataloguing in Publication Data

A catalogue record for this book is available
from the British Library

ISBN 1-85075-526-4

CONTENTS

ACKNOWLEDGMENTS

I would like to express my deep appreciation to those who have assisted me in the bringing of this project to completion. I am especially indebted to Dr John M.G. Barclay of the Faculty of Divinity of the University of Glasgow for his supervision of the research for my earlier thesis, *Chiasmus in the Pauline Corpus*, of which this volume is a revision. His patient guidance, incisive thinking and helpful criticisms have greatly enriched my own understanding of Pauline studies.

The congregation of my present church, Dunrossness Baptist Church in Shetland, have also been most understanding in allowing me the time needed to complete this work.

Finally, it would be wrong not to acknowledge the part played by my family. Throughout, my parents have given their constant support, and my wife, Morag, with our son, David, have encouraged and helped me in more ways than they will ever know.

ABBREVIATIONS

AB	Anchor Bible
AJSL	*American Journal of Semitic Languages and Literatures*
ANRW	*Aufstieg und Niedergang der römischen Welt*
BAGD	W. Bauer, W.F. Arndt, F.W. Gingrich and F.W. Danker, *Greek–English Lexicon of the New Testament*
BBB	Bonner biblische Beiträge
BDF	F. Blass, A. Debrunner and R.W. Funk, *A Greek Grammar of the New Testament*
BHT	Beiträge zur historischen Theologie
Bib	*Biblica*
BNTC	Black's New Testament Commentaries
BSac	*Bibliotheca Sacra*
BST	The Bible Speaks Today
BTB	*Biblical Theology Bulletin*
EBib	Etudes bibliques
EKKNT	Evangelisch-Katholischer Kommentar zum Neuen Testament
ETSMS	Evangelical Theological Society Monograph Series
EvT	*Evangelische Theologie*
ExpTim	*Expository Times*
HNT	Handbuch zum Neuen Testament
HR	*History of Religions*
HSCP	Harvard Studies in Classical Philology
HTKNT	Herders theologischer Kommentar zum Neuen Testament
ICC	International Critical Commentary
IDBSup	G.A. Buttrick (ed.), *Interpreter's Dictionary of the Bible*, Supplementary Volume
JBL	*Journal of Biblical Literature*
JETS	*Journal of the Evangelical Theological Society*
JR	*Journal of Religion*
JSNT	*Journal for the Study of the New Testament*
JSNTSup	*Journal for the Study of the New Testament*, Supplement Series
JTS	*Journal of Theological Studies*
KEK	H.A.W. Meyer (ed.), Kritisch-exegetischer Kommentar über das Neue Testament
LB	*Linguistica Biblica*

MNTC	Moffatt NT Commentary
NCB	New Century Bible
Neot	*Neotestamentica*
NICNT	New International Commentary on the New Testament
NIGTC	The New International Greek Testament Commentary
NovT	*Novum Testamentum*
NovTSup	*Novum Testamentum*, Supplements
NTS	*New Testament Studies*
ÖTKNT	Ökumenischer Taschenbuch-Kommentar zum Neuen Testament
RB	*Revue biblique*
RivB	*Rivista biblica*
RNT	Regensburger Neues Testament
RSR	*Recherches de science religieuse*
SBLDS	Society of Biblical Literature Dissertation Series
SCL	Sather Classical Lectures
SJT	*Scottish Journal of Theology*
SNTSMS	Society for New Testament Studies Monograph Series
SNTW	Studies of the New Testament and its World
ST	*Studia theologica*
SymBU	Symbolae biblicae upsalienses
TBl	*Theologische Blätter*
TDNT	G. Kittel and G. Friedrich (eds.), *Theological Dictionary of the New Testament*
THKNT	Theologischer Handkommentar zum Neuen Testament
TNTC	Tyndale New Testament Commentaries
TPINTC	Trinity Press International New Testament Commentaries
WBC	Word Biblical Commentary
WMANT	Wissenschaftliche Monographien zum Alten und Neuen Testament
ZKT	*Zeitschrift für katholische Theologie*
ZNW	*Zeitschrift für die neutestamentliche Wissenschaft*

Chapter 1

MATTERS OF BACKGROUND AND ISSUES OF METHODOLOGY

1.1. *Introduction*

The main purpose of this study is to show how the identification and analysis of chiasmus in the Pauline letters is a far more valuable and precise tool in the exegete's hands than many have previously realized. However, some of the earlier work in this whole field has left an unfortunate legacy that makes it essential to approach it very carefully indeed.

Thus, until recently, the perception has been widespread that the study of chiasmus in the New Testament is little more than the esoteric pursuit of a few enthusiasts, whose exuberance in the 'discovery' of chiasms of astonishing complexity in almost every page of the New Testament seems to know no limits. It is not surprising that this has provoked an often justifiable backlash of scholarly scepticism among the more cautious, who feel that many such chiastic patterns tell us more about the ingenuity of the commentator than about the intention of the original author.

The result has been a regrettable obscuring of the fact that the study of chiasmus has a legitimate, but often underrated, place in the field of New Testament rhetorical analysis in general, and in the Pauline letters in particular. Of paramount importance, therefore, is the discipline of working within defined parameters and using objective controls. With these in position, it is possible to propose a reasonable methodology for the identification of chiasmus, and for its subsequent use in exegesis.[1]

---

1. Five examples are explored in this study: two from Ephesians, and one each from Galatians, Colossians and Romans. Questions of authorship within the Pauline corpus do not affect the identification of an individual chiasmus, but clearly impinge on its exegesis, particularly in the matter of the wider Pauline use of vocabulary and concepts. For the purposes of this thesis, 'the Pauline corpus' is taken to include all those letters ascribed to 'Paul'. In the specific case of Ephesians and Colossians, the position adopted is that, on the balance of probability, Paul is not the author of

1.2. *The Classical and Semitic Background of Chiasmus*

In view of the way that the term 'chiasmus' is understood at this time, it is intriguing that it is not truly one of ancient rhetoric,[2] only coming into more widespread use since the Renaissance or later.[3] Lausberg notes that the *word* is used by Isocrates (d. 338 BC),[4] but the first clear reference to it as a technical term of rhetoric occurs as late as around the fourth century AD in Hermogenes,[5] who uses it of, but limits it to, the crosswise interchange of the clauses in a four-clause sentence.[6]

However, the theory of figures in ancient rhetoric is confused by the fact that many have both a Greek and a Latin name. Furthermore, different authorities have different names for the same figure.[7] Thus more than one of the *figurae elocutionis* exhibit features that would now be called 'chiastic' by most contemporary biblical scholars. The most notable, perhaps, are *commutatio* and its allied *figurae*.[8]

The way that Di Marco approaches the use of terminology may only add to the confusion. For example, he lists both *inclusio* and *regressio*,[9]

Ephesians, but is possibly the author of Colossians.

2.   H. Lausberg, *Handbuch der literarischen Rhetorik* (2 vols.; Munich, 1960), p. 893.

3.   A. Di Marco, 'Der Chiasmus in der Bibel 1. Teil', *LB* 36 (1975), pp. 21-97, 23.

4.   Lausberg, *Handbuch*, p. 361 n. 1.

5.   So G.A. Kennedy, *New Testament Interpretation through Rhetorical Criticism* (Chapel Hill, NC, 1984), p. 28; Hermogenes, *On Invention* 4.3. My edition is H. Rabe (ed.), *Rhetores Graece* (Bibliotheca Scriptorum Graecorum et Romanorum Teubneriana, 6; Leipzig, 1913), p. 181.

6.   See further Lausberg, *Handbuch*, p. 361 n. 1.

7.   Kennedy, *Interpretation*, p. 28.

8.   *Commutatio* consists of a contrast built on the crosswise repetition of two word-stems with change of word order and, for example, case. Thus, 'in pace bellum quaeritas, in bello pacem desideras'; 'in otio tumultuaris, in tumultu es otiosus' (Cicero, *Rhetorica ad C. Herennium* 4.15. My copy is H. Caplan [ed.] [Loeb Classical Library, 1954], p. 282). It may occur in balanced clauses, or in sentences where it is first expressed in a variety of types of subordinate clause and repeated in its inverted order in the principal clause. See Lausberg, *Handbuch*, pp. 395-97 for fuller discussion. There are a number of other terms for the same *figura*, including *contentio*, and in Quintilian, ἀντιμεταβολή, who cites the widely quoted example 'Non ut edam vivo, sed ut vivam edo'. Quintilian, *De Institutione Oratoria* 9.3.85.

9.   Di Marco, 'Chiasmus 1. Teil', p. 23.

which are discussed in Lausberg as figures of repetition,[10] representing them pictorially (for the word 'x') as /x...x/ and /...x/x.../. Thus, while it may be true that every chiasmus is necessarily an example of *inclusio*, not every example of *inclusio* is chiastic.[11] Likewise, only a chiasmus with an even number of elements will show *regressio*, but not every example of *regressio* is chiastic.

Perhaps not surprisingly, there was disagreement even among the ancients as to precise definitions: Aristarchus of Alexandria differentiated *hysteron proteron* (which he defined in terms of inversion of *ideas*)[12] from chiasmus (according to him, inversion of *words*) whereas Crates of Pergamum took them as equivalents.[13]

The same lack of clarity over terminology has continued into the present century among classicists, making inquiry into chiastic-like patterns difficult. For example, Whitman,[14] like others, supports the recognition of widespread use of *hysteron proteron* in long passages in Homer,[15] but differentiates it from ring composition. He sees *hysteron proteron* as a 'device' (his term) that combines inversion of the order of the elements with balancing by opposites, whereas ring composition uses the same inversion technique, but balances by similarity or identity. However, balance by both similarity and opposites is encompassed in most contemporary understandings of chiasmus.

Other modern writers on the classics also describe chiastic patterns (although, like Whitman, without using that specific term). Thus Norwood describes the plan of a 'normal Pindaric ode' as a recognizable five-element chiasmus:

---

10. Lausberg, *Handbuch*, pp. 317-18 and 314 respectively. Di Marco also includes *reduplicatio* and *anadiplosis*, for which Lausberg suggests that *inclusio* is an equivalent term.

11. Including, e.g., the ABA pattern in which there is no inversion of order of elements.

12. Included by Di Marco as an equivalent term for chiasmus ('Chiasmus 1. Teil', p. 23), but discussed by Lausberg (*Handbuch*, pp. 440-41) as a *figura per transmutationem*.

13. See J.W. Welch (ed.), *Chiasmus in Antiquity: Structures, Analyses, Exegesis* (Hildesheim, 1981), p. 255.

14. C.H. Whitman, *Homer and the Heroic Tradition* (Cambridge, MA, 1953), p. 254.

15. See S.E. Bassett, Ὕστερον πρότερον Ὁμηρικῶς (HSCP, 31; Cambridge, MA, 1920).

He begins with gods and prayer, proceeds to details about the victor, his family and his native city, then narrates a brief legend more or less clearly relevant to the occasion, next goes back to the victor, and ends with prayer.[16]

Myres[17] finds chiasmus in Herodotus, but uses the term 'pedimental composition', apparently arising from his observation of the form of pedimental sculpture of Greek temples, in which there is usually a centrepiece and pendant side panels, highly symmetrically disposed about the centre, even down to the directions in which the figures are pointing.[18]

It might be helpful to give even one example of what most biblical scholars would recognize as chiasmus from Homer's *Odyssey*.[19] It was noted by Aristarchus in the Oxyrhuncus Papyrus 1086 (a fragment of a commentary from c. 150 BC).[20] In the conversation between Odysseus and his mother Anticleia's shade in the underworld, Odysseus asks the shade a series of questions:

a   How she had died,
b   Was it by a long disease,
c   Or by the gentle arrows of Artemis?
d   He asks about his father,
e   And about his son;
f   He asks whether a stranger had assumed royal power,
g   And about his own wife, where does she stay

to which Anticleia responds in exactly the reverse order:

g   She stays in your halls;
f   No man has taken your royal honours;
e   Telemachus farms the estate,

16. G. Norwood, *Pindar* (SCL, 19; Berkeley, 1945), p. 72.
17. J.L. Myres, *Herodotus, Father of History* (Oxford, 1953), p. 81.
18. Myres, *Herodotus*, p. 81. For other examples of chiastic-like patterns in classical writers, see C. Exum and C.H. Talbert, 'The Structure of Paul's Speech to the Ephesian Elders (Acts 20:18-35)', *CBQ* 29 (1967), pp. 233-36, 234, and C.H. Talbert, 'Artistry and Theology: An Analysis of the Architecture of Jn 1,19–5,47', *CBQ* 32 (1970), pp. 341-66, 360. There is also a good discussion of the classical Greek and Latin background to chiasmus in D.R. Miesner, 'Chiasm and the Composition and Message of Paul's Missionary Sermons' (Unpublished ThD thesis, Concordia Seminary in Exile [Seminex] in Cooperation with Lutheran School of Theology at Chicago, 1974), esp. pp. 60-69.
19. *Od.* 11.170ff.
20. See also Welch, *Chiasmus*, p. 254.

d   And your father remains in the countryside, longing for your return.
c   Artemis did not slay me with her gentle arrows,
b   Nor did a sickness,
a   But I died of longing for you.

It is the contention of this study that Kennedy's conclusion is valid: chiasmus, whether simple or elaborated can be found in Greek as early as Homer, although it is ignored by classical rhetoricians and literary critics alike.[21] Although no evidence is offered here, it might be speculated that the development and use of chiasmus was regarded as a *compositional technique*, although one that was never systematically studied by the ancients.[22]

Chiasmus is frequently mentioned in the many literary studies of Old Testament and other Semitic texts that are flourishing at the present time,[23] where there is certainly now little disagreement about its presence.[24] Indeed, it was Lund's view that chiasmus in the New Testament emerged from the blend of Semitic and Greek cultures, the chiastic principle supposedly being 'a cultural heritage from the Semites, the gift of the East to the West'.[25] In the light of the widespread presence of chiastic-like *figurae* in classical writing, it would be difficult to substantiate such a claim.

Bailey has made an interesting study in this area,[26] tracing chiasmus[27]

21. Kennedy, *Interpretation*, pp. 28-29.

22. So B. Standaert, 'La rhétorique ancienne dans Saint Paul', in A. Vanhoye (ed.), *L'apôtre Paul: Personnalité, style et conception du ministère* (Leuven, 1986), pp. 78-92, 86.

23. It is my impression that, in these studies, it is seen more often (though not exclusively) as a literary feature, whereas in the Pauline letters (which may be better described as 'rhetorical' rather than 'literary' in nature) it is more of a rhetorical device.

24. No attempt is being made in the present study to pursue this aspect of the subject. My own introduction to the area was through N.W. Lund, 'The Presence of Chiasmus in the Old Testament', *AJSL* 46 (1930), pp. 104-26; N.W. Lund, *Chiasmus in the New Testament: A Study in Formgeschichte* (Chapel Hill, NC, 1942) (which, despite its title, devotes more than 20 percent of its contents to chiasmus in the Old Testament); Welch (ed.), *Chiasmus*, contains essays from a number of contributors on the presence of chiasmus in a range of ancient linguistic types, with a useful, though not exhaustive, bibliography. These works emphasized, for me, the need for a far more cautious approach than they adopt.

25. Lund, *Chiasmus*, p. viii.

26. K.E. Bailey, *Poet and Peasant and Through Peasant Eyes: A Literary-Cultural Approach to the Parables of Luke* (Grand Rapids, 1983).

27. Although he prefers to speak of an 'inversion principle' when more than four

through categories of Hebrew parallelism. He builds up an elaborate classification of types of literary structures present in the New Testament, although many of his examples are from the Old Testament. He concludes that, in prose sections, the type using inversion as an overall outline is perhaps the most common, and the most universal.[28]

As in the classics, discussion of chiasmus in the biblical literature has been fragmented,[29] with the by now familiar proliferation of terms for what would be widely recognized as 'chiasmus'; these terms include 'inverted parallelism',[30] 'introverted parallelism',[31] 'regression',[32] 'envelope figure',[33] 'correspondence',[34] and a number of others.[35]

The essential point that is becoming increasingly clear is that chiasmus belongs to no single ancient culture, but is present in many. The simple conclusion to be drawn is that there can be no *a priori* reason to rule out its presence in the Pauline letters.

1.3. *Paul and the Cultural Context of Chiasmus*

At the present time, perhaps as a reaction to the 'idealism' of much previous scholarship,[36] there is considerable interest in the Pauline letters (and, indeed, in all the New Testament documents) in their contemporary sociological and cultural milieu. Work on sociological insights is led by those like Theissen, who explored the social setting of the Corinthian situation, and Meeks.[37] Within the area in general, one 'particularly and

members are involved (Bailey, *Poet*, p. 49).

28. Bailey, *Poet*, pp. 44-75, 49.

29. See further H.van D. Parunak, 'Transitional Techniques in the Bible', *JBL* 102 (1983), pp. 525-48, 525-26.

30. J. Breck, 'Biblical Chiasmus: Exploring Structure for Meaning', *BTB* 17 (1986), pp. 70-74.

31. J. Jebb, *Sacred Literature* (London, 1820), p. 53.

32. Used by E. Galbiati, *La struttura letteraria dell' Esodo* (Rome, 1956).

33. M.E. Boismard, *Le prologue de S. Jean* (Paris, 1953), pp. 103-108.

34. T. Boys, *Tactica Sacra* (London, 1824).

35. See further the lists in Di Marco, 'Chiasmus: 1. Teil', pp. 22-23; Welch, *Chiasmus*, p. 10.

36. So, e.g., C. Tuckett, *Reading the New Testament: Methods of Interpretation* (London, 1987), p. 136.

37. G. Theissen, *The Social Setting of Pauline Christianity* (Edinburgh, 1982); W.A. Meeks, *The First Urban Christians: The Social World of the Apostle Paul* (New Haven, 1983). A useful survey of earlier work may be found in R. Scroggs, 'The Sociological Interpretation of the New Testament. The Present State of

potentially fruitful application of this interest in the Graeco-Roman world is the study of ancient rhetoric in relation to the New Testament',[38] giving rise to rhetorical criticism, to which 'astonishingly little attention' has been paid.[39] Betz's commentary on Galatians[40] has stimulated more awareness, but it remains one of a small number of major commentaries to attempt to analyse a Pauline epistle entirely in terms of a recognized ancient rhetorical model.[41]

As far as the study of chiasmus in the Pauline letters (and indeed in the wider New Testament) is concerned, rhetorical criticism is still, comparatively speaking, in its infancy, with much more potential for exploitation. It is only in very recent study that the nature and consequences of the failure to recognize 'the pervasiveness of rhetorical culture throughout Mediterranean society during the Hellenistic period'[42] have begun to be grasped, especially in the relationship between the oral and written culture of the times.

It is, therefore, appropriate at this point to ask if it is reasonable to

Research', *NTS* 26 (1980), pp. 164-79.

38. S. Neill and N.T. Wright, *The Interpretation of the New Testament: 1861–1986* (Oxford, 1988), p. 368; cf also R. Morgan with J. Barton, *Biblical Interpretation* (Oxford, 1988), pp. 214ff.

39. Neill and Wright's phrase, *Interpretation*, p. 368: an exaggeration now, but an observation which was probably true when they wrote it. We may cite J. Weiss, *Beiträge zur paulinischen Rhetorik* (Göttingen, 1897); R. Bultmann, *Der Stil der paulinischen Predigt und die kynisch-stoische Diatribe* (Göttingen, 1910) as important early works. An excellent introduction to the field is provided by H.D. Betz, 'The Problem of Rhetoric and Theology according to the Apostle Paul', in A. Vanhoye (ed.), *L'apôtre Paul: Personnalité, style et conception du ministère* (Leuven, 1986), pp. 16-48, and a more recent survey of the direction of current rhetorical criticism in C.C. Black, 'Keeping up with Recent Studies, XVI: Rhetorical Criticism and Biblical Interpretation', *ExpTim* 100 (1989), pp. 252-58.

40. H.D. Betz, *Galatians: A Commentary on Paul's Letter to the Churches in Galatia* (Hermeneia; Philadelphia, 1979).

41. Other works, e.g., V.K. Robbins, *Jesus the Teacher* (Philadelphia, 1984), consider aspects of the Gospels (in this instance, Mark) that can be discussed in the context of classical Greek literary models. The growing awareness of the rhetorical nature of the Pauline letters is reflected in D.F. Watson, 'The New Testament and Greco-Roman Rhetoric: A Bibliography', *JETS* 31 (1988), pp. 465-72. See, too, the significant collection of essays in D.F. Watson (ed.), *Persuasive Artistry: Studies in New Testament Rhetoric in Honor of George A. Kennedy* (JSNTSup, 50; Sheffield, 1991).

42. V.K. Robbins, 'Writing as a Rhetorical Act in Plutarch and the Gospels', in Watson (ed.), *Persuasive Artistry*, pp. 142-68, 144.

expect sophisticated chiasmus in Paul, and to what extent it would be appreciated by those to whom he wrote.

Paul's own educational background is not a major issue in this context. Hengel concludes that it is likely that Paul received his elementary education in a Greek-speaking Jewish school, but that his rhetorical art is not orientated on classical literary models.[43] However, even if Hengel were mistaken and Paul experienced a thorough Greek education, with its emphasis on the study of rhetoric,[44] he would not have encountered 'chiasmus' as a *figura elocutionis*, since, as we have seen, it was not recognized in the manuals of ancient rhetoric.[45]

The ancient educational system available to the privileged among Paul's readers, both Greek and Roman, made even its youngest pupils much more aware of the movement and structure of a passage than moderns are. Thus, in both systems, a child was not deemed to have learned its alphabet until it could be recited both from *alpha* to *omega* (A to X in Latin—Y and Z were looked on as 'foreign'), and also from *omega* to *alpha*, and then both ways at once, *alpha-omega, beta-psi...mu-nu*.[46] This could not but help contribute to chiastic awareness.[47]

Throughout classical education, too, learning by heart was given a prominent role. As the pupils progressed through the stages of schooling, ever-increasing attention had to be devoted to the *scriptio continua*. Thus, in the Greek system,[48] during the period of the μειράκιον (from 14 to 21 years), the grammarian's instruction was based on poetry, with Homer in the first place. At the beginning of the Christian era the treatment of an author had four stages. Textual criticism (διόρθωσις) was

---

43. M. Hengel, *The Pre-Christian Paul* (London, 1991), pp. 38 and 58 respectively.

44. See H.I. Marrou, *A History of Education in Antiquity* (London, 1956), p. 174 for its description.

45. Although the term is not used as such, he would have been aware of chiastic-like phenomena. Thus, it is interesting that, on the basis of Jeremias's study, for example (J. Jeremias, 'Chiasmus in den Paulusbriefen', *ZNW* 49 [1958], pp. 145-56), it can be seen that Paul used *commutatio* easily and effectively.

46. See Marrou, *Education*, p. 151 for the Greek system and pp. 269-70 for the Latin. S.F. Bonner, *Education in Ancient Rome: From the Elder Cato to the Younger Pliny* (London, 1977), p. 168 makes the same point.

47. So A. Stock, 'Chiastic Awareness and Education in Antiquity', *BTB* 14 (1984), pp. 23-27, 24.

48. See Marrou, *Education*, p. 154 for Greek education, p. 271 for Roman schools.

followed by expressive reading (ἀνάγνωσις). To do this, the *scriptio continua* had to be broken down, words separated, punctuation determined, phrases and sentences found, questions distinguished, lines made to scan. The third stage was that of literal and literary explanation (ἐξήγησις) of both form and content, with finally the ultimately moral judgment (κρίσις) of the text.[49] To sustain this level of attention to the text, it is little wonder that it effectively had to be learned by heart. It is not, of course, suggested that everyone had access to this kind of education, but even the most elementary steps in education encouraged an 'ambilateralism'[50] in thinking, and any reading ability demanded a much closer scrutiny of the text than in current Western education.

In our Western culture training from earliest days leads to thinking and writing in a 'left to right' fashion. However, this left-to-right system is not natural. Among children learning to write, it is common to find inversion of letters,[51] and even whole words, giving rise to the phenomenon of mirror writing. This incipient 'ambilateralism' has to be 'corrected' by training. In biblical times the Greek-speaking Hebrew, or the Hebrew- (or Aramaic-) speaking Greek was living in a culture where, depending on the language being used, writing and reading was sometimes from left to right, and sometimes from right to left. Indeed, even Greek itself at one time was sometimes found written from left to right in one line and from right to left in the next.[52]

Paul and his New Testament contemporaries would have found it difficult indeed to escape an awareness of rhetoric in the culture of their day because of its all-pervasive presence in almost every form of oral and written communication.

> In addressing a Greek audience, even when he pointedly rejected 'the wisdom of this world', Paul could not expect to be persuasive unless

---

49. Stock, 'Awareness', p. 24. The two systems (Greek and Roman) actually appear to have been very similar by the NT era.

50. See further R. Norrman, *Samuel Butler and the Meaning of Chiasmus* (London, 1986), p. vii, who defines 'ambilateralism' as 'an unwillingness or inability to distinguish between left and right, and a general preference for symmetry over asymmetry', features that he seeks to demonstrate in the author Samuel Butler.

51. Thus 'b' is written as 'd'; in fact, almost any letter may be inverted, including 's', 'c', etc.

52. The phenomenon known as βουστροφηδόν, which occurred in early Greek writing, e.g., in Solon's Laws.

there was some overlap between the content and the form of what he said and the expectations of his audience.[53]

Whether chiasmus is described as a *figura* with its roots in *commutatio*, or as a compositional technique, or is seen more broadly as a cross-cultural phenomenon, it is part of that cultural environment.[54]

1.4. *Methodological Questions in the Identification of Chiasmus*

1.4.1. *Preliminary Matters and the Focus of Interest of the Present Study*

The fact that an adequate methodology for identifying, verifying and using chiasmus as an exegetical tool has yet to emerge is at the root of many of the unresolved problems. Those that are discussed below are the result of the detailed analysis of a number of chiasms typical of many that others have suggested.[55] The subjects that need to be addressed resolve themselves into three groups: issues of principle as to what constitutes a valid chiasmus, along with its commonly observed characteristics; matters that relate to the procedure for identifying well-founded examples of chiasmus; and the function of chiasmus, both in relation to the text and to the argument. Implications for exegesis are then considered.

Because of the hesitancy that has surrounded this area of research, it is prudent, in the pursuit of objectivity, to use quite strict parameters and a significant degree of rigour. It is possible to find both *good* and *poor* examples of most rhetorical forms, including chiasmus, the weaker instances approximating to, rather than exactly matching, the definition. The first priority is to establish the presence and characteristics of a number of clear examples. Only after these are widely accepted should the scope of the enquiry be widened to include other, less precise examples that, in the present circumstances, might be better described as 'chiastic-like' or 'tending towards chiasmus'.

53. Kennedy, *Interpretation*, p. 10.
54. In this connection, M. Hengel, *Judaism and Hellenism* (trans. J. Bowden; 2 vols.; Philadelphia, 1974), I, pp. 81-83, 312, has shown that the influence of Hellenistic rhetoric can be found even in Palestinian Judaism.
55. I approached this question in a slightly different way in my earlier thesis ('Chiasmus in the Pauline Corpus' [unpublished PhD Thesis, Glasgow University, 1992], pp. 24-58) where the history of research into New Testament chiasmus is surveyed and weaknesses in procedure highlighted by the actual analysis of a number of examples.

The focus of interest of this study is chiasmus of intermediate length. These typically involve around 10-20 elements that may encompass perhaps 7-15 verses. These parameters have been chosen because they represent a significant development of the debate beyond the now widely accepted micro-chiasmus with its four-member pattern akin to *commutatio*, but do not extend it to include macro-chiasmus.[56]

In the simplest micro-chiasms, there is little new that can be added to work already done. Jeremias[57] has shown that Paul made quite extensive use of chiasms of four elements. There are few problems with such chiasmi, but, equally, little that is useful in exegesis, although, in a number of examples, such as Philemon 5, some difficulties may be clarified:[58]

A   ἀκούων σου τὴν ἀγάπην
B   καὶ τὴν πίστιν
B′ ἣν ἔχεις πρὸς τὸν κύριον Ἰησοῦν
A′ καὶ εἰς πάντας τοὺς ἁγίους.

By laying this out as a chiasmus, we see that love (in A) is directed towards the saints (in A′), and faith (in B) towards the Lord Jesus (in B′), thus explaining the otherwise awkward problem of faith being directed towards the saints.

Another widely accepted example is that shown by Robinson in Mt. 7.6:

A   Μὴ δῶτε τὸ ἅγιον τοῖς κυσίν,
B   μηδὲ βάλητε τοὺς μαργαρίτας ὑμῶν ἔμπροσθεν τῶν χοίρων,
B′ μήποτε καταπατήσουσιν αὐτοὺς ἐν τοῖς ποσὶν αὐτῶν
A′ καὶ στραφέντες ῥήξωσιν ὑμᾶς.

While pigs trample under foot (καταπατέω), they do not tear in pieces (ῥήγνυμι), this being much more typical of dogs. Thus, the fourth line is associated with the first, and only the third with the second.[59]

56. The distinction between 'micro-' and 'macro-chiasmus' is made by M. Dahood, 'Chiasmus', *IDBSup*, p. 145. This usage is not to be confused with H. Lausberg, *Elemente der literarischen Rhetorik* (Munich, 1963), pp. 128-31, who distinguishes 'Klein-Chiasmus' and 'Groß-Chiasmus', the former description being limited to a chiasmus of individual words within a sentence, and the latter used to refer to chiasmus involving groups of clauses.

57. Jeremias, 'Chiasmus', pp. 145-56.

58. Jeremias, 'Chiasmus', p. 146. Jeremias also gives some examples where two or three themes are presented in the order AB or ABC, but which are then worked out in reverse order, BA or CBA ('Chiasmus', pp. 152-56).

59. T.H. Robinson, *The Gospel of Matthew* (MNTC; London, 1928), pp. 61-62.

Many modern commentaries[60] point out similar chiasms in the Pauline letters, usually only in passing, and with the minimum of comment.[61] If, however, there is no more to the study of chiasmus in the Pauline letters than this, then it would deserve only a footnote in a study of Paul's use of rhetorical devices.

At the other end of the scale, macro-chiasmus is alleged to cover whole sections of a book,[62] or even a whole book. Perhaps the best known example of this is Bligh's analysis of Galatians,[63] which purports to identify a whole series of interlinking chiastic structures[64] that encompass the entire letter in a 'chiastic composition of what some readers will find quite unbelievable complexity'.[65] Such macro-chiasms continue to be identified. A recent example in the area of Pauline studies is provided by Myers's paper that suggests that Romans 3–8 is chiastically organized with a series of sometimes interlocking patterns.[66]

60. There are very few references to chiasmus in earlier commentaries. J.A. Bengel (*Gnomon Novi Testamenti* [Tübingen, 1742]) makes some use of it, finding, e.g., a seven-member chiasmus in Rom. 3.9–6.12. It was also used by J. Forbes, *Analytical Commentary on the Epistle to the Romans* (Edinburgh, 1868); J. Weiss, too, noted a few Pauline examples in passing (*Das Urchristentum* [Göttingen, 1917], e.g., at p. 310).

61. An interesting, if imprecise, illustration of this trend within the Pauline letters can be seen in two recent major commentaries on Romans. In that of C.E.B. Cranfield (*A Critical and Exegetical Commentary on the Epistle to the Romans* [ICC; 2 vols.; Edinburgh, 1975]) no mention (always a dangerous claim to make!) is made of chiasmus. In that of J.D.G. Dunn (*Romans* [WBC, 38A, 38B; Dallas, 1988]) several chiasms are suggested (e.g., pp. 78, 130, 698), although none of them are particularly significant. In a similar vein, V.P. Furnish, *II Corinthians* (AB, 32A; New York, 1984) mentions a four-member chiasmus in passing in 2 Cor. 2.15, 16 (*II Corinthians*, p. 177) but R.P. Martin, *2 Corinthians* (WBC, 40; Waco, TX, 1986) lists 'chiasmus' no less than ten times in his 'Index of Principal Topics' (p. 515: others appear in the text, e.g. 1.11b, pp. 13-14, but not in the index), although again they are typically ABBA patterns and do not often affect exegesis.

62. Among the most ponderous (and unlikely) is Lund's analysis of Mt. 4.25–8.1, requiring some 9 pages of tabulation to show not just a chiasmus containing a second level within, but a third level within the second level! (Lund, *Chiasmus*, pp. 241-50.)

63. J. Bligh, *Galatians in Greek: A Structural Analysis of St Paul's Epistle to the Galatians* (Detroit, 1966).

64. What he calls 'wheels within wheels' (Bligh, *Galatians in Greek*, pp. 2-3).

65. So M. Ward, Review of Bligh, *Galatians in Greek*, *ExpTim* 79 (1967), p. 15, whose review is more sympathetic than most.

66. C.D. Myers, 'Chiastic Inversion in the Argument of Romans 3–8', *NovT* 35

1.4.2. *Defining Chiasmus and Describing its Characteristics*

The need for a broadly based and widely acceptable definition of chiasmus is apparent. A number, of course, have already been suggested, all of which include the same two basic ideas of balance of elements about a central point within a given unit of material, and inversion of order of those elements.[67] The requirement of inversion of order of the elements rules out the ABA pattern as chiastic, and means that, in principle, a chiasmus must have a minimum of four elements to make inversion of order possible.[68]

Because the terminology associated with parallelism[69] can sometimes be rather vague, and may not always now be used in a uniform way,[70] a more precise way forward would be to identify chiasmus as a device that employs bilateral *symmetry*[71] about a central axis, leading towards a clear and simple description.

A working definition of chiasmus, therefore, might be as follows: chiasmus may be said to be present in a passage[72] if the text exhibits bilateral symmetry of four or more elements about a central axis, which may

(1993), pp. 30-47. Myers does have some valid points to make, but I am not convinced by his overall analysis, and continue to find the concept of macro-chiasmus fraught with difficulties. See further 1.4.3 d below.

67. Definitions offered by all of the following make these points: Dahood, 'Chiasmus', *IDBSup*, p. 145; Di Marco, 'Chiasmus 1. Teil', pp. 22-23; Jeremias, 'Chiasmus', p. 145; Exum and Talbert, 'Structure', p. 234; N.W. Lund, 'The Presence of Chiasmus in the New Testament', *JR* 10 (1930), pp. 74-93, 74; R.E. Man, 'The Value of Chiasm for New Testament Interpretation', *BibSac* 141 (1984), pp. 146-57, 146; Stock, 'Awareness', p. 23; Welch, *Chiasmus*, p. 13.

68. *Contra* Breck, 'Structure', p. 70, who specifically includes the ABA pattern as chiastic. Suggested occurrences of ABA patterns in the Pauline corpus can be found in, e.g., J.J. Collins, 'Chiasmus, the "ABA" Pattern and the Text of Paul', in *Studiorum Paulinorum Congressus Internationalis Catholicus 1961* (Rome, 1963), II, pp. 575-83.

69. As pioneered by R. Lowth, *De sacra poesi Hebraeorum praelectiones academicae* (Oxford, 1821).

70. Terms associated with parallelism include direct, standard, synonymous, step, antithetical, inverted, introverted, incomplete, and so on, depending on the context and the author.

71. Norrman, *Chiasmus*, I, p. 276 discusses chiasmus in this way. Vanhoye, too, has a long note on 'structures symétriques' (A. Vanhoye, *La structure littéraire de l'épitre aux Hébreux* [Paris, 1963], pp. 60-62).

72. A non-specific term to cover chiasmus at both the 'micro-' and 'macro-' level.

itself lie between two elements, or be a unique central element,[73] the symmetry consisting of any combination of verbal, grammatical or syntactical elements, or, indeed, of ideas and concepts in a given pattern. Such a description corresponds well with the consensus of current opinion, and thus serves as a reasonable definition that sets initial limits on the characteristics of the phenomenon into which this study inquires.[74]

In addition, there are a number of features that are said to be commonly observed in chiasms of intermediate length. The point must be carefully made that these are characteristics[75] that are *frequently* but not *necessarily* present. On the basis of his experience, Lund[76] had suggested seven 'laws governing chiastic structures'. He has been rightly criticized for his use of the word 'law',[77] which gives them far too much weight. In fact, their usefulness at all is not beyond question, especially if any attempt is made to use them as diagnostic tests for the presence of chiasmus. Such characteristics as may be present are of interest only after a chiasmus has been identified. With some hesitation, therefore, in this study four of Lund's seven 'laws'[78] are more carefully drafted, and

73. *Contra* Breck, 'Structure', p. 71, who argues that the term 'chiasmus' must be reserved for structures with a unique central element. He suggests, without adequate argument, that the widely accepted ABBA pattern is not chiasmus but 'inverted parallelism'. For him, 'the uniqueness of the chiastic structure lies in its focus upon a *pivotal theme*'. Breck's argument does not appear to have found support.

74. There are still some, however, who would want to reserve the term for four-element patterns only, e.g., Bailey, *Poet*, p. 49.

75. Their description even as 'characteristics' needs to be tested in practice, and their validity will be re-assessed in the concluding chapter.

76. Lund, *Chiasmus*, pp. 40-42.

77. T.W. Manson, Review of Lund, *Chiasmus*, *JTS* 45 (1944), pp. 81-84, 82.

78. Those which are omitted are (a) 'The centre is always the turning point'. (This is taken as self-evident. By definition, the passage turns back on itself in some way at the centre in order for any kind of symmetry to be present); (b) 'The law of shift from centre to extremes', where an idea at the centre of one system recurs at the extremes of a corresponding system, with the deliberate intention of interlinking the two systems. (This, if it occurs at all, would be found only in highly elaborate patterns, none of which I have found persuasive.) (c) The 'tendency of certain terms to gravitate towards certain positions within a given system'. He gives, as examples, quotations which he claims tend to occur at the centre of a system, and even individual terms like 'body' when it denotes the Church. (I find this totally unconvincing, and on many occasions suspect that Lund, with this preconceived notion, places a quotation at the 'centre' of a supposed chiasmus, and then 'creates' a chiastic pattern around it.)

are suggested as being worth considering as possible characteristics, with a further two, (e) and (f) added:

a. Chiasms frequently exhibit a shift at, or near, their centre. This change can be very varied in nature: a change of person of the verb, a new or unexpected idea suddenly introduced, and so on. Usually, after the 'shift', the original thought is resumed. For this reason, in this study, the phrase 'shift and reversion' is preferred to Lund's simple term. This immediately highlights the problem associated with all such characteristics. Many passages have 'shifts', but are obviously not chiastic; in a chiasmus 'shifts' that are not at its centre will occur, marking, for example, points of development in an argument.

b. Chiasms are sometimes introduced or concluded by a frame passage. Lund himself makes no comment on this, but by looking at examples which he later gives, a 'frame-passage' is a spring-board from which to launch into the chiasmus, or a section which acts as a tail-piece to a chiasmus without itself being part of the chiastic pattern.

c. Passages which are chiastically patterned sometimes also contain directly parallel elements.[79]

d. Identical ideas may occasionally be distributed in such a fashion that they occur in the extremes and at the centre of a given system.

e. Balancing elements are normally of approximately the same length. On the few occasions when this is not the case, some explanation seems to be called for.

f. The centre often contains the focus of the author's thought. It will be suggested that this is a particularly powerful feature with obvious implications for exegesis.

---

79. This observation replaces Lund's seventh law (Lund, *Chiasmus*, p. 41), which is not very clearly stated. In a chiasmus $ABC \ldots C'B'A'$, it is sometimes apparent that a given pair of elements (say, B and B$'$) can each be resolved into two sub-elements, B_1 and B_2, and B_1' and B_2', where the sub-elements occur without inversion of order. This gives $AB(B_1B_2)C \ldots C'B'(B_1'B_2')A'$. In this case, there is no inversion of order of the sub-elements. This is seen in practice in later chapters, e.g., in 2.3 below.

1.4.3. *Requirements and Constraints in the Identification of Chiasmus*
In keeping with the quest for objectivity, Welch's appeal is well worth reproducing:

> If any aspect of the chiastic analysis is to produce rigorous and verifiable results, the inverted parallel orders, which create the chiasms upon which that analysis is based must be evidenced in the text itself and not imposed upon the text by Procrustean design or artifice of the reader. Therefore, one's predominant concern is over objectivity. In striving for objectivity, it is reasonable to require significant repetitions to be readily apparent, and the overall system to be well balanced. The second half of the system should tend to repeat the first half of the system in a recognizably inverted order, and the juxtaposition of the two central sections should be marked and highly accentuated... Key words, echoes, and balancing should be distinct and should serve defined purposes within the structure.
>
> Nevertheless the objective criteria alone do not tell the whole story. Evidence of chiasmus is not entirely objective and quantifiable. For example, chiasmus operates by definition within literary units. Yet defining what consitutes such a literary unit and determining where it begins and ends is often a predominantly subjective matter especially where multiple structures operate simultaneously... Furthermore, wherever synonyms, cognates, antitheticals or logically proximate terms appear in a chiastic system, substantial subjective judgment is again involved in the process of deciding which terms in the first portion of the system match (if at all) with particular terms in the second portion of the system. One also recognizes that any significant chiasm must embrace each of the predominant words and concepts appearing in the system (for what is omitted from a diagrammed arrangement is often as critical as that which is included, in terms of evaluating both the ancient author's creative success and the modern exegete's conceptual clarity in respect to any proposed chiasm.) But here again, subjectivity is inevitably involved in deciding which elements are in fact predominant and must, therefore, be judged indispensable.[80]

In the light of Welch's plea, three requirements are suggested, without the fulfilment of which an alleged pattern could not be accepted as chiastic:

> a. The chiasmus will be present in the text as it stands, and will not require unsupported textual emendation in order to 'recover' it.[81]

---

80. Welch, *Chiasmus*, p. 13.
81. Thus, Bligh finds a chiasmus in Gal. 4.3-10 which is 'greatly improved' if 4.10 is placed before the last clause of 4.9! (*Galatians in Greek*, p. 43).

b.   The symmetrical elements will be present in precisely inverted order.
c.   The chiasmus will begin and end at a reasonable point.

Nothing, perhaps, needs to be said about the first of these, but the second is a little more problematical. Many examples of chiasmus are suggested in which there is a greater or smaller degree of perturbation in the order of the elements in the second half.[82] However, if any disturbance at all in the order of the elements is allowed, the problem becomes that of deciding at what point a perturbation becomes so severe that the pattern fails as a chiasmus.[83] In the present atmosphere this is a case for erring, if any way, on the side of caution in order to exclude doubtful structures.

The third requirement has been left deliberately vague at this stage. It is difficult to define what a 'reasonable point' would be in many instances because of the variety of possible situations that might be encountered. Sometimes a chiasmus will equate with a 'rhetorical unit' (corresponding to the *pericope* in form criticism),[84] although a complicating factor is the possible presence of a frame passage which, while not strictly part of the chiastic pattern, might be said to belong to the same 'rhetorical unit'. However, if it were necessary to incorporate material from a clearly different preceding or subsequent unit before the symmetry could be produced, that chiasmus would be suspect.[85] Equally,

82. As an extreme example, we may cite the chiastic pattern proposed by Welch (*Chiasmus*, p. 212) for the book of James, with the elements of the first half labelled A, B, C, D, E, F, G, H, I, J, K, L, M, but the order of the elements in the second half, working out from the centre, are, according to his analysis, K′, L′, E′, D′, B′, I′, H′, C′, A′, F′, J′ and G′. I find this totally unconvincing and, although he admits that this might best be seen as a rudimentary chiasm, this presentation is particularly disappointing in view of his appeal for care and objectivity in the face of scepticism about sophisticated chiasmus.

83. See Y.T. Radday, 'Chiasmus in the Old Testament', in Welch (ed.), *Chiasmus*, pp. 50-117, for discussion and examples of a statistical technique that measures the degree of perturbation. Even if the basis of Radday's method is sound, this merely says that a near-perfect chiasmus (already identified, of course, *before* the application of the statistical analysis) is a near-perfect chiasmus. It gives no indication of when an alleged pattern is not viable.

84. Kennedy, *Interpretation*, p. 33.

85. As a short example of this (upon which little actually turns, other than the demonstration of the *principle*), attention might be drawn to Amos 5.4b-6a, which both Lund (*Chiasmus*, p. 42) and Bailey (*Poet*, p. 48) use. It can be portrayed as:

one would be very cautious about a chiasmus that ended, say, in the middle of a clause.[86] As with all these observations, this requires testing and will be reviewed in the light of the examples that will be produced in the next five chapters.

There are other constraints, too, that must be considered.

d. 'Chiasmus by headings' will be discouraged as they can create what may be no more than an illusion of chiastic balancing.[87] This is, perhaps, not quite so relevant for the present study since it is more typically, though not uniquely, found in macro-chiasms. The problem associated with headings is that, by definition, they must be both theologically and interpretatively selective.[88] The key question is how well the chosen

---

A 'Seek me and live; B but do not seek Bethel; C and do not enter into Gilgal; D or cross over to Beersheba; C' for Gilgal shall surely go into exile; B' and Bethel shall come to nought. A' Seek the Lord and live.' Here, there is no natural break in the passage at Amos 5.6a. Indeed, it seems clear that Amos 5.4, 5 forms one rhetorical unit, and 5.6, 7 forms the next. Neither Lund nor Bailey offer any justification for this.

86. As in the example from Turner (N. Turner, *Style*, Vol. 4 in J.H. Moulton, *A Grammar of New Testament Greek* [Edinburgh, 1976], p. 98): see 3.2.1 below.

87. I am conscious that 'chiasmus by headings' may be more acceptable in other kinds of writing in the NT outside of the Pauline letters. As two attractive examples, we may cite the seven-member chiasmus suggested in J. Marcus, *The Mystery of the Kingdom* (SBLDS, 90; Atlanta, 1986), pp. 221-23 that he accepts as providing a helpful outline of Mk 4.1-34: A Narrative introduction (4.1, 2); B Seed parable (4.3-9); C General statement (4.10-12); D Explanation of parables (4.13-20); C' General statements (4.21-25); B' Seed parables (4.26-32); A' Narrative conclusion (4.33-34); the second is Welch's analysis (*Chiasmus*, p. 239) of Lk. 15.11-32: A One son takes his inheritance; conversation between father and son (15.11, 12); B One son goes out; his conduct (15.13-16); C The well-being of the father's servants recalled; 'I perish' (*apollumai*) (15.17); D I will say 'I have sinned' (15.18, 19); E At the point of *crisis*, the father runs to meet his son and is compassionate (15.20); D' The son says 'I have sinned' (15.21); C' The father instructs the servants to make well; the lost (*apolos*) is found (15.22-24); B' One son refuses to go in; his conduct (15.25-30); A' One son promised his inheritance: conversation between father and son (15.31, 32). This leads to a much more satisfactory exegesis than the commonly found exposition of the passage as the parable of the prodigal son, with an addendum about the elder brother. The central purpose can now be seen as an illustration of the compassion of the father, equally shown to both sons, each of whom commits his own sins, and to each of whom is given a position of equivalent weight in the chiastic pattern.

88. The problem is well illustrated in Myers, 'Inversion', p. 38, where he suggests that Rom. 3.24-26 is chiastically balanced by Rom. 5.1-11. He lays this out as:

heading reflects the *author's* focus of interest rather than the *commentator's*. This produces a potentially circular argument: headings are interpretatively selected to create or bolster a chiasmus; it is then argued from the chiasmus that the selective choice of heading reflects the true interests of the author! Indeed, in the more extreme cases, the heading may be so bland as to be virtually meaningless.[89] As a matter of procedure, therefore, no headings are assigned to elements in the examples presented in this study.

e. The selective use of a commonly occurring word in a passage to produce a chiasmus is often a questionable procedure. This problem does arise in some chiasms of intermediate length. Thus, when Lund analyses Eph. 5.22-33 as a chiasmus, in order to produce his pattern, he parallels 'wives' in 5.22 with 'wife' in 5.33, but not with 'wife' in 5.23, 5.24, 5.25, 5.28 or 5.31 and so forth.[90] Closely related to this is the situation where some parallels are highlighted and others are ignored, making the whole exercise appear suspiciously subjective. Reasoned consideration needs to be given to circumstances where obvious parallels are ignored.

f. The existence of non-balancing elements in an otherwise well-developed symmetrical pattern must be very carefully accounted for. This concept will be developed more fully below, since such deviation may, in fact, be very significant exegetically. To allow even one such

---

A '...*justified... by his blood...at the present time...*' (3.24-26); B '...our *boasting...*' (3.27); C '...a person is *justified by faith...* ' (3.28); C' '...since we are *justified by faith...* (5.1); B' '...we *boast...*' (5.2, 3); A' '...now...we have been *justified by his blood.*' (5.9). Welch's point above that what is omitted from an arrangement is often as critical as what is included is very pertinent here! If a sufficiently large section of material is chosen, it is often possible to find words and ideas that occur in an apparently inverted order without there ever truly being a chiasmus present.

89. Bligh's analysis of Galatians again provides many examples of these. Thus, in his primary chiasm, he uses as his heading for Gal. 1.11–2.10 'Paul's Two Ways: Before and After Conversion', which he then balances with Gal. 5.11–6.11, headed 'The Way of the Flesh and the Way of the Spirit' (*Galatians in Greek*, p. 4). Bligh's analyses are only occasionally discussed in Galatian studies, and have not been widely accepted. Thus, e.g., C.K. Barrett ('The Allegory of Abraham, Sarah and Hagar in the Argument of Galatians', J. Friedrich *et al.* [eds.], in *Rechtfertigung: Festschrift für Ernst Käsemann zum 70. Geburstag* [Tübingen, 1976], pp. 1-16, 3-5) discusses, but rightly rejects as unlikely, Bligh's Sixth Tertiary Chiasm (Gal. 4.11-30: Bligh, *Galatians in Greek*, pp. 44-45).

90. Lund, *Chiasmus*, pp. 198-99.

non-balancing pair may arguably be seen as a compromise with the stated priority of objectivity and clarity of parallels. However, as will be discussed later, it is often the paradoxical presence of *asymmetries* in a pattern, built by definition on *symmetry*, that draws the reader's attention to the content of those elements, giving them consequently more prominence.

g. Laying out a chiastic pattern in an exegetical vacuum in the present sceptical climate invites rejection. A vitally important part of the process of the identification of a chiasmus is the provision of reasonable proof of its presence. A chiasmus, if it is to be defended as being of the author's making, must be capable of being demonstrated to others, rather than existing only in the mind-set of its 'discoverer'. The failure to grasp this essentially simple point is one of the greatest weaknesses of so much of the work done in this field to date. The assumption is made that a chiasmus is readily discernible,[91] when the reality for most is that the *basis* for such a claimed chiastic pattern is obscure to the point of complete opacity. Unless the chiasmus is of the simplest possible type, exegetical evidence must be presented to support its presence. Indeed, with more and more chiasms being 'discovered', exegesis has to play an increasingly significant part in distinguishing between alternative, or competing, chiastic analyses of the same passage.

As more confidence is gained in the understanding of the nature of New Testament chiasmus, there may be a case for relaxing some of these constraints, since it is possible so to overemphasize them that a new kind of strait-jacket is created that would again effectively hamper the development of this field of study.[92]

It is important, too, to give some attention to the question of when a possible chiasmus is rejected as being not well-founded. It needs to be clearly stated that this point is not reached when the pattern is first laid out, but comes only after the nature of all the proposed parallels have been discussed and explored. The validity of a chiasmus depends on the *cumulative impact* of a number of criteria.[93] Because readers bring their

91. So Welch, *Chiasmus*, p. 211.

92. See further Welch, *Chiasmus*, p. 13.

93. The essential point made by D.J. Clark, 'Criteria for Identifying Chiasm', *LB* 35 (1974), pp. 63-72, 66. Clark's article, based on Dewey's conclusion that Mk 2.1–3.6 forms an ABCB′A′ chiasmus (J. Dewey, 'The Literary Structure of the Controversy Stories in Mark 2.1–3.6', *JBL* 92 [1973], pp. 394-401), suggests that five types of criteria operate in the establishing of a chiasmus: content, form or

own preconceptions to a subject, it is sometimes very difficult to suspend judgment when a different way of looking at a passage is proposed, especially if it is immediately seen that it may involve much wider issues.

1.4.4. *Procedures for Identifying Chiasmus*

The process for identifying chiasmus is inevitably complex, and the one discussed here is unavoidably circular. This does not mean that all study of chiasmus is impossible,[94] but a sober appreciation of the inherent problems may help to avoid some of the more obvious pitfalls. Proper interpretation of each part (in this case, the individual element) depends on a proper appreciation of the whole. However, appreciation of the whole can only be built upon interpretation of the parts. To some extent, this can be developed into a *self-correcting procedure*, so that, in the course of going round the 'circle', corrective adjustments can be made. Kennedy makes a similar point in his description of the determination of a rhetorical unit. For him, it involves a certain amount of 'experiment', specifically, in his case, looking for signs of opening and closure.[95]

In practical terms for chiasmus, this translates into a two-step methodology. The first stage is to identify a pattern which is potentially chiastic. This usually involves giving as much careful and detailed attention to the text as was expected in the educational system of the day (as outlined in 1.3 above), primarily in terms of vocabulary and syntax, and then in terms of content. As a general rule, the greater the number of objective balances of vocabulary and syntax in potentially corresponding elements, the more likely there is to be an authentic chiasmus present.

Thus, as an example, and without wishing to argue from the particular to the general, an *inclusio* may indicate that further analysis will reveal greater symmetry. Likewise, a sudden change in a unit of text may turn out to be the shift and reversion at the centre of a chiasmus. It is worth repeating that, at this stage, there is necessarily a measure of trial and

---

structure of a pericope, language (use of 'catchwords'), setting, and theology. His conclusions are of limited use here because his discussion is based on the Gospel example, with the result that some of his criteria (e.g., the 'setting' of incident A 'inside' (Mk 2.1-12) and incident A′ 'outside' (Mk 3.1-6)) are relevant only to the narrative, pericope-based style of the Gospels.

94. Tuckett concludes that a certain amount of circularity is inherent in all literary study: *Interpretation*, p. 70.

95. Kennedy, *Interpretation*, pp. 33-34.

error. The self-correcting process means that what may initially appear to be a parallel may need to be left to the side if it does not 'nest' with other parallels. In the same way, a series of strong parallels may prove in the end not to be present in inverted order, with the resulting conclusion that the embryonic pattern is not workable.

The second step is then to test the suggested pattern at the conceptual level by exegesis in order to validate the hypothesis. There are many occasions on which scholarly opinion will point to repetitions, parallels and contrasts, to shifts of emphasis, or apparent discontinuities and so on in a passage. While those scholars are not thinking in terms of a chiasmus, these insights may well reinforce the hypothetical pattern at the conceptual level. It is at this point that the evidence must be weighed and the decision taken as to whether the so-called chiasmus is actually present, or is a product of the commentator's ingenuity, artificially imposed upon the text. No matter how careful the inquiry, it is unlikely that absolute certainty will be reached, and most cases will result in a balance of probability.

1.5. *The Functions of Chiasmus*

Watson[96] suggested a dual functionality for chiasmus: as both a *structuring* and an *expressive* device. It may, however, be helpful to discuss chiasmus more broadly: first in relation to the text, and then in relation to the argument.

1.5.1. *The Functions of Chiasmus in Relation to the Text*
It is possible to classify many of the views about its functions in the text under three headings, which are not intended to be mutually exclusive.

a. Chiasmus functioned as an art form[97] lending beauty[98] as well as a pleasing sound to a passage[99] and giving variety,[100] particularly in language types where there exists the possibility of exploiting flexibility of

---

96. W.G.E. Watson, 'Chiasmus in Biblical Hebrew Poetry', in Welch (ed.), *Chiasmus*, pp. 118-68, 145.

97. So Manson, 'Review', p. 82; Stock, 'Awareness', p. 23; Myres, *Herodotus*, p. 64; *et al.*

98. Miesner, 'Chiasm', p. 44.

99. Jeremias, 'Chiasmus', p. 145.

100. Dahood, 'Chiasmus', *IDBSup*, p. 145.

word order[101] and where it was a widely accepted way to write for aesthetic effects.[102]

b. It acted as a mnemonic device.[103] There may be an inherent problem if this second approach is over-emphasized in the present context, since it suggests that Paul was consciously aware that his writing was subsequently going to be committed to memory. If this were the case, it might have been reasonably anticipated that chiasmus would be found in passages devoted to the more important themes, perhaps of a doctrinal or liturgical nature, rather than in those dealing with more prosaic matters, but this may well not be borne out in practice.

c. Chiasmus functions in the text as a structuring device that helps to divide one section of material from another. Parunak[104] underlines the degree to which the modern Western reader is bombarded by graphical signals embedded within the written text—including the use of italics, footnotes, chapter headings, paragraph indentations and so on. Many of these are absent in the ancient texts where, commonly, a *scriptio continua* is used. Chiasmus is one of the devices that serves to divide a section of undifferentiated text from that around it. He suggests rather cryptically that 'chiasm signals its own conclusion',[105] since, if the reader has already encountered ABC, the occurrence of C′B′A′ will indicate the completion of the unit. A corollary to this is that chiasmus also serves to unify material within a section, thus making that section stand out.[106] Parunak's case is persuasively made.[107]

101. See further Norrman, *Chiasmus*, p. 2.

102. Talbert, 'Artistry', pp. 365-66.

103. Whitman, *Homer*, p. 98; Breck, 'Chiasmus', p. 73; Talbert, 'Artistry', p. 365; Miesner, 'Chiasm', p. 44; *et al.*

104. H.van D. Parunak, 'Oral Typesetting: Some Uses of Biblical Structure', *Bib* 62 (1981), pp. 153-68; cf., too, Stock, 'Awareness', p. 23; Welch, *Chiasmus*, p. 12.

105. Parunak, 'Typesetting', p. 156.

106. Parunak, 'Typesetting', pp. 162-63.

107. Standaert has an interesting point to make that chiasmus was one of three models of compositional technique in antiquity. The first is the rhetorical model of introduction, narration, argumentation, peroration and conclusion. The second is the dramatic model with its δέσις leading towards the denouement of the λύσις. The third is the widely found chiastic model, evidence for which can be gleaned from occasional remarks, but which was never systematized in the work of the ancients. (Standaert, 'Rhétorique', pp. 86ff.) The use of chiasmus as a *compositional technique* (as over against its function as a *structuring technique* within a composition) merits more attention.

If Parunak is correct, then Lund's concept of the frame passage before and after a chiasmus needs to be re-examined. While it might be possible to envisage a short introduction to a chiasmus, the idea of a frame passage at the end of a chiasmus would defeat its structuring purpose, since there would be no way of telling how long or short that might be.

Parunak's thesis also raises, but does not address, the difficult problem of how readers (and especially hearers) could tell that they were dealing with a chiasmus. In considering this, Western twentieth-century presuppositions must not be imported into our thinking. While chiasmus does undoubtedly occur in English, it is not as common as to be immediately perceived by even native-born English speakers.[108] The fact that modern readers of New Testament Greek may struggle to identify a chiastic structure may say more about the modern cast of mind than about the presence and relevance of chiasmus. It may well be, therefore, that the readers (or even the hearers) of a particular epistle of Paul's would be aware of the presence of the chiasmus because of a much more highly developed consciousness of chiastic patterns resulting from its prevalence in the languages of their day. The chiastic form, however, was not restricted to language alone: it had its counterpart in the visual arts, in, for example, the conventional bilateral symmetry of pedimental decoration.[109] Because the use of extended chiasms is not covered in the manuals of rhetoric, it is not possible to prove that there was such a heightened awareness, other than obliquely.

It still remains difficult, however, to imagine how anything beyond a short chiasmus could be detected by a *listener*, even if the ancients could perform what seem to moderns to be prodigious feats of memory. Whitman is very conscious of this problem, especially when symmetries are separated by a great many lines as in the Iliad. He cannot, of course, give a totally adequate account of it, but concludes that

> the human mind is a strange organ, and one which perceives many things without conscious or articulate knowledge of them, and responds to them

108. Its function in English appears to be largely decorative ('Fair is foul, and foul is fair', Macbeth, Act 1, scene 1), although it may be highly elaborate as in Dylan Thomas's, 'Author's Prologue to his Collected Poems', consisting of 102 lines which exhibit a completely regular overall chiastic rhyme scheme. In other instances it seems little more than a curiosity: 'Old king Cole was a merry old soul, and a merry old soul was he.'

109. Talbert, 'Artistry', p. 364.

> with emotions necessarily and appropriately vague. An audience hence
> might feel more symmetry than it could possible analyze or describe.[110]

This is well said, but must remain conjectural.[111] Talbert, too, tries to deal with the problem and suggests four possibilities: the architectonic scheme was the secret of the author; only a few would become aware of the pattern after study; it was intuitively felt by most, but not consciously perceived until after reflection; it was generally recognized at the conscious level at the time of reading. He himself chooses the third option,[112] which may well be the most attractive.

This difficulty, however, may not be as acute as is sometimes thought, particularly in relation to the Pauline letters. Irrespective of whether these epistles were primarily intended to be heard or read, they were transmitted, and were solely available, in written form. Even if they were then heard only, the likelihood is that they were read aloud again and again 'and thus took on the qualities of a frozen oral text in which a hearer might remember passages yet to come'.[113] Talbert's point is well made that chiasmus may have been intuitively felt, but not consciously perceived until after reflection.[114] There can be little doubt that both

---

110. Whitman, *Homer*, pp. 255-56.

111. The closest contemporary analogy may be that of the musically-aware listener's appreciation, not only of recurring themes within a major piece of music, but even of the development and variations on the themes. Such appreciation may well transcend the purely conscious level. Cf. Talbert, 'Artistry', p. 365 n. 104.

112. Talbert, 'Artistry', pp. 363-65.

113. Kennedy, *Interpretation*, pp. 5-6, although I am unsure about his rather sweeping conclusion that the 'rhetorical qualities inherent in the text were originally intended to have an impact *on first hearing*' (italics mine). While this may well be true of some simpler facets of the rhetorical quality (e.g., hyperbole, or apostrophe etc.), other rhetorical techniques, although clear in the mind of the orator, may have demanded considerable reflection on the part of the hearer before a full appreciation of them was possible, as in, for example, the interpretation of a complex metaphor.

114. An oblique confirmation of this may be found in the fact that a number of passages in which chiasms have recently been identified have earlier been the subject of much debate regarding sometimes highly speculative hymnic structures, as, for example, Col. 1.15-20 and Wright's paper (N.T. Wright, 'Poetry and Theology in Colossians 1.15-20', *NTS* 36 [1990], pp. 444-68). Although it is true that a passage may be hymnic and chiastic, it is possible that sometimes those seeking to reconstruct hymns are doing so because of an intuitive awareness of movements and balances within the passage that are present as a result of its chiastic, rather than hymnic, nature. More evidence of this will be presented in subsequent chapters, and the subject raised again in the concluding chapter.

Paul and the recipients of the letters 'lived in a socio-linguistic world shaped by the conscious rhetoric of Hellenism'.[115] To that extent, it is to be expected that an audience, even with only a limited amount of education, would nonetheless be aware of many of those rhetorical features that were in everyday use.[116]

1.5.2. *The Functions of Chiasmus in Relation to the Argument*

It is in this area above all others that an adequate methodology is imperative, because of the increasing awareness of the usefulness of chiasmus in exegesis.[117] The problem, if indeed there is one, is assessing what might reasonably be expected in terms of exegesis resulting from the identification of a given chiasmus.

It may appear obvious, but nevertheless needs to be carefully stressed, that the identification of a chiasmus is not a way of defining the content of a passage. If the hypothesis is valid that one of the prime functions of chiasmus may be as a basic structuring device in a passage,[118] then what it produces is a pattern that describes primarily the *movement of thought rather than the thought itself*; it is a dynamic, fluid concept that provides the framework of the passage[119] into which other patterns may well be interwoven. Thus, it needs to be remembered that the Pauline authors may well wish to make more points in a passage other than that which is highlighted by the central elements; likewise, there may be more parallels in the passage, other than those formed by chiastic partners. Within almost any Pauline passage there is a richly coloured and complex tapestry of thought with contrasts, parallels and echoes often overlaid.[120]

115. S.M. Pogoloff, 'Isocrates and Hermeneutics', in Watson (ed.), *Persuasive Artistry*, pp. 338-62, 350.

116. See further 1.3 above.

117. A. Di Marco, 'Der Chiasmus in der Bibel 4. Teil', *LB* 44 (1979), pp. 3-70, 55-56. See further Man, 'Value', pp. 146-57, who describes its exegetical value in terms of comparison and contrast, emphasis, the point of a passage, clarification of meaning, and the purpose of a book.

118. Without denying that it may have other functions as well.

119. I am attracted by Talbert's regular description of chiasmus as providing the 'architecture' of the passage—see Talbert, 'Artistry' where it is used throughout. Another useful metaphor might be to see the chiasmus as forming the *skeleton* of the passage; the *body* is only seen when the skeleton is enfleshed by the use of other material.

120. Indeed, Talbert goes so far as to suggest that a text can show evidence of

Thus, the relationship between form and content is not a simple one.[121] It seems clear that form will not be divorced from content, inasmuch as the use of chiasmus may be particularly appropriate in a passage, say, where a series of antitheses are being developed, or in which there is a circular sweep of movement of thought. Of course, such themes can be developed without the use of chiasmus. Other themes where there are no antitheses can still be accommodated by the chiastic mould. Form, in this instance, cannot constrict content. If a suggestion were to be made to describe the relationship between form and content in this case, it would be that *form enhances content*. The symmetries that emerge in a chiasmus have the effect of making the combined impact of element X with its chiastic partner X′ more than the impact of X and X′ taken in isolation.[122]

In terms of the advancing of his argument, it must be remembered that Paul is involved in the matter of *persuasion* as he tries to move his readers from their present position to where he wants them to be. The use of chiasmus is one of the means to that end of persuasion,[123] and this study shows how he uses it to great effect, often with consummate skill. However, to develop a chiasmus in which the second half precisely mirrors (in thought and language) the first would be a somewhat sterile endeavour. Its function in terms of the argument would effectively be limited to reinforcement. Thus, paradoxically, in a device which depends for its definition on symmetry, it is often the asymmetries that emerge from the pattern that drive the argument forward. Part of the task of exegesis is to identify those asymmetries, and to suggest what prompts their introduction.

Another kind of asymmetry in a chiasmus occurs when no clear parallel can be seen between a single pair of elements in an otherwise viable pattern. There are a number of possible explanations:

---

more than one architectural pattern. This means that it is not necessary to discredit one such pattern if there is good support for more than one (Talbert, 'Artistry', p. 363). He also suggests evidence for this in the classics.

121. *Contra* the oversimplified and quite misleading opening aphorism of Breck's paper, 'Form expresses content, therefore content determines form' (Breck, 'Chiasmus', p. 70).

122. Cf. Talbert, 'Artistry', p. 366: 'Form is most definitely the ally of meaning...'

123. At this level, the study of chiasmus is but one element in the much wider study of Pauline rhetoric.

a.   The author has accidentally or unintentionally created the imbalance. It would appear that this could never be proved.

b.   The author has been unable to sustain the pattern. This, of course, is theoretically possible, but may be considered to be unlikely.

c.   Another consideration has over-ridden the need or desire to maintain symmetry throughout. The author may have been distracted, or have gone off at a point.

d.   There may be some cultural aversion to perfect symmetry. There is evidence for this in both Jewish and Graeco-Roman culture.[124]

e.   The asymmetry or imbalance may have been deliberately used as an emphasizing device. 'In this case the emphasized item is highlighted precisely because it does not fit into the expected symmetrical scheme.'[125] The author produces his effect by the unexpected absence of parallelism.

The use of the unexpected is part of classical rhetorical theory, in, for example, *lexis*, where an archaic or rare word is used for its effect, or in the unexpected statement of a *hyperbole*.[126] In an apparently carefully constructed chiasmus, the disturbance in the order caused by a weakly paralleled pair (or even, in the extreme case, a pair in which no parallel can be discerned) draws attention to that pair, and forces examination of the reasons why the writer should allow such intrusion into an otherwise symmetrical pattern.[127]

124. See further G.A. Smith, *The Early Poetry of Israel* (London, 1912), pp. 17-18; Bassett, *Homer*, p. 14; see also the discussion in Talbert, 'Artistry', pp. 361-62. It could be argued that this same principle might be invoked to explain the disturbance of the order of the elements in some patterns. It still seems best at this stage, however, to exclude such examples from consideration because of the intractable problem of defining to what extent disorder is permissible for a pattern still to be viable.

125. So Parunak, 'Typesetting', pp. 165 and 167-68. He describes this phenomenon as the 'broken chiasm'.

126. Cf. Kennedy, *Interpretation*, p. 26.

127. This particular explanation must be used particularly carefully in practice, and confined only to examples where the remaining parallels are very clear indeed, and, possibly also, where the imbalance is near the centre rather than at the distant edges of a chiastic pattern. The danger in its over-use is that it becomes a 'catch-all' for any weakly paralleled elements, lending an unjustified veneer of verisimilitude to a pattern that may not otherwise merit the description 'chiastic'.

Increasing attention is being paid to the argumentative role of figures in rhetorical criticism.[128] In order that there may be a figure present, both a discernible structure (independent of content) is required, and a use that is different from the normal manner of expression, and that, consequently, attracts attention.[129] In addition, a given figure may not always produce the same effect in argumentation.[130] Kennedy is sure that they are functional devices, integral to the purpose of the speaker or writer.[131] There seems little doubt that chiasmus at this intermediate level is pregnant with possibilities in terms of argumentation. What seems more difficult, however, is to predict in advance of the study of a given example what those possibilities are.

1.6. *The Use of Chiasmus in Exegesis*

1.6.1. *The Nature of the Relationship between Corresponding Chiastic Elements*

The ways in which the two halves of a chiasmus relate to one another form the basis for its usefulness in exegesis, and can range from the simple and obvious to the subtle and complex. These can be summarized under three headings.

a. *The Balance of Syntactically Similar Elements*. If repeated a number of times in a chiasmus, the effect can be striking. However, the parallel should be more than trivial or incidental. This means that the balance will usually consist of more than just, say, a final clause balanced by a final clause, with greater significance being lent if there are additional grammatical correspondences (e.g. in word order).

b. *The Balance of Key-words or Catch-words*. The word may be unusual in the particular context and, in order to carry conviction, will not normally occur too frequently within the suggested chiasmus. The same word may be repeated; two different words that share a common root or background may be used; they may occur as opposites, and so

128. See further C. Perelman and L. Olbrechts-Tyteca, *The New Rhetoric: A Treatise on Argumentation* (Notre Dame, 1969), especially at pp. 166-79.
129. Perelman, *Rhetoric*, p. 168.
130. Perelman, *Rhetoric*, p. 172.
131. Kennedy, *Interpretation*, p. 29.

on. Sometimes, a subjective judgment must be made as to what is significant in a given context.[132]

c. *The Balance of Concepts or Ideas*. This is by far the most complex and potentially rewarding relationship in terms of exegesis. The balancing of concepts may be further described in three different ways: repetition (which is sometimes perhaps better described as recapitulation), contrast and expansion (in which one element may complete or complement its partner).[133] In a given pair of elements, more than one of these features may be present. Thus, a brief recapitulation of its chiastic partner may be followed by expansion, and so forth.

In a single chiasmus, there may be elements which show any or all of these different kinds of balance, and an individual pair of elements may be balanced by, say, both syntactical and conceptual features. Indeed, it strengthens a chiasmus when it can be shown that such balancing is occurring at more than one level.

It is in the area of the balancing of ideas where most problems occur, with the major difficulty once more being that of subjective judgment. It is usually inevitable, as Clark recognizes, that, in the case of parallelism of content, there is 'some measure of abstraction' involved. 'Parallelism of content, then, is to be seen as a cline[134] with varying degrees of strength and persuasiveness rather than as a feature which is definitely either present or absent.'[135] Radday suggests that the problem may be more apparent than real 'as long as such differences merely reflect different levels of perception *justifiably* arising out of the underlying texts'.[136]

Having said this, however, it will frequently be found that there is more than one thought expressed in a given element, and more allusions (or even parallels) to it within the whole pattern than those in its chiastic partner.

132. Thus, as was pointed out in 1.4.3 e above, when Lund, *Chiasmus*, pp. 198-99, chooses to highlight 'wives' in Eph. 5.22 and 5.33 in a chiasmus that spans the whole of 5.22-33, he has undoubtedly chosen a key word in the author's vocabulary of the passage, but one that occurs in 5.23, 24, 25 and 28 as well!

133. Cf. Welch, *Chiasmus*, p. 10, who suggests that 'the author may compare, contrast, juxtapose, complement or complete each of the flanking elements'. His five categories can be reduced to three without loss.

134. By which term he means a 'scale'.

135. Clark, 'Criteria', p. 65.

136. Italics mine. Radday, 'Chiasmus', p. 111.

1.6.2. *Chiasmus as an Exegetical Tool*
Four areas of potential interest may emerge, though not necessarily all in the one chiasmus.

a. *The Role of the Centre.* By the very fact of its being the 'turning point' of a chiasmus, ideas deployed there enjoy a special prominence,[137] and attention tends to focus on it.[138] As such, these ideas characteristically may have any of three functions: forming the climax of the argument,[139] indicating its purpose, or acting as an apophthegmatic summary of its contents. In each of these instances this way of looking at the centre may reinforce existing exegetical judgments about the author's purpose, or may suggest the need for re-evaluation, or even re-interpretation, of the author's focus of interest.

b. *The Nature of the Relationship between the Individual Elements.* It may happen that an unusual term in a given element can be better understood by reference to the context of its chiastic partner. Likewise, two chiastically paired elements, linearly separated by a number of others, may reveal that they stand in vivid contrast when examined, one in the light of the other, as chiastic partners.

c. *The Shape of the Argument within the Chiasmus.* The chiastic pattern often reveals the 'skeleton' of the movement of the author's thought, and is, therefore, a useful tool for describing how a case is built up.[140]

d. *The Role of the Chiasmus in the Wider Argument.* It is obvious that a given chiasmus is only one rhetorical unit in a larger context. Particularly if a new focus of interest is suggested as a result of the exegesis of the chiasmus, it is important to see how this relates to the remainder of the epistle.

While there is an intrinsic value, useful in itself, in the identification of

137. So Parunak, 'Typesetting', pp. 165-66.
138. A.B. Spencer, *Paul's Literary Style: A Stylistic and Historical Comparison of II Corinthians 11.16–12.13; Romans 8.9-39 and Philippians 3.2–4.13* (ETSMS; Jackson, MS, 1984), p. 284.
139. So Stock, 'Awareness', p. 23; Welch, *Chiasmus*, p. 10; Bailey, *Poet*, pp. 54-55; *et al.*
140. Though with the caveat again that the chiasmus is frequently overlaid by other parallels and allusions.

a chiasmus, in that it shows how Paul uses patterns and combinations of language and ideas in both formulating and advancing arguments, its importance is greatly enhanced if it brings additional exegetical insights, although it must be recognized that these may vary in significance from example to example.[141]

1.7. Conclusion

It is evident that the current interest in rhetorical analysis has led to a much greater awareness of the use of rhetorical devices in the Pauline letters. Often included as one of the 'figures', more attention is being paid to chiasmus, although to date, in general, 'figures and their functions seem to have little impact on scholars writing *exegetical commentaries* on the NT'.[142] This may have been due, in part at least, to the absence of an accepted methodology.

The way that chiasmus has been investigated has often been less than satisfactory. The reasons for this are both historical and methodological. Historically, for much of this century, the debate about chiasmus has been polarized between the incautious enthusiasm of its exponents[143]

---

141. Typical of an increasing number of studies is Wright's recent paper that seeks to advance the debate on Col. 1.15-20. He argues for an ABBA pattern as its structure, without any need to delete any of its parts, and dealing with the text as it stands. He uses the chiasmus as an exegetical tool and suggests, for example, that his pattern allows for a satisfactory explanation of 'the notorious τῆς ἐκκλησίας of 18b' which 'at a stroke... rehabilitates 18b as part of the original poem'. ('Poetry', pp. 447-48. See p. 457 for further exegetical implications of the chiasmus.) Thompson also has recently argued for the presence of a chiasmus (a modification of a chiastic pattern suggested by Parunak, 'Techniques', p. 436) in Rom. 14.13-21, and used it to highlight the importance to Paul's argument of the concept of ἡ βασιλεία τοῦ θεοῦ, a phrase that Thompson put at the centre of his pattern. (M. Thompson, *Clothed with Christ: The Example and Teaching of Jesus in Romans 12.1–15.13* [JSNTSup, 59; Sheffield, 1991], pp. 200-207.)

142. A.H. Snyman, 'On Studying the Figures (*schēmata*) in the New Testament', *Bib* 69 (1988), pp. 93-107, 98. It should be said, though, that this judgment is becoming less valid year by year.

143. Huge numbers within the Pauline letters alone have been suggested. Welch, *Chiasmus*, pp. 349-51, lists more than 60; Di Marco's list (albeit with some brief comments) covers some 23 pages! ('Chiasmus 4. Teil', pp. 9-32) Many more have been suggested since these works were published. I find many of those that are not simple micro-chiasms to be quite improbable, and many more completely implausible.

and the legitimate scepticism of their critics who, in their negative reactions, may have failed to see the possibilities that might flow from such study.

Methodologically, the absence of accepted criteria for the identification of a chiasmus has greatly hindered advances in the field. The procedures put forward in this study will undoubtedly need further refinement, but they are an attempt to put such definitions, conditions and constraints in place that will bring a degree of objectivity to the subject. By working within defined parameters, it should be possible to develop some well-founded examples of chiasmus, and, therefore, to begin to draw out conclusions of much greater significance for exegesis.

Chapter 2

EPHESIANS 1.3-14 : A NEW APPROACH TO AN OLD PROBLEM

2.1. *Introduction*

2.1.1. *The Question of Authorship*

Despite many years of discussion, the matter of the authorship of Ephesians remains disputed. While it is beyond the scope of this study to rehearse the arguments that point in one direction or another, a working hypothesis must be established, affecting not so much the production of the chiastic outline of the section, as the procedure to be adopted in exegesis. Only if the author is taken as Paul does it becomes permissible to investigate the use of terms in Ephesians through their occurrence in other undisputed Pauline epistles, since there can be no certainty that an otherwise unknown author would use language in the same way as Paul. There are still those who follow Percy's line and argue for the authenticity of Ephesians;[1] others defend Pauline authorship but ascribe some features of its style/theology to the influence of a secretary.[2] At present, however, the consensus is that the epistle is pseudonymous,[3] this case resting on linguistic, syntactical and theological differences[4] between Ephesians and the undisputed Paulines, as well as on the special relationship that Ephesians appears to have with Colossians, and the later point

1. E. Percy, *Die Probleme der Kolosser- und Epheserbriefe* (Lund, 1946); a more recent defence is that of M. Barth, *Ephesians* (AB; 2 vols.; New York, 1974), pp. 36-50.

2. E.g., A. van Roon, *The Authenticity of Ephesians* (Leiden, 1974), pp. 438-39 etc.

3. The position, for example, of A.T. Lincoln, *Ephesians* (WBC, 42; Dallas, 1990), pp. lix-lxxxiii, who also provides a useful bibliography and survey of recent discussion.

4. These include the realized eschatology of Ephesians, the dwindling of the expectation of the imminent parousia, the new value given to marriage, a more thoroughly worked out ecclesiology, and so on.

of view from which the author sometimes appears to be writing. Those defenders of Pauline authorship can usually give some reason for these differences, but their cumulative weight is such that the position adopted in this study is that, on balance, the author of Ephesians is likely to be other than Paul.[5]

2.1.2. *The Problem of Ephesians 1.3-14*

Eph. 1.3-14 presents the commentator with difficulties of significant dimensions in the middle of a chapter of problems. It is apparent that it constitutes part of an introduction to a letter without parallel in the remainder of the New Testament. In most of the Pauline epistles the pre-script is followed immediately by an introductory thanksgiving. While it is true that in 2 Corinthians the thanksgiving is replaced by a eulogia, there is not much similarity to that of Ephesians. Furthermore, in Ephesians the 'eulogia' of 1.3-14 does not replace the more commonly found thanksgiving, but precedes it, as the author turns to thanksgiving in 1.15-23. Were this the only problem, however, Eph. 1.3-14 would be little more than a curiosity—an unusual introduction to a New Testament letter.[6] However, for a long time there has been an ongoing interest in, and debate about, the structure of Eph. 1.3-14, with a striking lack of consensus as to what precisely it constitutes.[7]

Some give up the struggle;[8] some lose patience.[9] However, it can strike yet others quite differently: 'One is struck by the fullness of its tone, by its liturgical majesty, by its rhythm perceptible from beginning to end'.[10]

---

5. But see 7.5 below for a possible link that might be worthy of exploration between the chiasmus in Eph. 1.3-10 and the question of authorship.

6. This is the title of P.T. O'Brien's useful article, 'Ephesians 1; An Unusual Introduction to a New Testament Letter', *NTS* 25 (1979), pp. 504-16.

7. Summed up by O'Brien: 'in the light of the style and structure, how is the pericope to be classified: as a hymn, liturgical piece or prose prayer etc?' ('Introduction', p. 507).

8. 'The twelve verses... baffle our analysis. They are a kaleidoscope of dazzling lights and shifting colours', so, e.g., J.A. Robinson, *St Paul's Epistle to the Ephesians* (London, 2nd edn, 1909), p. 19.

9. For E. Norden, it is 'das monströseste Satzkonglomerat... das mir in griechischer Sprache begegnet ist.' (*Agnostos Theos: Untersuchung zur Formengeschichte religiosöser Rede* [Stuttgart, 4th edn, 1956], p. 253)—a widely quoted comment on Eph. 1.3-14.

10. So C. Masson, *L'épître de Paul aux Ephésians* (Neuchâtel, 1953), p. 149.

Cambier rightly concludes that 'This section is famous for its literary quality and for its doctrinal richness, but it also presents exegetical difficulties that people have often tried to illuminate: those have to do with the strophic division and the grammatical constructions'.[11]

These different observations, however, give a first indication of the problem facing us. There are two closely related questions to be addressed: the matters of the content of the passage and of the form into which that content is shaped. While they cannot be divorced from each other, it is convenient to focus primarily, at this stage, on the *form* of the passage, and to look briefly at some of the many attempted structural analyses of the section.

2.2. *Some Attempted Solutions to the Problem of the Structural Analysis of Ephesians 1.3-14*

2.2.1. *Solutions Involving Hymnic Structures*
This type of approach is of interest in this study only insofar as it begins the process of differentiating the passage from its surroundings. The variety of 'reconstructions', and the complete lack of unanimity about their results may make the whole procedure suspect. Westcott fore-shadowed what was soon to become a popular path for scholars to tread, entitling Eph. 1.3-14, 'A Hymn of Praise to God'.[12] However, having detected a 'rhythmical structure',[13] he made little further use of this. Around the same period Innitzer[14] suggested that the passage had 'a possible poetic form',[15] describing it later as a hymn of praise veiled in the plain dress of rhythmic prose.[16]

Many more attempts have been made to find a convincing hymnic

---

Barth notes Norden's verdict and then becomes engaged in 'an attempt... to make visible the distinctness, the beauty, and the sense of the several limbs of the "monster"' (Barth, *Ephesians*, p. 77). It is interesting, too, that Nestle-Aland also divides 1.3-14 into four separate sentences.

11. J. Cambier, 'La bénédiction d'Eph 1.3-14', *ZNW* 54 (1963), pp. 58-104, 58.

12. B.F. Westcott, *St Paul's Epistle to the Ephesians* (London, 1906), p. 4.

13. Westcott, *Ephesians*, p. 5.

14. T. Innitzer, 'Der "Hymnus" im Epheserbrief 1.3-14', *ZKT* 28 (1904), pp. 612-21.

15. Innitzer, *Hymnus*, p. 616.

16. Innitzer, *Hymnus*, p. 619.

structure.[17] Some have thought that the key to the hymn lay in the participles,[18] although their resulting analyses are not the same. Others look elsewhere for the significant words or phrases around which it seems possible to 'reconstruct' the hymn, such as the recurring phrase εἰς ἔπαινον (τῆς) δόξης.[19] The best analysis, however, may be that of Cambier[20] whose long, and in many ways impressive, article results in a structure that tries to combine the sequence of ideas contained in the passage with an emphasis on its formal characteristics (using the same phrase, primarily, as Fischer: εἰς ἔπαινον δόξης αὐτοῦ). Many of his comments are worth noting, and are relevant for this present study. Thus, he pleads that, before trying to distinguish literary form from content, it will be important to discover the movement and progressive development of the author's thought, writing in a style that lies *between* Greek and Hebrew poetry, so that it cannot be read as a Greek poem. The passage has a rhythmical nature, more pronounced at the beginning than at its end.[21]

Attempts are still being made to find the elusive hymn, with one of

17. Cambier, 'Bénédiction', p. 59 lists at least 11.

18. Including E. Lohmeyer, 'Das Proömium des Epheserbriefs', *TBl* (1926), pp. 120-25; G. Schille, *Frühchristliche Hymnen* (Berlin, 1962), pp. 66-67; M. Dibelius, *An die Kolosser, Epheser an Philemon* (Tübingen, 3rd rev. edn, 1953), p. 60; C. Maurer, 'Der Hymnus von Epheser 1 als Schlüssel zum ganzen Briefe', *EvT* 11 (1951–52), pp. 151-72, 154.

19. E.g., K.M. Fischer, *Tendenz und Absicht des Epheserbriefes* (Göttingen, 1973), pp. 111-12, whose reconstruction is a good example of the difficulties raised by the whole approach. These begin with deciding what constitutes a 'hymn'. For some reason, he feels that 'So wie der Text jetzt vorliegt, kann es kein Hymnus sein' (Fischer, *Tendenz*, p. 112). This does not deter him, however, from an ambitious 'reconstruction' which involves unsupported transpositions in the text, and the complete omission of over 80 of the words of Eph. 1.3-14! (See further C.C. Caragounis, *The Ephesian Mysterion* [Lund, 1977], p. 43, who calls it an 'over-enthusiastic chase'.)

20. Cambier, 'Bénédiction', pp. 58-104.

21. Cambier, 'Bénédiction', p. 60. It is noted, in passing, that at a number of places Cambier finds ABA′ patterns. Of the five he suggests, the clearest example is that in 1.10b, which he portrays as follows: τὰ πάντα | ἐν τῷ Χριστῷ | τὰ ἐπὶ τοῖς οὐρανοῖς καὶ τὰ ἐπὶ τῆς γῆς. Here, it could be argued that τὰ πάντα (A) is clarified and expanded in τὰ ἐπὶ τοῖς οὐρανοῖς καὶ τὰ ἐπὶ τῆς γῆς (A′) ('Bénédiction', p. 83). He himself makes little use of these observations, and they do not seem to play much part in determining the wider structure.

the most recent being that of Grelot.[22] However, Sanders's earlier conclusion is still valid that every attempt to provide a strophic structure for Eph. 1.3-14 fails, and places in very grave doubt the thesis that we have to do here with the quotation of the hymn.[23] Thus, the wide variety of views about such basic matters as the number of strophes, what is primary material and what are secondary additions, and the lack of consensus even on the theme of such a hymn tends to show that, if there is one here, it must have been so altered that its original form is beyond recovery.[24]

2.2.2. *Solutions Focusing on the 'Jewishness' of the Passage*
Another more recent line of inquiry is well represented by Sanders, who draws attention to the 'Jewishness' of the opening lines of Eph. 1.3, 4: 'This is very strictly in the style of the Jewish (particularly Qumranian) and early Christian berachah/hodayah... Also, closing with the phrase εἰς ἔπαινον τῆς δόξης αὐτοῦ hints at a doxology, a fitting close for a berachah.'[25]

22. P. Grelot, 'La structure d'Ephésiens 1,3-14', *RB* 96 (1989), pp. 193-209.

23. J. Sanders, 'Hymnic Elements in Ephesians 1–3', *ZNW* 56 (1965), pp. 214-32, 227. This same conclusion is quoted with approval by Lincoln, *Ephesians*, p. 15.

24. Perhaps more fundamentally, I am not sure how much agreement there is either on what would constitute the definition of an early Christian hymn, or what sort of structure such a 'hymn' would have, anyway! P.T. O'Brien, *Colossians, Philemon* (WBC, 44; Waco, TX, 1982), pp. 32-33, is sure that we should not think in terms of the Greek poetic forms, but of something more akin to that of a creed that might include a wide range of material. Among the criteria that differentiate a passage from its surroundings, stylistic and linguistic considerations may betray the presence of a hymn. See further R.P. Martin, *Carmen Christi: Philippians 2:5-11 in Recent Interpretation and in the Setting of Early Christian Worship* (SNTSMS, 4; Cambridge, 1967), pp. 12-13, and M. Barth, 'Traditions in Ephesians', *NTS* 30 (1984), pp. 3-25, esp. 9-10, who both include chiasmus as one of the rhetorical devices that may be present in a hymn.

25. Sanders, 'Hymnic Elements', p. 224. Others who find such traits include C.L. Mitton, *Ephesians* (NCB; London, 1981), p. 3; J.C. Kirby, *Ephesians, Baptism and Pentecost* (London, 1968), p. 25; R. Schnackenburg, *Der Brief an die Epheser* (EKKNT; Neukirchen-Vluyn, 1982), pp. 43 and 47-48; Cambier, 'Bénédiction', p. 62; Caragounis, *Mysterion*, pp. 39-40 (though he has reservations on how clearly it conforms to Jewish precedents); Barth, *Ephesians*, p. 97; F.F. Bruce, *The Epistles to the Colossians, to Philemon, and to the Ephesians* (NICNT, Grand Rapids, 1984), p. 252; O'Brien, 'Introduction', *passim*; Lincoln, *Ephesians*, pp. 10-12; *et al.*

Kuhn[26] too has drawn attention to the possibility that there might be links between the Semitic style of Ephesians 1–3 in general, and the language of Qumran, including long, loosely joined sentences with ranks of relative clauses and prepositional phrases. Kuhn also observes that, in general terms, there are many more indications of Semitic style in Ephesians than in all the other letters of the Pauline corpus.

There is currently a broad measure of agreement that the passage exhibits Semitic features in both style and content. This may be helpful to the extent that it may finally be possible to abandon attempts to fit the passage into the mould of Greek poetry. It may be best to agree with those like Schnackenburg who see the passage as reflecting Jewish usage.[27]

2.3. *Grammatical Patterns in Ephesians 1.3-10*

It will be argued that there are, within Eph. 1.3-14, some differences of perspective that are significant pointers for the way that the passage will be analysed in this study. These are noted by Barth, who, having concluded that the contents of what he calls the 'great benediction' are primarily the grace, action and the revelation of God, continues, 'Still, v. 7 and the prose vv. 11-13 seem to constitute an exception. They mark a transition from objective presentation to personal application.'[28]

Caragounis, who makes a highly detailed semantic study of the passage, reaches a very similar conclusion:

> Syntactically, the grammatical subject of all the Event clauses till vs10 is God, with the only exception of vs7. But suddenly in vs11, the grammatical subject is changed to 'we' though the constructions become passive... It does imply something... which is of considerable importance in a semantic consideration... Up to vs10, God... was in the center of focus. With vs11, however, God is backgrounded and 'we' is pushed into the foreground.[29]

It will be suggested that the change of perspective after 1.10 has enough significance to justify treating the passage *as though* it consisted of two

---

26. K.G. Kuhn, 'Der Epheserbrief im Lichte der Qumrantexte', *NTS* 7 (1960), pp. 334-46.

27. Schnackenburg, *Epheser*, p. 43.

28. Barth, *Ephesians*, p. 98.

29. Caragounis, *Mysterion*, pp. 34-35. See also, Schille, *Hymnen*, pp. 65-73, who argues that 1.11-13 is a prose interpolation into a pre-Pauline hymn.

sections, dividing after the word γῆς in 1.10,[30] and that 1.7 has a special significance for the proposed chiasmus.

Among all that has been written about this passage, its grammar has frequently been noted as being of interest. O'Brien furnishes a typical list:

> an accumulation of relative clauses, participial and infinitival construc-
> tions, a large collection of prepositional expressions (including 15
> instances of ἐν, most of which are ἐν (τῷ) Χριστῷ or its equivalents, ἐν
> αὐτῷ and ἐν ᾧ) and instances of synonymous words linked together with
> the genitive case, as well as other genitival constructions.[31]

There is, however, much more to be said, particularly in regard to the symmetrical disposition of its verbs and verbal parts.

The change of perspective of 1.7 is highlighted by the fact that this contains the only verb not in the third person in 1.3-10, and the only present indicative active, ἔχομεν. Furthermore, on either side of this are the only two aorist indicative active verbs, ἐχαρίτωσεν (1.6) and ἐπερίσσευσεν (1.8). There are two adverbial aorist participles in the passage, again symmetrically disposed about the 'centre' provided by 1.7, προορίσας in 1.5 and γνωρίσας in 1.9. Symmetry can be main-tained still further by noticing that we can group the only aorist indica-tive middles with the only infinitives: ἐξελέξατο with εἶναι (1.4) and προέθετο (1.9) with ἀνακεφαλαιώσασθαι (1.10). The only verbal parts that remain to be accounted for are those in 1.3 (and the adjectival participle in 1.6 which is clearly functioning as a noun in the phrase ἐν τῷ ἠγαπημένῳ).

The hypothesis is, therefore, that 1.3 constitutes an introduction to a chiasmus, with an unusually high degree of grammatical symmetry that stands independently of content, the structure of which may be repre-sented as follows:

---

30. I shall suggest, with perhaps the majority of scholars, that ἐν αὐτῷ looks forward to 1.11-12 (*Pace* Nestle-Aland; see, too, Lincoln, *Ephesians*, pp. 17-18, who argues that it rightly belongs to 1.10 to make the whole phrase stand in apposi-tion to, and be epexegetic of, τὰ πάντα ἐν Χριστῷ), but for the sake of conve-nience the first section will be referred to as '1.3-10', and the second as '1.11-14'.

31. O'Brien, 'Introduction', p. 506; Barth, *Ephesians*, p. 100 has a similiar list.

Introduction

1.3 Εὐλογητὸς ὁ θεὸς καὶ πατὴρ τοῦ κυρίου ἡμῶν Ἰησοῦ Χριστοῦ, ὁ εὐλογήσας ἡμᾶς ἐν πάσῃ εὐλογίᾳ πνευματικῇ ἐν τοῖς ἐπουρανίοις ἐν Χριστῷ,

A { {A₁ 1.4 καθὼς ἐξελέξατο ἡμᾶς ἐν αὐτῷ πρὸ καταβολῆς κόσμου,

{A₂ εἶναι ἡμᾶς ἁγίους καὶ ἀμώμους κατενώπιον αὐτοῦ (ἐν ἀγάπῃ),

B   (   ) 1.5 προορίσας ἡμᾶς εἰς υἱοθεσίαν διὰ Ἰησοῦ Χριστοῦ εἰς αὐτόν, κατὰ τὴν εὐδοκίαν τοῦ θελήματος αὐτοῦ,

C   1.6 εἰς ἔπαινον δόξης τῆς χάριτος αὐτοῦ ἧς ἐχαρίτωσεν ἡμᾶς ἐν τῷ ἠγαπημένῳ.

D   1.7 Ἐν ᾧ ἔχομεν τὴν ἀπολύτρωσιν διὰ τοῦ αἵματος αὐτοῦ, τὴν ἄφεσιν τῶν παραπτωμάτων,

C′   1.7c κατὰ τὸ πλοῦτος τῆς χάριτος αὐτοῦ, 1.8 ἧς ἐπερίσσευσεν εἰς ἡμᾶς (ἐν πάσῃ σοφίᾳ καὶ φρονήσει)

B′   (   ) 1.9 γνωρίσας ἡμῖν τὸ μυστήριον τοῦ θελήματος αὐτοῦ, κατὰ τὴν εὐδοκίαν αὐτοῦ

A′ { {A₁′ ἣν προέθετο ἐν αὐτῷ 1.10 εἰς οἰκονομίαν τοῦ πληρώματος τῶν καιρῶν,

{A₂′ ἀνακεφαλαιώσασθαι τὰ πάντα ἐν τῷ Χριστῷ, τὰ ἐπὶ τοῖς οὐρανοῖς καὶ τὰ ἐπὶ τῆς γῆς·

The beginning and ending of each element emerges from the 'flow of syntax' of the passage.[32]

There may actually be further degrees of symmetry within the passage. Thus both B and B′ end with similar κατά phrases, and both C and C′ consist of phrases followed by relative clauses introduced by ἧς.

This leads to the hypothesis of a final chiastic pattern that may be represented as follows:[33]

---

32. This useful phrase is Lincoln's (*Ephesians*, pp. 15-16). The phrases ἐν ἀγάπῃ and ἐν πάσῃ σοφίᾳ καὶ φρονήσει are presented in brackets because of the possibility of their being construed as the last phrases in these clauses, or as the first phrase of the subsequent clauses. Any conclusion as to where the phrases properly belong does not affect my argument at this stage, and will be dealt with later.

33. For convenience, a copy of each of the principal chiastic patterns proposed in chs. 2–6 is included in the Appendix at the end of this study.

Introduction

         1.3 Εὐλογητὸς ὁ θεὸς καὶ πατὴρ τοῦ κυρίου ἡμῶν Ἰησοῦ
         Χριστοῦ, ὁ εὐλογήσας ἡμᾶς ἐν πάσῃ εὐλογίᾳ πνευματικῇ
         ἐν τοῖς ἐπουρανίοις ἐν Χριστῷ,

{A₁   1.4 καθὼς ἐξελέξατο ἡμᾶς ἐν αὐτῷ πρὸ καταβολῆς
A {   κόσμου,
{A₂   εἶναι ἡμᾶς ἁγίους καὶ ἀμώμους κατενώπιον αὐτοῦ
         (ἐν ἀγάπῃ),

{B₁   (   ) 1.5 προορίσας ἡμᾶς εἰς υἱοθεσίαν διὰ Ἰησοῦ
B {   Χριστοῦ εἰς αὐτόν,
{B₂   κατὰ τὴν εὐδοκίαν τοῦ θελήματος αὐτοῦ,

{C₁   1.6 εἰς ἔπαινον δόξης τῆς χάριτος αὐτοῦ
C {
{C₂   ἧς ἐχαρίτωσεν ἡμᾶς ἐν τῷ ἠγαπημένῳ.

D   1.7 Ἐν ᾧ ἔχομεν τὴν ἀπολύτρωσιν διὰ τοῦ αἵματος
         αὐτοῦ, τὴν ἄφεσιν τῶν παραπτωμάτων,

{C₁′   1.7c κατὰ τὸ πλοῦτος τῆς χάριτος αὐτοῦ,
C′ {
{C₂′   1.8 ἧς ἐπερίσσευσεν εἰς ἡμᾶς (ἐν πάσῃ σοφίᾳ καὶ
         φρονήσει)

{B₁′   (   ) 1.9 γνωρίσας ἡμῖν τὸ μυστήριον τοῦ θελήματος
B′ {   αὐτοῦ,
{B₂′   κατὰ τὴν εὐδοκίαν αὐτοῦ

{A₁′   ἣν προέθετο ἐν αὐτῷ 1.10 εἰς οἰκονομίαν τοῦ
A′ {   πληρώματος τῶν καιρῶν,
{A₂′   ἀνακεφαλαιώσασθαι τὰ πάντα ἐν τῷ Χριστῷ,
         τὰ ἐπὶ τοῖς οὐρανοῖς καὶ τὰ ἐπὶ τῆς γῆς·

It is possible, of course, that this pattern has been *imposed* on the passage, and that it is no more than accidental that it has this level of symmetry. However, such numbers of *coincidences* are unlikely in a passage of such length and showing such a high degree of syntactical symmetry. It seems to be just as reasonable to postulate the presence of *design* (which, in turn, may theoretically be conscious or unconscious on the part of the author),[34] and, indeed, a design through which the passage

34. It is very difficult to conceive of any procedure that could be set up to test whether these chiasms are the product of conscious design, or are 'felt' in some way by an author for whom this style of writing is 'natural'. Simple micro-chiasms present little problem in this regard, but it appears to me to be more likely that chiasms

begins to reveal a markedly elegant grammatical pattern that has not been shown before.

Indeed, this conclusion may be further reinforced when the only four sub-components of the chiasmus that contain no part of a verb are examined. Two of them begin with an identical prepositional phrase—κατὰ τὴν εὐδοκίαν (B_2 and B_2'), and the other two end with an identical genitival phrase—τῆς χάριτος αὐτοῦ (C_1 and C_1').

Once this basic framework has been established, a number of other parallels may be seen. The problem now becomes one of distinguishing those which may be significant from those which are fortuitous, or which are required by the rules of grammar. The following suggestions are offered as being worthy of consideration:

a. In each of the components of the chiasmus containing part of a verb, the position of the verb in its clause is exactly the same in both of its occurrences. (This only holds true if both the bracketed phrases belong to the clauses in which they are presently placed, or, indeed, if they are both moved to their alternative positions. Again, exegesis may clarify this.)

b. There may be a deliberate patterning of the way in which some of the components of the chiastic structure end. Thus, A_1 and A_1' both end with nouns in the genitive; B_2 and B_2' both end with αὐτοῦ; C_1 and C_1' both end in the phrase τῆς χάριτος αὐτοῦ; C_2 and C_2' both end in phrases with ἐν and the dative.[35]

Such an analysis draws attention to the exceptionally high order of syntactical symmetry present in this passage, a symmetry that is confined to 1.4-10, and is markedly absent from 1.11-14.

The presence of chiastic structures in the Pauline letters in which the chiasmus is formed by parts of speech has already been identified by Jeremias, who notes a considerable number of examples in which 'the

of the length and relative complexity dealt with in this study are the product of a particular compositional technique.

35. Again, these observations are dependent on precisely how the bracketed phrases are assigned. Without prejudging the exegesis, I simply note that the highest degree of symmetry is attained with respect to the endings of the various elements when the two 'moveable' phrases are construed as components ending their respective clauses. There is, however, no reason for expecting the passage to exhibit that highest degree of symmetry.

disposition of a part of a sentence varies chiastically according to rhetorical principles'.[36] However, as has been seen, his examples are very simple and usually provide no more than an ABBA pattern, based on a sentence which may have, for instance, the word order: first subject—first verb—second verb—second subject. It is this same *principle* that appears to be operating in Eph. 1.4-10, in a somewhat analogous fashion, but at a length and level of complexity that none of his examples attain.

2.4. *Further Investigation of the Chiasmus within Ephesians 1.3-10*

The next step in the study of this chiasmus is more complex. The hypothetical chiastic pattern must now be tested to see the degree, if any, to which the content corresponds to the form. This will involve a reasonably detailed examination of the passage, in an effort to discern the flow of the author's thought.

2.4.1. *Introduction*
Eph. 1.3 has already been described as the frame passage to the chiasmus. There is now quite a wide consensus that this verse begins with a phrase (Εὐλογητὸς ὁ θεός) that is steeped in the Jewish tradition of the *berakah*,[37] a prayer ascribing blessing to God. Rooted in the Old Testament (e.g. Gen. 14.19; 24.27; 1 Kgs 8.14-61), found in the Old Testament Apocrypha (Tob. 13.1–14.1), used in the Synagogue and in daily life,[38] the *berakah* is an outburst of praise and prayer. There are other examples of it in the New Testament (2 Cor. 1.3, 4; 1 Pet. 1.3-5), and in its opening phrases, at least, the author is using language that would be familiar to anyone of Jewish background. Indeed, it may be that the earliest Christians took over this form for use in epistolary introductions.[39] The threefold use of the cognates εὐλογητός... εὐλογήσας... εὐλογία[40] lends a particular emphasis to the idea of blessing. It is what this spiritual blessing encompasses that will be made explicit in the subsequent verses.

The phrase ἐν τοῖς ἐπουρανίοις is a rather striking one that, in this

36. Jeremias, 'Chiasmus', p. 145.
37. See 2.2.2 above.
38. See Kirby, *Ephesians*, pp. 87-89 for examples.
39. So Furnish, *2 Corinthians*, p. 116.
40. Cambier, 'Bénédiction', p. 62; Barth, *Ephesians*, p. 77; *et al.*

precise form, occurs only in Ephesians (at 1.3, 20; 2.6; 3.10; 6.12), although ἐπουράνιος occurs fourteen other times in the New Testament in other contexts. There are two problems associated with it: viz., whether it is masculine or neuter, and whether it is to be distinguished from οὐράνιος in meaning. The majority view is that it points to blessing 'in the heavenly places' rather than 'among the heavenly beings'. Schlier's view of the ἐπουράνια, as comprising a number of heavens where various powers are found, is less likely, since this seems to be too dependent on gnostic cosmological theories that belong to a later age,[41] or to Odeberg's idea that 'ἐπουράνιος includes that which elsewhere is expressed by that term *and* the term signifying its opposite, viz. ἐπίγειος'.[42] This latter idea seems somewhat fanciful, and has not attracted much support. Mitton has an interesting translation of the same phrase as 'in God's heavenly counsels', but without presenting any evidence for such a paraphrase.[43] It may be best to conclude that there is no fundamental difference between ἐπουράνιος and οὐράνιος.[44]

Finally, this verse has the first of the many uses of the much-discussed phrase ἐν Χριστῷ (or ἐν αὐτῷ or ἐν ᾧ referring to Christ) in the passage. In this case believers appear to be blessed in Christ, ἐν Χριστῷ being read along with ὁ εὐλογήσας. Barth's explanation is attractive, that in Gen. 18.18 where 'in Abraham' all the nations of the earth will be blessed, 'Abraham is at the same time the beneficiary, the beginning, the model and the instrument of the blessing in which all nations are to participate'.[45] This seems to cover well the range of the role of Christ portrayed by the various usages of the phrases ἐν Χριστῷ and so forth in the remainder of the passage.

Eph. 1.3 serves its purpose well of acting as an introduction to what follows. It sets the stage for the development of the concept of 'the sum of all that is called spiritual blessing' (from ἐν πάσῃ εὐλογίᾳ πνευματικῇ, 1.3). While some underline the Trinitarian nature of the verse,[46] this may be better seen as a function of later theological

---

41. H. Schlier, *Christus und die Kirche im Epheserbrief* (BHT, 6; Tübingen, 1930), pp. 5-6 and also in *Der Brief an die Epheser: Ein Kommentar* (Düsseldorf, 7th edn, 1971), pp. 45-48.

42. H. Odeberg, *The View of the Universe in the Epistle to the Ephesians* (Lund, 1934), p. 9.

43. Mitton, *Ephesians*, p. 47.

44. So too Lincoln, *Ephesians*, pp. 20-21.

45. Barth, *Ephesians*, p. 78.

46. E.g., Cambier, 'Bénédiction', p. 62; J.R.W. Stott, *The Message of*

development than as part of the author's purpose. It is the construction of the platform from which to launch into the theme, and as such may provide a good example of a frame passage.[47]

2.4.2. A (1.4) and A' (1.9b, 10)

The chiasmus itself is constructed in a sweeping arc that runs from past eternity to future eternity. It begins in the eternal counsels of God (πρὸ καταβολῆς κόσμου, A₁, the only occurrence of this phrase in the Pauline letters) and ends in those same eternal counsels (οἰκονομία τοῦ πληρώματος τῶν καιρῶν, A₁').[48]

'God' is the implied subject of both ἐξελέξατο (A₁) and προέθετο (A₁'), with both verbs clearly conveying the idea of God's *sovereign* action. Believers in A₁ are chosen 'in Christ'. Bruce neatly links this verse with A₁' by observing that 'As the fulfilment is experienced "in Christ", so it is in him that the purpose is achieved'.[49]

In A₁' it is possible to predicate ἐν αὐτῷ to προέθετο, or to the prepositional phrase which follows it (εἰς οἰκονομίαν τοῦ πληρώματος τῶν καιρῶν). Is the plan (οἰκονομία) a plan 'in him', or is the action implied by προτίθημι an action 'in him'? The word order may play a part in this, and ἐν αὐτῷ should perhaps be linked closely with προέθετο.

But what is the meaning of προτίθημι? Most commentators follow similar paths and translate it with a term like 'set forth',[50] 'arranged, established'.[51] Emphasizing the middle voice 'to set before oneself' leads to a translation like 'planned',[52] but Barth approaches it differently, wanting to give the prefix its full temporal force. He suggests that the same word in Rom. 1.13 means 'to resolve' and in Rom. 3.25, 'to fore-ordain, appoint, set forth, offer'.[53] Here, however, he maintains that the context strongly suggests that the temporal sense is in the foreground.

Ephesians: God's New Society (BST; Leicester; 1979), p. 33; *et al.*

47. See 1.4.2 above.

48. Caragounis, *Mysterion*, p. 61: 'The eulogy has spanned the great temporal gap from eternity past to eternity future'; Bruce, *Ephesians*, p. 254 notes that the passage moves 'from eternal election to eternal glory'.

49. Bruce, *Ephesians*, p. 254.

50. Mitton, *Ephesians*, p. 55.

51. Schnackenburg, *Epheserbrief*, p. 57, who uses *festsetzen*.

52. Bruce, *Ephesians*, p. 261.

53. This is, of course, a controversial translation in the context of Rom. 3.25— see further, for example, Dunn, *Romans*, p. 170.

He draws attention to the four other occurrences of πρό as a preposition or prefix in Eph. 1.3-14 (although there are only two in 1.3-10: 1.4 and 1.5). He concludes that it should be possible to render the phrase in terms of God's favour being *set first* in Christ.[54] If this interpretation can be sustained, there would be a marked correlation in content between A_1 and A_1'. Due account must be taken of the charge of circular reasoning in the premise that there are strong temporal overtones in A and A', and then using these temporal overtones to suggest, with Barth, that προ- be given its full temporal weight. However, in this chiasmus care has been taken to show that the basic structure stands on the foundation of the grammatical symmetry of the passage, and it is argued, therefore, that it is legitimate to strengthen the links between A and A' by following Barth's line.[55]

Thus, A_1 makes the statement that believers have been chosen in Christ, and that this has happened in past eternity (before the foundation of the world). Then, if such an interpretation is sustainable, in A_1', the author affirms that God's favour has been set 'first'[56] in Christ as the plan for the fullness of time, calling to mind a future eternity. Christ thus becomes the exemplary elect, and election becomes first and essentially the election of the Son by the Father;[57] cf. 1 Pet. 1.20, and perhaps Lk. 9.35, 23.35 and the interesting comment in *1 Clem.* 64.1: 'God elected...the Lord Jesus Christ and through him us for his own people'. The following translation of 1.9b-10a is, therefore, tentatively offered: 'according to his favour which he first set in him[58] as a plan for the fullness of time...'

The parallelism between A_1 and A_1' is not dependent on such a translation of προέθετο, since it lies basically in the concepts of God's sovereign action, in the first instance in the past, and in the second for the future, and both accomplished in some sense ἐν αὐτῷ.

The phrase in A_1' (1.10a), εἰς οἰκονομίαν τοῦ πληρώματος τῶν καιρῶν, is a significant one. Barth[59] suggests that the only meaning for

54. Barth, *Ephesians*, pp. 76, 85.

55. Although I do not agree with Barth's paraphrase of 1.9-10, which, it seems to me, may be a case of translation, and the ensuing exegesis, being made to serve dogmatic presuppositions.

56. In the temporal understanding of the word, rather than understanding it as 'first in rank'—although this, too, is true in more general terms.

57. See Barth, *Ephesians*, p. 86.

58. Or, perhaps, 'on him'?

59. In a detailed study, Barth, *Ephesians*, pp. 86-88.

οἰκονομία of which Paul would be aware would be that of 'administration' or 'stewardship', based on the LXX and other Pauline usage in Col. 1.25 and 1 Cor. 4.1, 2, but this goes against his own suggestion that we are here dealing with pre-Pauline material,[60] and assumes that the same author was responsible for all the passages.

Barth advances a number of reasons against the usual translation of 'plan'. He suggests that the text would read κατὰ οἰκονομίαν rather than εἰς οἰκονομίαν if a fixed plan were meant. This is not clear, however. Indeed, in order to accommodate his own translation, Barth himself has to take considerable liberties with prepositions in the text (thus, ἐν αὐτῷ in 1.10 becomes '*under* him'!) εἰς *is* an appropriate preposition for a plan in the course of execution: God's favour first placed in Christ *leads towards* (εἰς, with the indicated end) the οἰκονομία.[61]

The traditional rendering of 'plan' is to be preferred, despite its relatively late use in this sense. The election of Christ is the essential prerequisite for God's plan; it is that which makes it possible or feasible. In this context εἰς οἰκονομίαν becomes an appropriate and comprehensible phrase, and 'the fullness of time' points to the occasion of the consummation of the purposes of God. It lies in the future as 'before the foundation of the world' lies in the past.

But what is the content of this 'plan'? That Eph. 1.9, 10 has eschatological and cosmological overtones can hardly be denied,[62] but there may be a danger in reading back into this present context ideas from later in the epistle, perhaps notably from 3.9-11, and to a lesser extent from 1.21-23. It will be suggested later in this chapter that there may be some evidence that Eph. 1.3-10 was actually pre-formed material, the language of which is sometimes developed and used in the rest of the epistle in a way that may not have been part of the intention of its original author. Although the evidence for this must wait, it is preferable, in the first instance, to understand the 'plan' in the immediate context of the chiasmus, rather than in the light of the rest of the letter.

Thus, the content of the plan may be the bringing to fruition of that which is specified for the first time in A, the choosing of those who believe ('us') to be holy and blameless before him, a plan for 'us' that will be completed in the fullness of time, but that was

---

60. Barth, *Ephesians*, p. 79.
61. Cf. BAGD on εἰς, para. 4d.
62. Barth, *Ephesians*, p. 87, and most commentators, and seen most clearly in the phrase τὰ ἐπὶ τοῖς οὐρανοῖς καὶ τὰ ἐπὶ τῆς γῆς, epexegetic of τὰ πάντα.

formulated before the foundation of the world, a plan for the uniting of τὰ πάντα, including humankind, to God in Christ.[63]

Some of the other more important words and phrases of A₂ and A₂′ ought to be considered briefly. It has been argued by some that the phrase ἁγίους καὶ ἀμώμους is tautological.[64] Even if it is, however, the effect of the whole is to stress the believers' standing before God by setting the positive concept of holiness (belonging to God) alongside the negative concept of being without blame or blemish.

It is extremely difficult to come to any firm conclusion about the most satisfactory meaning of ἀνακεφαλαιώσασθαι. It occurs here as the aorist *middle* infinitive. However, some translations apparently treat it as passive,[65] although it is true that there may be, on occasion, little difference between them. Its only other occurrence in the New Testament is at Rom. 13.9, where again it is in the middle, and where it is possible to give that voice some weight. The translation 'to sum up' seems clearly appropriate in this context. To argue on the basis of authorship that it should have the same meaning in Ephesians as in Romans may be to make too many assumptions. Barth[66] suggests that the prefix ἀνα- has, in fact, little force, and therefore that there is little difference between the simple and compound forms. This would lead to those translations like 'to sum up', 'to gather up' or 'to unite'.[67]

Despite such agreement, however, there may be more to be said. The term ἀνακεφαλαιόω plays a significant part in Irenaeus's complex theory of recapitulation. It is perhaps as a result of this theory as much as anything else that the Old Latin versions and the Vulgate translate it as 'recapitulare' or 'instaurare', 'to renew, restore'. There is obviously a theological attractiveness in the wider context of Ephesians to suggest that in 1.10 we are dealing with a doctrine of the renewal of, say, broken relationships between individuals, and more importantly, between individuals and God. Such a restoration may, indeed, be in view in, for example, Col. 1.20.

---

63. It is interesting to note, but beyond the scope of this study to discuss, the possible universalistic overtones of this statement. Cf. Sanders, 'Hymnic Elements', pp. 230-31, for example.

64. So Cambier, 'Bénédiction', p. 71; *et al.*

65. E.g., Barth, *Ephesians*, p. 76: 'All things are to be comprehended...'

66. Barth, *Ephesians*, pp. 89-92.

67. So RSV, NEB, C.J. Ellicott, *Ephesians* (London, 1855), pp. 12-13; Robinson, *Ephesians*, p. 145; Westcott, *Ephesians*, p. 14; Mitton, *Ephesians*, p. 55; Bruce, *Ephesians*, p. 261.

One other approach to ἀνακεφαλαιόω that has a little support is worth noting. This is that strand of thought that sees the term as being derived from κεφαλή (head) rather than from κεφάλαιον (main point, sum). Despite the strictures of those who deny that ἀνακεφαλαιόω is etymologically derived from κεφαλή, it may not be adequate to reduce this to terms of black and white. Schlier[68] certainly does argue persuasively that the concept of headship has a prominent place in ἀνακεφαλαιόω as it is used in Eph. 1.10.[69] Ellicott[70] is wrong in suggesting that the context of this verse is atonement rather than sovereignty—the sovereignty of God is very much to the fore in both A and A′. As such, overtones of headship are not at all out of place. Schlier recognizes the ambiguity of the term, and suggests that Eph. 1.22[71] can shed light on its use in 1.10. This is possible even if 1.3-10 had a prior literary history, because it might indicate that the author of Ephesians at least understood 1.10 in this fashion.

To some extent, the difficulties with ἀνακεφαλαιόω are difficulties of English rather than of Greek. With considerable hesitation, it is translated here as 'unite', although still with the feeling that the idea of 'headship' is not too far away. In English a choice has to be made between 'alternatives', both of which are held without tension in Greek. However unsatisfactory it may be, we may well have to live with the ambiguity of the term.

It has been suggested that there is a definite and marked parallelism of content between A and A′—God's sovereign action in past eternity in A, and in a future eternity in A′, his choosing 'us' in Christ before the foundation of the world, and the setting first of God's favour in Christ resulting in the plan for the fullness of time. It is clear, though, that the parallelism described thus far is between A_1 and A_1'. There is, however, also parallelism between A_2 and A_2' insofar as both describe the end result of God's action. Indeed, it is essentially the same conclusion described, in the first, in terms of the believers' standing before him, and in the second, in the more metaphysical terminology of the outcome of his plan—although it has been suggested that the content of that plan is as well described by A_2 as by A_2'. It is possible that there may be further evidence elsewhere in Ephesians of a theological connection between A_2

68. Schlier, *Epheser*, pp. 64-65.
69. *Contra* Schnackenburg, *Epheser*, p. 58; *et al.*
70. Ellicott, *Ephesians*, pp. 12-13.
71. καὶ αὐτὸν ἔδωκεν κεφαλὴν ὑπὲρ πάντα τῇ ἐκκλησίᾳ...

and A₂', notably in Eph. 3.8-12 where there are many echoes of the vocabulary of 1.4-10 (χάρις ...πλοῦτος τοῦ Χριστοῦ...οἰκονομία...μυστη-
ρίου...τὰ πάντα...γνωρισθῇ...ἐπουρανίοις ...σοφία...πρόθεσιν). It
will be suggested later that this in itself is noteworthy, but the point here
is the way in which the outworked purpose of God is linked with the
making known of his wisdom to the 'principalities and powers' (3.10)
and to our access to God's presence through Jesus (3.12).

The Position of ἐν ἀγάπῃ. No consensus has been reached by those
who assign ἐν ἀγάπῃ one way or the other on the basis of rhythmic or
strophic considerations. Some can be found who assign it to 1.4[72] and
some who assign it to 1.5.[73]

As with so many other aspects of this paragraph, the choice is not just
the 'simple' one of assigning it to A or B, but involves the related
question of identifying its antecedent if it does belong to A. Thus, are
believers 'chosen' ἐν ἀγάπῃ, or are they to be 'holy and blameless' ἐν
ἀγάπῃ? This part of the problem, however, will not arise if it is decided
that the phrase belongs to προορίσας in B.

There is least support for taking it with ἐξελέξατο. A number of the
modern scholars admit that it is possible, but choose one of the other
options.[74] On the other hand, there is good historical support for linking
it to προορίσας in B,[75] although its function here must be questioned.

Thus, it is difficult to follow the reasoning of those like Ellicott who
think that ἐν ἀγάπῃ reveals 'the transcendent principle of love which
informed the προορίσας of God'. It may be more convincing to argue
that the principle of love informed the original *choosing* by God! What
other motive could God have had for choosing 'us', other than that of
love? Once having been chosen in love to be holy and blameless before
him, being destined to sonship is the way in which this end is to be
achieved. It is, however, quite conceivable that the author has introduced
a deliberate ambiguity here, seeing love as being the key to *all* of God's
sovereign action, and strategically positioning the phrase at a point

72. So, e.g., Robinson, *Ephesians*, p. 143.
73. So, e.g., Schlier, *Epheser*, p. 52 n. 2.
74. Barth, *Ephesians*, pp. 79-80, as an example.
75. Among the Fathers, Theodore, Chrysostom and Origen; Ellicott, *Ephesians*,
p. 6; T.K. Abbott, *A Critical and Exegetical Commentary on the Epistles to the
Ephesians and to the Colossians* (ICC; Edinburgh, 1897), p. 8; Schnackenburg,
Epheser, pp. 45, 52; Cambier, 'Bénédiction', pp. 71-74.

where it equally looks back to the clause with ἐξελέξατο and forward to προορίσας. As the element of the chiasmus that deals with God's choosing and its outcome spills over into the element dealing with foreordination and its results, the phrase ἐν ἀγάπῃ stands, at the same time ending the first and introducing the second, uniquely connected to neither, but broadly connected to both.

Others, however, link it with 'holy and blameless'.[76] Such an understanding makes it likely that it is the believers' love that is in view, rather than God's love for them.[77] This, indeed, may be the most satisfactory option, with Lincoln suggesting that love is part of the goal that election is intended to achieve in those it embraces.[78]

2.4.3. *B (1.5) and B′ (1.9a)*

In this pair of elements the common theme is that of the privileges that come from the believers' special relationship with God. In the opening phrase of B_1, προορίσας ἡμᾶς, those in view are described as being 'destined, ordained' or 'predestined, preordained'. The precise choice of English translation for, and the implications of, προορίσας are both very fertile ground for theological discussion. This, however, need not occupy us.

There is a very considerable literature on μυστήριον in $B_1′$.[79] In the context of this study the relevant question is what the author means to convey by using the term, which may be translated as 'mystery' or 'secret'. For the great majority, it refers in some way to God's plan, although not all members of the group understand that plan in the same way.[80] In his detailed study of μυστήριον in Ephesians, Caragounis says that in this passage it is 'the all-comprehending eschatological purpose of God as made known to the author...'[81] For Lincoln[82] it is the summing

---

76. Westcott, *Ephesians*, p. 9; Robinson, *Ephesians*, p. 143; Bruce, *Ephesians*, p. 256 (perhaps); Barth, *Ephesians*, pp. 79-80; Lincoln, *Ephesians*, p. 17.

77. See, e.g., Bruce, *Ephesians*, p. 256.

78. Lincoln, *Ephesians*, p. 17.

79. See the extensive bibliography in Caragounis's monograph, for example.

80. So, e.g., Robinson, *Ephesians*, p. 31; Schnackenburg, *Epheser*, pp. 56-57; Schlier, *Epheser*, pp. 61-62; Mitton, *Ephesians*, pp. 54-55; F. Mussner, *Der Brief an die Epheser* (ÖTKNT, 10; Gütersloh, 1982), p. 47.

81. Caragounis, *Mysterion*, p. 141. C.E. Arnold, *Ephesians: Power and Magic. The Concept of Power in Ephesians in Light of its Historical Setting* (SNTSMS; Cambridge, 1989), pp. 126ff., reaches a similar conclusion.

82. Lincoln, *Ephesians*, p. 30.

up of all things in Christ. Lincoln regards the whole phrase κατὰ τὴν εὐδοκίαν...τῶν καιρῶν as qualifying γνωρίσας, and ἀνακεφα-λαιώσασθαι κτλ. as being appositional to, and therefore explicatory of, τὸ μυστήριον τοῦ θελήματος αὐτοῦ. This is unlikely because of the considerable distance between them.

It may be, however, that an unwarranted assumption has been made in directly linking the ideas of the mystery and the plan for the fullness of time. Keeping close to the context, the author makes it clear that the mystery is in fact the 'mystery *of his will'*. The syntax of the passage demands that it is not the *mystery* that is 'put forward' or 'set first' (προέθετο) in Christ, but his *purpose* (εὐδοκία, the natural antecedent of ἣν in 1.9), and it is this purpose that is subsequently described as the plan for the fullness of time.

At the same time, it must be recognized that there is, in some sense, a link between (a) the mystery and God's will (τὸ μυστήριον τοῦ θελήματος αὐτοῦ), (b) the fact that he has made known that mystery according to his purpose (γνωρίσας...κατὰ τὴν εὐδοκίαν αὐτοῦ) and (c) this purpose being legitimately described as the plan for the fullness of time. This is not the same, however, as concluding that the content of the mystery *is* that plan.

It is possible that the chiastic pattern may produce another suggestion for the content of the mystery from the balancing element of B_1': the fact of believers being destined for adoption through Christ Jesus. This, of course, is *linearly* distant, but *chiastically* close. In this case the phrase 'the mystery of his will' in B′ is used to recapitulate B, with the new thought added that this amazing action has been made known.

There is significant further evidence for this viewpoint from later use of μυστήριον in Ephesians (once again with the caveat that the idea will be developed that Eph. 1.3-10 may be preformed material used for the Ephesian author's own ends). The passage in question is the intriguing Eph. 3.1-6, where μυστήριον occurs twice. 'Paul' first claims that the mystery was made known to him (3.3, ἐγνωρίσθη μοι τὸ μυστήριον) in language reminiscent of 1.9, but now clearly goes on to define the μυστήριον in terms of the Gentiles being fellow-heirs (3.6, συγκληρονόμα).[83] In 3.1-6 he thus links the ideas of the privileges of

83. Meeks, *Urban Christians*, p. 168 etc. consistently sees the mystery as being 'the uniting of Jew and Gentile in one household'; see further the discussion in 3.6 below. Arnold, *Ephesians*, p. 127, argues that this is too restrictive a view of the content of the mystery, seeking instead an understanding of μυστήριον that covers

sonship first found in B_1 with that of the μυστήριον first found in B_1'.[84]

The term μυστήριον occurs for a third time in Eph. 3.9, where it is found specifically linked to the idea of the 'plan' in the phrase ἡ οἰκονομία τοῦ μυστηρίου, but now with a cosmic dimension to it. The terms οἰκονομία and μυστήριον are being used in a combination that is not seen in the original chiasmus. Even if it were to be assumed that the content of the mystery is best described by the 'plan for the fullness of time' (although I have reservations about this), then this is not the same as describing the *mystery* as having a *plan*. In other words, the two terms from the chiasmus are now combined in a way that allows them to carry implications that may not be present in their original use in the chiasmus.

Finally, in this section B_2 and B_2' ought to be examined briefly. The immediate parallelism is obvious, insofar as both begin with the identical phrase κατὰ τὴν εὐδοκίαν. Whereas in B_2 this is followed by τοῦ θελήματος αὐτοῦ (which, in the corresponding element B', actually forms part of B_1'), it is completed by the simple genitive αὐτοῦ in B_2'. The two terms εὐδοκία and θέλημα are close in meaning although the former may carry warm connotations that the latter lacks, so that God's θέλημα cannot be thought of as being something coldly arbitrary.[85] Outside of this chiasmus εὐδοκία does not occur frequently in Paul,[86] whereas θέλημα is widely used.[87] The two terms are used nowhere else in the Pauline corpus in close proximity, which makes their repeated conjunction in B and B' stand out even more. When θέλημα is used in Eph. 1.11, it is in conjunction with βουλή. Abbott[88] stresses the similarity

all its uses in Colossians and Ephesians. Such a procedure, however, makes assumptions about authorship and consistency of usage between possibly different authors that would be difficult to justify.

84. I am not, however, assuming that the 'us' of 1.3-10 describes both Jews and Gentiles. The right to inheritance, of course, is a major consequence of sonship. In B_1, Bruce (*Ephesians*, p. 257) calls adoption 'the believer's incorporation into the family of God'. It is an expression of the ultimate blessing, the final confirmation of having being chosen. (Arnold, *Ephesians*, p. 128, suggests, but does not develop the idea, that the concepts of election and the mystery are 'closely linked'.) Without this adoption, there is no possibility of being holy and blameless before him. The central element D will reveal how this is anchored in historical action.

85. Barth, *Ephesians*, p. 81; so, too, Abbott, *Ephesians*, p. 9; *et al.*

86. Only 4 other times: Rom. 10.1; Phil. 1.15; 2.13; 2 Thess. 1.11.

87. 20 other occurrences.

88. Abbott, *Ephesians*, p. 17.

of construction between B and B' by insisting that κατὰ τὴν εὐδοκίαν qualifies γνωρίσας here as it does προορίσας in 1.5. Its effect is, once again, to underline the sovereignty—but the *benevolent* sovereignty—of God.

2.4.4. *C (1.6) and C' (1.7c, 8)*
In these two elements God's grace moves sharply into focus. Those chosen by God do not merit what has happened, nor what is yet to happen, as a result of God's choosing. In C_1 what has happened should result in (εἰς) the praise of the glory of his grace, that is, it should lead to God's grace being given glory. This is to be preferred to the view of those who would make δόξης an adjectival attribute ('to the praise of his glorious grace'[89] or 'for the glorious praise of his grace'.[90] In C_1' it is the richness of that same grace that is being emphasized.

In both C_2 and C_2' χάρις is further qualified. Both begin with the genitive of the relative pronoun (ἧς) where another case might have been expected—the dative in the first instance, and the accusative in the second. It is perhaps best to regard ἧς as being attracted into the case of its antecedent.[91]

In C_2 the unusual and late verb χαριτόω is used. God has 'be-graced' his people;[92] there appears to be implied in the term an abundant demonstration of grace.[93] As if then to underline the point, the recipients are reminded that even this experience of grace is not because of any merit that those who experience it may have—they are 'be-graced' in the Beloved. Jesus is thus marked out as the supreme object of the Father's love.[94] The designation of Christ as ὁ ἠγαπημένος is not used elsewhere in the Pauline corpus, although it is found in later Jewish writings, and in early Christian literature outside of the New Testament.[95]

In C_2' it is the abundance of grace that is highlighted by the use of περισσεύω.

89. So RSV, Mitton, *Ephesians*, p. 51; *et al.*
90. So Bruce, *Ephesians*, p. 258.
91. Robinson, *Ephesians*, p. 144.
92. Bruce, *Ephesians*, p. 258.
93. Barth, *Ephesians*, p. 82.
94. Bruce, *Ephesians*, p. 258.
95. Robinson, *Ephesians*, pp. 229-33, has a long detached note on 'the Beloved' as a messianic title.

The Position of ἐν πάσῃ σοφίᾳ καὶ φρονήσει. As with the earlier example, there is a division of opinion as to the best way to construe the phrase ἐν πάσῃ σοφίᾳ καὶ φρονήσει. Among those who would take it with ἐπερίσσευσεν are Abbott ('the making known of the "mystery" is not the proof of the abundance of grace, but of its abounding in the particular matter of σοφία καὶ φρόνησις.'), Barth, Bruce, Schlier and Lincoln.[96] Among those who construe it with γνωρίσας are Mussner, Gnilka and Cambier, although Cambier chooses this partly on the basis of strophic considerations.[97]

As with the previous example, there is no way of finding a definitive answer to this question. Indeed, if Abbott is correct and it is the gifts of wisdom and insight that are in mind here as particular outworkings of God's grace, then the phrase has a special aptness as being the main point of C′, while at the same time preparing the way for B′. Without such an interpretation, C′ would be adding little, if anything, more to what has already been said in C. While repetitions may characterize Eph. 1.3-14 as a whole, it will be shown below that these 'repetitions' are found almost entirely in 1.11-14 rather than in the chiasmus itself.

It obviously suits my purposes best that both ἐν ἀγάπῃ and ἐν πάσῃ σοφίᾳ καὶ φρονήσει belong at the end of their respective clauses, rather than introducing a new element. If *both* were moved to their alternative positions, little would be lost in terms of the symmetry of the whole pattern; if *one* were moved, there would be some lessening of the degree of symmetry, but it would in no way so weaken the pattern as to render it void.

2.4.5. *The Central Element, D (1.7a, b)*

In even a casual reading of the passage, 1.7 stands out. It has the only verb in 1.3-10 that is *not* in the third person, and is also the only one in the present tense. It marks in the text

> a sudden transition from the election before the world's foundation to a specific event i.e. to Jesus Christ's death on the cross... Suddenly, men instead of God are the subject of a sentence. A statement about the present rather than a remote past or future is made.[98]

96. Abbott, *Ephesians*, p. 15; Barth, *Ephesians*, p. 84; Bruce, *Ephesians*, p. 260; Schlier, *Epheser*, p. 59; Lincoln, *Ephesians*, p. 17; *et al.*

97. Mussner, *Epheser*, p. 47; J. Gnilka, *Der Epheserbrief* (HTKNT; Freiburg, 1971), p. 77; Cambier, 'Bénédiction', pp. 82-85.

98. Barth, *Ephesians*, p. 83.

Schnackenburg, too, highlights the change by suggesting that now it is our historical redemption in Jesus Christ that is described in the divine plan of salvation.[99]

This element, in many ways, is an archetypal example of the 'shift and reversion' pattern often seen at the centre of a chiasmus,[100] with the change in the person of the verb that immediately reverts in the next element. With the concept of grace clearly flanking it, this element serves as the pivotal point between the events of that past eternity in view in A, and that future eternity envisaged in A'. Between these two 'poles' of history, the chiasmus is now 'grounded' or 'earthed' in the present with this deceptively simple statement of the believers' two possessions—redemption through the blood of Christ and forgiveness of sins. Like so much else in this chiasmus, what believers have is 'in Christ' and not by right. The blood of Christ is the means by which his people's redemption has been procured,[101] thus revealing what makes adoption possible. It is interesting that Paul links redemption and adoption in Rom. 8.23, having just before this linked the ideas of being set free from bondage (the goal of redemption) with the obtaining of the liberty of the *children* of God (Rom. 8.21).[102]

Thus, the death of Jesus (clearly envisaged in D in διὰ τοῦ αἵματος αὐτοῦ) is the 'central' (I use the word deliberately) event in the whole chiasmus. It brings about not only redemption and forgiveness, but also leads to the elect becoming holy and blameless, and being made sons. That same death makes possible the plan for the fullness of time, which will result in the reuniting of τὰ πάντα in Christ. This element, on which the others turn, is the key one for the understanding of the whole chiasmus. The climax to *history* may be in the reuniting of all things in Christ, but the central focus of the *chiasmus* lies in this element.

2.5. *The Structure and Function of Ephesians 1.11-14*

This section will show that, while Eph. 1.11-14 follows on very closely from the chiasmus, it is not part of it. The vocabulary of the chiasmus is used, particularly at the beginning and towards the end of these four verses, but often in a subtly different way. Mainly in the middle of the

---

99. Schnackenburg, *Epheser*, p. 54.
100. See 1.4.2 above.
101. Bruce, *Ephesians*, p. 259.
102. Mitton, *Ephesians*, p. 52.

section, new vocabulary and new ideas are introduced. These features, in turn, lead to the conclusion that it is possible to argue that the chiasmus is preformed material that is then used for the Ephesian author's own ends. This hypothesis, reinforced by an examination of the way that 'we' and 'you' are used throughout the whole passage, does not affect the validity of the chiasmus, but helps lend weight to the suggestion that the promotion of unity among believers is an important part of the author's purpose in writing.

It has already been noted how Barth, Schille and Caragounis find a change in the passage at 1.11. Caragounis neatly encapsulates it when he says that, up to 1.10, God has been the central focus of the passage (with the exception of 1.7). Now, however, 'God' is pushed into the background, and 'we' and 'you' into the foreground.[103]

2.5.1. *The Vocabulary and Syntax of Ephesians 1.11-14 in Relation to Ephesians 1.4-10*

One of the most obvious and striking features of 1.11-14 is the way that it uses a significant number of words, phrases and grammatical constructions that have already occurred in the chiasmus, as can be seen below by highlighting the common vocabulary:

$\{A_1$ 1.4 καθὼς ἐξελέξατο ἡμᾶς **ἐν αὐτῷ** πρὸ καταβολῆς
A { κόσμου,
$\{A_2$ **εἶναι ἡμᾶς** ἁγίους καὶ ἀμώμους κατενώπιον αὐτοῦ
  (ἐν ἀγάπῃ),

$\{B_1$ (   ) 1.5 **προορίσας** ἡμᾶς εἰς υἱοθεσίαν διὰ Ἰησοῦ
B { Χριστοῦ εἰς αὐτόν,
$\{B_2$ **κατὰ** τὴν εὐδοκίαν **τοῦ θελήματος αὐτοῦ,**

$\{C_1$ 1.6 **εἰς ἔπαινον δόξης** τῆς χάριτος αὐτοῦ
C {
$\{C_2$ ἧς ἐχαρίτωσεν ἡμᾶς ἐν τῷ ἠγαπημένῳ.

D 1.7 Ἐν ᾧ ἔχομεν τὴν **ἀπολύτρωσιν** διὰ τοῦ αἵματος
  αὐτοῦ, τὴν ἄφεσιν τῶν παραπτωμάτων,

$\{C_1'$ 1.7c κατὰ τὸ πλοῦτος τῆς χάριτος αὐτοῦ,
C' {
$\{C_2'$ 1.8 ἧς ἐπερίσσευσεν εἰς ἡμᾶς (ἐν πάσῃ σοφίᾳ καὶ
  φρονήσει)

103. Caragounis, *Mysterion*, pp. 34-35.

{B₁′ (   ) 1.9 γνωρίσας ἡμῖν **τὸ μυστήριον τοῦ**
B′ {   **θελήματος** αὐτοῦ,
{B₂′ κατὰ τὴν εὐδοκίαν αὐτοῦ

{A₁′ ἣν **προέθετο** ἐν αὐτῷ 1.10 εἰς οἰκονομίαν τοῦ
A′ {   πληρώματος τῶν καιρῶν,
{A₂′ ἀνακεφαλαιώσασθαι **τὰ πάντα ἐν τῷ Χριστῷ**,
       τὰ ἐπὶ τοῖς οὐρανοῖς καὶ τὰ ἐπὶ τῆς γῆς·

Of course, not all of these have the same importance, and some may be
of no consequence. When the remaining verses of the section are laid
out with the similarities in language highlighted, the following is found:

1.10c **ἐν αὐτῷ**. 1.11 Ἐν ᾧ καὶ ἐκληρώθημεν
προορισθέντες κατὰ **πρόθεσιν** τοῦ **τὰ πάντα** ἐνεργοῦντος
κατὰ τὴν βουλὴν **τοῦ θελήματος αὐτοῦ**,

1.12 εἰς τὸ **εἶναι ἡμᾶς εἰς ἔπαινον δόξης** αὐτοῦ τοὺς
προηλπικότας ἐν τῷ Χριστῷ.

1.13 Ἐν ᾧ καὶ ὑμεῖς ἀκούσαντες τὸν λόγον τῆς ἀληθείας, το
εὐαγγέλιον τῆς σωτηρίας ὑμῶν,
ἐν ᾧ καὶ πιστεύσαντες ἐσφραγίσθητε τῷ πνεύματι τῆς ἐπαγγελίας
τῷ ἁγιῳ,

1.14 ὅ ἐστιν ἀρραβὼν τῆς κληρονομίας ἡμῶν,
εἰς **ἀπολύτρωσιν** τῆς περιποιήσεως,
εἰς **ἔπαινον** τῆς **δόξης αὐτοῦ**.

(Note: No particular significance is intended in the layout adopted above,
other than to highlight the flow of syntax in 1.11-14 in an analogous way
to the chiasmus.)

It can be seen that there is some continuity in style in these two sections.
Attention may be drawn to the continued use of relative clauses,[104]
prepositional constructions and the frequent use of 'in Christ' and its
variants. What is missing, however, is the symmetrical elegance of construction that characterized the chiasmus. Indeed, the section becomes
repetitious, and is sometimes awkward.

It must be asked, therefore, why, if one person was responsible for
the whole, the need suddenly arose in 1.11, 12 and 14b to re-use so
much vocabulary from the chiasmus. Such repetitions as occur within
the body of the chiasmus itself (κατὰ τὴν εὐδοκίαν and τοῦ
θελήματος αὐτοῦ in B and B′, and τῆς χάριτος αὐτοῦ in C and C′)

104. The use of ἐν ᾧ in 1.11 and 1.13 (2×) is a repetition not so much of
significant vocabulary as of a syntactical style.

are accommodated by the constraints of the chiastic pattern, and help to lend it clarity of shape.

2.5.2. *The Content of Ephesians 1.11-14*

In fact, it has been suggested that this section begins with the last two words of 1.10 (ἐν αὐτῷ) but in a markedly clumsy construction. Of those who specify whether this phrase properly belongs to 1.10 or 1.11, Lincoln is one of the few who assigns it to 1.10.[105] For the majority, the phrase seems to represent a drawing of breath before the vast sentence continues on its way.

With ἐκληρώθημεν in 1.11 we come to a word that is used only here in the New Testament.[106] The word can be traced through the idea of casting a lot, to that of the appointment of an officer by lot, to the more general use 'to assign something', or in the passive, 'to be in possession'. Thus, it may contain the idea of the elect having the good fortune to be chosen by God, in which case the election and predestination of 1.4 would now be described by a new word. (The Peshitta version actually uses the same word here as it uses in 1.5.) Alternatively, we could see in it the idea of those chosen being given a share. In the LXX the Hebrew concept of 'lot', share' and 'inheritance' are frequently combined and sometimes even identified.[107] The third option is that it is taken with the sense that they have been appropriated, becoming, as it were, God's property. Among others, both Abbott and Schnackenburg link κληρόω with κληρονομία in 1.14.[108]

It may well be that this word is specifically used because of its richness—which cannot be conveyed in translation. Whether any one of Barth's options is selected, or another combination of them, it is obvious that the conceptual context is once more the realm of God's sovereign action, an area strongly reminiscent of the beginning of the chiasmus.

Abbott's warning is well given that καί should not be translated as if it were καὶ ἡμεῖς. 'Also' belongs to the verb: its purpose was 'also' carried out.[109] The effect of this, however, is to increase the sense of

---

105. Lincoln, *Ephesians*, pp. 17-18. Barth, *Ephesians*, p. 76, also places it in 1.10, but gives no reasons.

106. I make use of Barth's extended discussion in what follows (*Ephesians*, pp. 92-94).

107. Num. 18.24; 26.56; Josh. 12.7; 14.2; etc.

108. Abbott, *Ephesians*, pp. 19-20; Schnackenburg, *Epheser*, p. 61.

109. Abbott, *Ephesians*, p. 19.

tautology in the passage when this phrase is placed alongside καθὼς ἐξελέξατο ἡμᾶς ἐν αὐτῷ in 1.4. Indeed, Robinson says bluntly of the whole phrase ἐν αὐτῷ ἐν ᾧ καὶ ἐκληρώθημεν προορισθέντες that it is practically a restatement in the passive voice of ἐξελέξατο ἡμᾶς...προορίσας ἡμᾶς.[110]

It may be suggested that the phrase προορισθέντες κατὰ πρόθεσιν τοῦ τὰ πάντα ἐνεργοῦντος is needed to act as a counter to any implication of choice by chance or lot. On the other hand, it may occur because the juxtaposition of ἐξελέξατο and προορίσας in the chiasmus is remembered. But, replete as it is with overtones from the chiasmus, it adds little to what has already been said there—except, perhaps, in the idea of God accomplishing all things.

In this connection it is an interesting question as to whether or not τὰ πάντα in 1.10 are to be identified with τὰ πάντα of 1.11. This has not been widely discussed. As far as its use in 1.10 is concerned, Mitton makes the point that, while the phrase is neuter, it may be merely a very emphatic way of insisting that the reconciling power of Christ is effective in all circumstances, in heaven (that is, in reconciling people to God) as well as on earth (that is, in all the relationships of human life). Although the neuter plural is used, the emphasis in 1.3-10 is certainly on the uniting of all *people*.[111] However, even if it were taken in its strictly literal sense of 'all things' in both these verses, can 'uniting all things' (as in 1.10) be said to be the same as 'accomplishing all things' (as in 1.11)? Even if there is an albeit veiled reference to a grand cosmological design in 1.10, as seems to be the majority view, then there remains the problem of equating 'all *powers*' (which is then the implication of τὰ πάντα) in 1.10 with τὰ πάντα of 1.11, along with a suitable translation of ἐνεργοῦντος. The latter can only be reasonably translated by terms such as 'works, accomplishes' and so forth, with the result that to understand τὰ πάντα in 1.11 in terms of 'all powers' is not appropriate. The phrase τὰ πάντα appears to have different implications in the two neighbouring verses.

The phrase κατὰ τὴν βουλὴν τοῦ θελήματος αὐτοῦ in 1.11 brings to mind the very similar κατὰ τὴν εὐδοκίαν τοῦ θελήματος αὐτοῦ in B. As long ago as Abbott's time, there was disagreement as to the distinction, if any, between βουλή and θέλημα.[112] The effect of the

110. Robinson, *Ephesians*, p. 146.
111. Mitton, *Ephesians*, pp. 56-57.
112. Abbott, *Ephesians*, p. 20.

conjunction of the two terms is to produce a further labouring of the point,[113] with the addition of nothing new.[114] In this case it might be speculated that the use of κατὰ τὴν βουλήν has arisen because of the influence of the similar sounding καταβολῆς of A.

Thus, in 1.10c-11 no fewer than six words or phrases have been taken directly, or derived, from the chiasmus, and have been put together in a different way to form a section that says little new of substance. Of the six, *all* come from A, B, B′ or A′. The only exception is ἐν ᾧ, which comes from D, and is perhaps the least significant anyway.

In 1.12 every word of the infinitival phrase εἰς τὸ εἶναι ἡμᾶς εἰς ἔπαινον δόξης αὐτοῦ has already occurred in the chiasmus. They are again, however, put together quite differently here. It is difficult to be certain whether the antecedent of the phrase is the participle προορισθέντες or the main verb ἐκληρώθημεν. There is little that hangs on the point since the phrase expresses the purpose of the believers having been chosen or predestined.

In the earlier chiasmus, the elect are chosen ἐν αὐτῷ to be holy and blameless. The fact of having been chosen brings an ethical obligation to live in a certain way, linked with the elect's destiny for adoption διὰ Ἰησοῦ Χριστοῦ εἰς αὐτόν. This whole divine strategy is seen as being εἰς ἔπαινον δόξης αὐτοῦ, with the riches of God's grace again being stressed in 1.7. However, in 1.12 (indeed, in the whole of 1.11-14) there is notably *no reference* to the grace of God, which figured so centrally in the chiasmus. Instead of the idea of the whole strategy being to the praise of the glory of his grace, believers themselves are to be, in an absolute sense, εἰς ἔπαινον δόξης αὐτοῦ. The concept of the trans-formed life (ἁγίους καὶ ἀμώμους) has receded, and in its place has come the thought that the believers' being chosen and destined leads them, by dint of the act itself, to be to the praise of his glory. The same words as occurred in the chiasmus have here been made to carry a rather different meaning.

Up to this point in 1.12 the impression is left that we are dealing with a rather inelegant restatement of the main thrust of elements A and B of the chiasmus, but while much of its vocabulary is derived from that chiasmus, it does not convey quite the same message.[115]

---

113. So Mitton, *Ephesians*, p. 57.

114. It might be argued that the similar phrase in B is also tautological.

115. Thus, if we had only Eph. 1.11, 12, our view of the basis and purpose of election and predestination would be somewhat different.

It should be noted that there are other approaches to 1.12. Abbott understands εἰς ἔπαινον δόξης αὐτοῦ as a parenthesis.[116] He wishes to take τοὺς προηλπικότας as the predicate of εἶναι, but gives no convincing reason for doing this and ends up with a translation that seems to make already difficult Greek even more clumsy: 'That we, to the praise of His glory, should be those who have before had hopes in Christ'. He may be trying to force uniformity of usage upon a passage where it is not present.

Schnackenburg notes Abbott's interpretation (which is actually followed by Gnilka),[117] but disagrees with it, drawing attention to the parallels with 1.4, and going on to suggest that the purpose of being chosen is not just some kind of cultic praise of God, but carries with it the implication of a life that should conform to the will of God. In this sense all of Christian existence should lead to the glorification of God. In 1.12, though, this is not explicitly expressed and can only be seen by inference.

In 1.12 we find the only New Testament occurrence of προελπίζω, 'to hope before, to be the first to hope',[118] thus bringing to the passage the new concept of 'hoping' in Christ. The idea of hoping in Christ is one that is not unknown to Paul, but is not widely used in this sense in the undisputed letters.[119]

The majority of scholars (*pace* Abbott and Gnilka) take προηλπικότας as standing in apposition to ἡμᾶς. For the first time, too, comes the apparent (and significant) differentiation between believer and believer, since there are some who have a 'priority' of hoping over others. Salvation is now viewed from humankind's standpoint, as it were. Up to this point the divine initiative has consistently been stressed: what believers have has been from God, as a result of his actions and prerogative. Even when the subject of the verb briefly changes from 'God' to 'we' in 1.7 with ἔχομεν, what 'we' have was κατὰ τὸ πλοῦτος τῆς χάριτος αὐτοῦ. Now, however, it is 'we' who have directly hoped in Christ.

Eph. 1.13 has, at its beginning, some *formal* similarities to element D in the chiasmus. As well as beginning with the same phrase, it also has a

---

116. Abbott, *Ephesians*, p. 21.

117. Schnackenburg, *Epheser*, pp. 61-62; Gnilka, *Epheserbrief*, p. 83.

118. The precise significance of the prefix will be discussed below when we examine which group is intended by 'we' and 'you' in this passage.

119. See 1 Cor. 15.19; Rom. 15.12 (citing LXX) with ἐπί; 1 Thess. 1.3 ἐλπίς + genitive, for example.

verbal part (here, of course, a participle) with two direct objects. The main verb is apparently absent in this elliptical clause, unless it is argued that ὑμεῖς is the subject of ἐσφραγίσθητε, in which case the second ἐν ᾧ would be regarded as picking up the sentence that has been broken to insert the emphatic phrase ἀκούσαντες τὸν λόγον...τῆς σωτηρίας ὑμῶν.[120]

In element D the believers' salvation is presented in history—redemption through Christ's blood and forgiveness of sins. The historical event (the death of Jesus) with its historical effects on 'us' came at the turning point of a passage that until then had been looking largely to the past.

In 1.13a the historical event of salvation is also present, described this time in terms of hearing—whether the word of truth, or the good news of salvation—these being applied emphatically to 'you'. Once more, this occurs after a section where the temporal references are backward looking. The concept of 'hearing' as an event linked with, but prior to, faith is one that is found elsewhere in Paul (as in Rom. 10.14; Gal. 3.2; 1 Thess. 2.13, for example), as are also somewhat similar descriptions of the gospel and its effects (e.g., Rom. 1.16; 1 Cor. 1.18; Gal. 2.5; Col. 1.5, 6).

The syntax of 1.13b is rather obscure. There is the question of the antecedent of the phrase ἐν ᾧ. This may pick up the same phrase as in the broken construction of 1.13a (ἐν Χριστῷ in 1.12). Otherwise, theoretically, it could be εὐαγγέλιον or even λόγον. There is also the problem of whether it looks forward to πιστεύσαντες or ἐσφραγίσθητε. It may be that it should be taken with ἐσφραγίσθητε, mainly because of the absence of the idea of believing 'in' (ἐν) Christ in Paul (although the related phrase διὰ τῆς πίστεως ἐν Χριστῷ Ἰησοῦ does occur in Gal. 3.26—and also in Eph. 1.15, which may well weaken this argument).

What has been conveyed now, therefore, is the thought that, having heard and believed, those addressed are sealed in Christ with 'the Holy Spirit of promise' or, more likely, 'with the promised Holy Spirit'. Very similar language can be found in 2 Cor. 1.22 where the three elements of sealing, the guarantee (ἀρραβών, Eph. 1.14) and the Spirit are all present.

It is noticeable that the *language* of the chiasmus has been left behind in 1.14, and a whole range of new ideas introduced: the use of

---

120. ἡμεῖς (אA K L Ψ) is read for ὑμεῖς and ἡμῶν (K Ψ) for ὑμῶν in a few MSS, possibly under the influence of ἡμᾶς in 1.12, although they are poorly attested variants.

προελπίζω, the ideas of hearing and believing, what is heard, the sealing with the promised Holy Spirit, and now the Spirit as a guarantee. Almost the only connection with the chiasmus (although a weak one) is the thought that these ideas are rooted firmly 'in Christ'. However, as the end of the passage approaches, the language of the chiasmus comes into view again, although obliquely at first with κληρονομία, which is a corollary of the concept of υἱοθεσία in B. Mitton is right that here it is the future aspect of the term that is emphasized. The gift of the Spirit is enjoyed *now* as part of the believers' inheritance, the other part of which awaits when this life is ended.[121] It should be noted in passing that the second person of 1.13 has been replaced again by the genitive of the first personal pronoun (ἡμῶν).

The translation of the next phrase εἰς ἀπολύτρωσιν τῆς περιποιήσεως is obscure, and therefore much discussed. The details of that discussion, while interesting, need not detain us. Mitton translates it as 'until we acquire possession of it'; Bruce, 'until the redemption of God's possession'.[122] Probably the majority suggest a translation something like that of Bruce. There seems to be general agreement that the phrase has a future reference. This stands in contrast to the use of ἀπολύτρωσις in element D, where it is something that the elect now have, and is used in an absolute sense.

The final phrase of the section, εἰς ἔπαινον τῆς δόξης αὐτοῦ, returns once more to the vocabulary of the chiasmus, here of C, though, as in 1.12, with no mention of χάρις. While God's grace appears to be the primary object of praise in 1.6 (and an important feature of the chiasmus), it is God's glory itself that is in the forefront here.

2.5.3. *The Function of Ephesians 1.11-14*
The key to the function of 1.11-14 is to be found in the relationship between 'we' and 'you'. All personal references in the chiasmus are in the first person. The second person comes into view only from 1.13. The questions may be stated as follows: are there two distinct groups in mind (referred to respectively by 'we' and 'you'), and is the term 'we', in particular, used consistently throughout to refer to one specific group? Is it possible to identify who 'we' and 'you' are? Abbott, Bruce, Westcott, Ellicott and Stott all take 'we' to refer to 'all we Christians' from 1.3-11, but in 1.12 think that 'we Jewish Christians' are in mind,

---

121. Mitton, *Ephesians*, p. 62.
122. Mitton, *Ephesians*, p. 64; Bruce, *Ephesians*, p. 263.

with 'you Gentile believers' coming into view in 1.13.[123] Mitton thinks that it is 'we Christians' up to 1.11, and thereafter either 'we first-generation Christians' or 'we Jewish Christians'. He suggests that there may not, in fact, be much difference between the two, because most of the first-generation Christians would have been Jews, and most of the subsequent generations Gentile.[124] Robinson has a slightly different perspective on the question. He suggests that 'we' in 1.12 could either be 'we Jewish Christians' or 'we, the Jewish people', pointing for a moment to the Jewish priority,[125] whereas Schnackenburg suggests that the author is turning from addressing 'we Christians in general' to 'you Christians in particular'.[126]

In trying to resolve this matter, it is of the greatest importance to ask what impression the passage would make upon those to whom it was sent. From 1.3-10 they would see themselves along with the author as one group, through the use of the simple terms 'we' and 'us'. But, as soon as they came to προηλπικότας, the recipients would realize that they were not necessarily included in that group. This holds true no matter what detailed interpretation is placed on προελπίζω, as its inevitable inference is to put distance between those addressed and the author's 'group'.[127]

It is probable, therefore, that the author intends the readers to understand this in terms of 'we Jews', although no explanation can be offered of why he does not make this clearer.[128] The term 'Jew' does not occur at all in Ephesians, although the 'Gentiles' are specifically mentioned in 2.11, 3.1, 6, 8 and 4.17, while in 2.11 and 3.1 the phrase 'you Gentiles' is actually used.[129]

The Gentile readers are immediately reassured, however, with the

---

123. Abbott, *Ephesians*, p. 21; Bruce, *Ephesians*, pp. 264-65; Westcott, *Ephesians*, pp. 15-16; Ellicott, *Ephesians*, pp. 14-15; Stott, *Ephesians*, pp. 45-46.

124. Mitton, *Ephesians*, pp. 57-59.

125. Robinson, *Ephesians*, pp. 34-35.

126. Schnackenburg, *Epheser*, p. 63.

127. *Pace* Schnackenburg, *Epheser*, p. 62, who thinks that the prefix προ- simply intensifies the meaning of the root without introducing a strong temporal sense.

128. Especially as, in the undisputed letters, Paul is not reticent about using the term 'Jew' or 'Jewish' about himself (e.g. Rom. 3.9; Gal. 2.15 etc.)—although, of course, the authorship question complicates this.

129. That there is a significant, wider emphasis in Ephesians on the relationship between Jewish Christians and Gentile Christians will be suggested in 3.6.1 and 3.6.2 below.

emphatic καὶ ὑμεῖς of 1.13. They, too, are included in the gospel of salvation, and this is highlighted by their sealing with the Holy Spirit, whose presence with Gentile Christians had earlier so impressed Peter (Acts 10.44-47). The Spirit is the guarantee of 'our' (now, that is, Jewish Christian and Gentile Christian) inheritance, and the Gentile Christian will be 'to the praise of his glory', just as the Jewish Christian (1.12). Armed with this new insight, the Gentile Christian readers can look again at the chiasmus with fresh understanding, the eyes of their hearts now enlightened (1.18), knowing now that 'the riches of his glorious inheritance in the saints' (1.18) are for them too, and that Jesus is the head over all things (1.22: ἔδωκεν κεφαλὴν ὑπὲρ πάντα τῇ ἐκκλησίᾳ).[130]

2.5.4. *The Hypothesis of the Preformation of the Chiasmus*
While it is quite widely accepted that the two major criteria for distinguishing preformed material are those of distinctive stylistic and linguistic features,[131] these need not be determinative in the present context because of (a) the position of the chiasmus very near to the beginning of the letter, and (b) the fact that the author may be consciously echoing material from the chiasmus in later passages.

The hypothesis rests on the *cumulative effect* of the following observations, most of which have already been noted.

a. Eph. 1.3-10 constitutes a unit defined by the limit of the chiasmus, and introduced by language familiar to us from other examples of the Jewish *berakah*. That unit can be seen as being theoretically capable of having an independent existence.[132]

b. There appears to be a deliberate and conscious echoing of the language of 1.3-10 in 1.11-14, including possibly an attempted summary of some of the points of the chiasmus in 1.11. At the same time, however, that language conveys a subtly different message. Even at this stage, some of the principal emphases of the chiasmus drop out of view (notably 'grace'). New material is added, especially in 1.12b-14a, but the section ends with more echoes of the language of the chiasmus. This

---

130. I still feel that there may be a very remote allusion here to ἀνακεφαλαιόω in the chiasmus.

131. See, e.g., O'Brien, *Colossians*, p. 33.

132. It is, of course, absurd to deduce from this that every such discrete unit may have had a prior existence!

reads like an author adapting preformed material and refocusing it by inserting new ideas.

c. The refocusing in 1.11-14 may, in some cases, contribute to some of the most intractable syntactical obscurities in Eph. 1.3-14, beginning with the awkward ἐν αὐτῷ ἐν ᾧ καί of 1.10c, 11, continuing with the clumsy threefold use of ἐν ᾧ clauses, to the highly obscure phrase εἰς ἀπολύτρωσιν τῆς περιποιήσεως in 1.14.

d. In the remainder of the letter, some of the key ideas of the chiasmus (especially election and predestination) never specifically re-emerge, while others (particularly those of uniting τὰ πάντα in Christ, the mysterion, the fulfillment of the plan of God) are further developed.

Such theories about the preformed nature of the chiasmus are not beyond challenge, most notably because it must be admitted that there is not any great stylistic variation between the chiasmus and the remainder of the letter. It is possible that the author of the letter consciously retains the style in which the chiasmus is written as appropriate to its theme, especially as this kind of writing is apparently known from Qumran texts.[133] The whole matter is further complicated by the possible relationship between Ephesians and Colossians, with the years of arguments about interdependency and priority of one over the other. Thus, if the priority of Colossians could be established beyond reasonable doubt, and if it could be shown that Eph. 1.3-10 depended on parts of Colossians, then the whole idea of preformed material in Eph. 1.3-10 would become untenable.

At the risk of repetitiveness, it must be very carefully underlined that *the validity of the chiasmus is not dependent on its being preformed.* If it is not preformed material, then it is more difficult, but clearly not impossible, to give a coherent account of the relationship between the carefully constructed chiasmus and the more obscure and convoluted 1.11-14. Thus, it might be suggested, for instance, that in 1.11-12a the author recapitulated an earlier theme before introducing the new material of 1.12b-14 as a development of it.

2.6. *The Use of the Chiasmus in the Remainder of Ephesians*

A number of scholars suggest that Eph. 1.3-14 has a very important role in the rest of the letter.[134] This need not conflict with the position

---

133. See further Lincoln, *Ephesians*, p. 12.

134. We might draw attention to Maurer, 'Hymnus', pp. 151-72 whose article is

adopted in this study that 1.11-14 actually contains the first development of a theme of the chiasmus, that of the uniting of τὰ πάντα in Christ.[135]

Thus, echoes of the language of the chiasmus are often found later in the letter, although the vocabulary may be used in a different context. A case in point is the use of τὰ ἐπουράνια in 1.20, 2.6, 3.10 and 6.12—used in this sense only in Ephesians in the Pauline corpus. Another example is πλοῦτος: in 1.7 it is the riches of his grace; in 1.18, the riches of his glorious inheritance; in 2.7, the riches of his grace; in 3.8, the riches of Christ; and in 3.16, the riches of his glory—a term used on only eight other occasions in the rest of the Pauline corpus, four of which are in Romans.[136]

Other themes in the chiasmus—or themes that might be described as being incipient within it—are developed, sometimes considerably so. Into this category would come the theme of unity among believers of different backgrounds in the present church (2.11-22; 4.1-16), the will and purposes of God (ch. 3) and the grace of God (2.1-10).[137] Equally significant, too, are those ideas that figure prominently in the chiasmus but are then left behind, including the concepts of election and predestination (although, of course, there is a close relationship between the will and purposes of God, and those concepts).

The case for the ongoing use of the chiasmus must not be overplayed, however. In some sections there are not many allusions to its themes, for example, in 5.21–6.9 (although some of its language is echoed

less useful than its title suggests because of his insistence that Ephesians is pervaded by Gnostic motifs; Sanders, 'Hymnic Elements', pp. 230-32; Barth, *Ephesians*, pp. 53ff.; Schlier, *Epheser*, pp. 72-73, among others.

135. See 3.6.1 and 3.6.2 below.

136. There is, of course, another way of looking at this. The preponderance of terms that occur only in Ephesians, or which are used more extensively in Ephesians than in the wider Pauline corpus, may simply be confirmation of the fact that Ephesians was not written by Paul. On the other hand, it would be an interesting exercise to compute the number of such words or allusions occurring later in the letter that relate to this chiasmus, in order to try to quantify the extent to which its language has coloured the remainder of the letter. Theoretically, it may be possible to show that the use of a preformed chiasmus can account for some of the linguistic peculiarities that have led many to suggest that the letter is not Pauline. Having said this, however, I recognize that there are more than linguistic peculiarities that lead to questions about authorship. See 7.5.1 below.

137. I do not mean to imply that these are the only, or even necessarily the most important, themes of these sections, but simply that there is a thread that seems to run through them.

occasionally), unless the paraenetic section is seen in terms of the practical outworking of the elect being chosen to be holy and blameless, with the thread of unity supporting its injunctions,[138] allied with love.

2.7. *A Possible* Sitz im Leben *for the Chiasmus*

It has already been indicated that there is a significant group who find the form of the chiasmus to be reminiscent of that of the Jewish *berakah*, the outburst of praise and blessing of God. That it originated in a Jewish Christian community might be further indicated by its initial emphasis on election and predestination. This was a problem for Jewish Christians—why some of God's people responded to the gospel while others did not. The answer lies, the chiasmus suggests, in God's sovereign actions of election and predestination (cf. Rom. 9–11). Love and grace are the keynotes of these actions, which are accomplished in Christ. The choosing in Christ before the foundation of the world of this group of (former) Jews, and their presentation holy and blameless, well merits the description of 'the plan for the fullness of time', in the same way as their adoption into Christ through him is a mystery.

What we cannot know is how familiar this preformed chiasmus may have been to the Christians of the author's day. One attractive possibility is that it was quite well known. Indeed, it may already have been understood in terms of *all* Christians,[139] rather than just *Jewish* Christians. Whether or not this was the case, the author then sees its possibilities for adaptation for the situation to be addressed in the letter, with the need to recognize, but minimize, the distinction between 'we' and 'you'. Thus, the chiasmus becomes the basis for a significant part of what is to be communicated to the readers, and the author continues to draw on its language, even when it is used in a different context. The effect of the whole is to remind the readers continually that we bless a God who operates from eternity past to eternity future, whose actions are firmly centred in the historical death of Christ, and who will unite τὰ πάντα in him.

138. Sanders, 'Hymnic Elements', p. 230.
139. With 'we' being understood as 'all we Christians'.

2.8. *Conclusion*

When Eph. 1.3-10 is identified as a chiasmus prefaced by a short introductory verse, hitherto unsuspected symmetries are revealed in the
grammar and syntax that give the passage a surprising degree of elegance. That grammatical symmetry is then shown to support an equally
highly structured parallelism of content which may suggest a new way
of understanding the substance of μυστήριον and may expand our
understanding of God's οἰκονομία.

Eph. 1.11-14 is not part of the chiasmus, but is closely (if somewhat
inelegantly) joined to it. Its structure and subtly different use of the
vocabulary of the chiasmus may suggest that the chiasmus had an existence prior to its incorporation in this letter, although the acceptance or
rejection of this further hypothesis is a matter independent of the validity
of the chiastic pattern.

The language and style of 1.3-10 is in keeping with its being in the
form of a Jewish *berakah*, and a coherent, if speculative, account can be
given of its original purpose.

There are a number of clear advantages to this analysis of Eph. 1.3-14
over the many attempts to find a strophic structure.[140] Thus, there is no
need to resort to hypothetical textual emendations to 'recover' a structure: the text is dealt with as it stands. The chiastic pattern does not
depend on a subjective analysis of contents; in this instance (albeit a very
unusual case) it rests on objective grammatical parallels. This example of
chiasmus illustrates well some of its more frequently observed characteristics: an introduction or frame passage, a clear shift and reversion at the
centre, and a mixture of directly and antithetically parallel statements.

---

140. Theoretically, of course, it could be a 'hymn' with a chiastic pattern; chiasmus occurs in prose and poetry alike.

Chapter 3

EPHESIANS 2.11-22: A CHOICE OF CHIASTIC PATTERNS

3.1. A Further Passage Containing 'Hymnic Traits'

One feature that Eph. 2.11-22 shares with Eph. 1.3-14 is that there have been a significant number of attempts to find a hymnic element within it.[1] However, the same kind of reservations stand about these as in the case of Eph. 1.3-14, notably, the lack of consensus, both about the length of the hymn and about its strophic arrangement, along with the extent to which the text has to be altered to 'recover' the hymn.

A single quotation from Sanders serves to illustrate this graphically:

> It is not entirely clear where within this framework the author's interpolations are to be seen... Schille[2] considers ὁ ποιήσας... λύσας to be one line and places ἐν τῇ σαρκὶ αὐτοῦ τὸν νόμον τῶν ἐντολῶν ἐν δόγμασιν καταργήσας vv. 14f. in parallelism to it. This would seem, however, to overlook the strong parallelism between ὁ ποιήσας.../ καὶ... λύσας, where one also notes that a participle falls first at the beginning of the line, next at the close—a not uncommon hymnic trait. The references to τὴν ἔχθραν are probably with Haupt[3] and Schille[4] to be omitted from the original, since they disturb the formal structure as is almost certainly διὰ τοῦ σταυροῦ v. 16, which may be considered a 'Paulinism'. If διὰ τοῦ σταυροῦ falls out, then so does, quite likely, ποιῶν εἰρήνην v. 15 on formal grounds.

He now concludes that we may say 'with a considerable degree of certainty' that 2.14-16 is an early Christian hymn!'[5]

---

1. Helpful bibliographies of discussions of the hymnic nature of 2.14-16 or 2.14-17 or 2.14-18 are found in Barth, *Ephesians*, p. 261 and Schnackenburg, *Epheser*, pp. 106-107, for example. The former accepts the presence of a hymn, the latter denies it.

2. Schille, *Hymnen*, pp. 24-25.

3. E. Haupt, *Der Brief an die Epheser* (Göttingen, 1902), pp. 78-80.

4. Schille, *Hymnen*, p. 27.

5. Sanders, 'Hymnic Elements', p. 218.

In fact, however, a large degree of uncertainty appears to surround
the whole process. This sense of unease is only increased when some
who support the evidence of hymnic elements in Eph. 2.11-22 then
deny their presence in 1.3-14,[6] and *vice versa*,[7] making the application
of the criteria for the identification of hymns appear much less well-
founded and cetainly not 'more or less fool-proof' as, for example,
Barth would maintain.[8]

There are, of course, other approaches to the passage. One such is
Schnackenburg's, who treats 2.14-18 as a three-part unit within 2.11-22,
laying out parts 1 and 2 (2.14-15a[9] and 2.15b-16 respectively) in three
columns. The third section (2.17, 18) is laid out in a somewhat similar
fashion. What he produces thereby is not so much a structure as a dia-
grammatic representation of the dynamics of the passage that senses the
tension in the first two parts between 'once' and 'now', the 'two' and
the 'one', 'enmity' and 'peace', and stresses the central role of Christ
who stands in the middle. In the third section everything that is negative
is laid out on the left, with its positive outcome portrayed on the right-
hand side. These are some of the parallels and contrasts that emerge
from the chiastic pattern, but they are sustained over a longer section
than he suggests. The identification of the whole of 2.11-22 as a chiasmus leads to a better appreciation of the author's flow of thought.

Lincoln offers another approach to the structure of the passage,[10]
included here because he specifically prefers his own scheme to that of
the 'somewhat contrived'[11] identification of a chiasmus in the passage.
He focuses on the ποτὲ...νῦν contrast, in which he finds the pre-
Christian past (explicitly or implicitly) referred to in 2.11, 12 and 13, set
over against the Christian present in 2.13 and, implicitly, in 2.19. He
suggests that some aspects of the contrast are completed in 2.11-13, but
that, for others, 2.14-18 intervenes before other aspects mentioned in
2.12 are reversed in 2.19. He calls this *schema* 'a major structural element in the thought of Eph. 2:11-22, particularly since it shapes the key

6.   Notably and strongly, Sanders, 'Hymnic Elements', p. 232.
7.   Schnackenburg, *Epheser*, pp. 43ff., although he stops short of referring to
the strophic or thematic division of the section that he proposes as a 'hymn'.
8.   Barth, 'Traditions', p. 9.
9.   Erroneously labelled '16a' in my copy.
10.   Lincoln, *Ephesians*, pp. 124-34.
11.   Lincoln, *Ephesians*, p. 126, in relation to the chiasmus suggested in Kirby,
Ephesians, pp. 156-57—see further 3.2 below.

summarizing verse', 2.19.[12] He still has to admit, however, that it is supplemented by other material, with 2.14-18 providing an excursus on how the readers' changed situation was accomplished by Christ, and 2.20-22 expanding the imagery for the new community of the church introduced in 2.19. The whole *schema* has as its purpose the highlighting of the present highly privileged situation of its members.[13] It will be argued in this chapter that 2.14-18 is not an excursus, but is very closely linked with 2.13 under the influence of Isa. 57.19, and in fact contains the central point of the passage that the law, the cause of the separation of Jew and Gentile, has been abrogated, making possible the creation of the one new man in Christ.

Lincoln is right insofar as the 'then...now' *schema* is a major structuring element for the passage, although it is only one such element. The parallels in the passage are best, although not wholly, displayed in the symmetries of a chiasmus. Lincoln may have fallen into the trap of imagining that we are faced with the *alternative* of choosing his *schema* or that of a chiasmus. It is my position that the skeletal structure is best portrayed as a chiasmus, which is then enfleshed at other levels by parallels, contrasts and other allusions beyond the chiastic pattern, thus lending the passage its dynamism.

Lincoln's attempted reconstruction of what he sees as hymnic material in 2.14-16 is no more convincing than any of the others. Of the 57 words in these verses, he suggests that 14 are three different glosses by the author. He would omit τοῦ φραγμοῦ, ἐν τῇ σαρκὶ τὸν νόμον τῶν ἐντολῶν ἐν δόγμασιν and διὰ τοῦ σταυροῦ. These omissions would greatly smooth the syntax, but must be questionable as a procedure to simplify awkward exegetical points. Nor is his suggestion persuasive that the 'hymn' originally had a cosmic context (the 'two' are the two parts of the cosmos, heaven and earth), with the purpose of the additions being to adapt the preformed material to the present situation.[14]

3.2. *Earlier Attempts at Identifying Chiasmus in Ephesians 2.11-22*

It is becoming increasingly necessary in this field to be able to examine competing chiastic patterns, with a view to suggesting which one best enhances the content of the passage. Eph. 2.11-22 is an unusual instance,

---

12. Lincoln, *Ephesians*, p. 125.
13. Lincoln, *Ephesians*, p. 126.
14. Lincoln, *Ephesians*, pp. 128-29 and 140-41.

in that there are at least five proposed chiasms in the literature, all of which encompass exactly the same unit of material: those of Lund, Kirby, Giavini, Turner and Bailey.[15] Kirby, Giavini and Bailey make no reference to any other chiastic pattern for this passage,[16] but it is interesting that they all, apparently independently,[17] conclude that the passage is chiastic, writing in 1968, 1970 and 1983 respectively, the first two before the current upsurge of interest in New Testament chiasmus.[18]

3.2.1. *Turner's Patterns*

Turner[19] views 2.11-22 as 'an elaborate triple chiasmus', although it yields, in effect, three separate chiasms. He suggests:

a. (2.11-13) A once; B Gentiles; C flesh; D uncircumcision; D′ circumcision; C′ flesh; B′ strangers; A′ now in Christ.

b. (2.13-17) A far off, near; B blood of Christ; C both one; D middle wall; E hostility; F his flesh; G law; G′ commandments; F′ new man; E′ peace; D′ reconcile; C′ one body; B′ cross; A′ far off, near.

c. (2.18-22) A Spirit; B Father; C strangers; D house of God; E built; F foundation; F′ corner-stone; E′ building; D′ holy temple; C′ built *together*; B′ God; A′ Spirit.

At first sight, this may appear to produce a highly symmetrical pattern. Particular care, however, must be taken when a passage uses vocabulary or ideas repeatedly, as it offers great scope to the ingenuity of the commentator to 'choose' parallel elements in such a way as to produce a pattern that is wholly artificial.[20] Little is to be gained by analysing Turner's patterns in detail, but if they are expanded into consecutive

15. Lund in *Crozer Quarterly* 20, p. 110 (listed in Welch, *Chiasmus*, p. 350, an article that I have been unable to trace, and to which no one else appears to make reference); Kirby, *Ephesians*, pp. 156-57; G. Giavini, 'La structure litteraire d'Eph. 2.11-22', *NTS* 16 (1970), pp. 209-11; Turner, *Style*, p. 98; Bailey, *Poet*, p. 63.

16. Turner cites his own structure, and is also aware of Giavini's.

17. Although I recognize that I cannot *prove* that they were unaware of Lund's article.

18. Neither Welch nor Di Marco, writing respectively in 1981 and 1979, and each producing extensive catalogues of NT chiasms suggested by a wide cross-section of scholars, list Kirby's, Giavini's or Turner's structures.

19. Turner, *Style*, p. 98.

20. See 1.4.3 e above.

elements using the Greek text, the atomistic nature of his chiasms clearly emerges.[21]

In his first chiasmus (2.11-13) some of the more serious weaknesses include the particularly poor balance of B and B'. In the Greek text of 2.11 the four words ποτὲ ὑμεῖς τὰ ἔθνη appear to be a closely linked phrase, which could perhaps be balanced neatly with νυνὶ δὲ ἐν Χριστῷ Ἰησοῦ. It is an odd procedure to split ποτέ from the rest of the phrase, and then be required to parallel τὰ ἔθνη with ξένοι, highlighting this single word from a long clause full of significant ideas in order to create B'. In addition, no matter how 2.12 is apportioned between C', B' and A', a structure always ensues in which B is very brief (ὑμεῖς τὰ ἔθνη), and B' inappropriately long (the most sympathetic division would make B': ὅτι ἦτε τῷ καιρῷ ἐκείνῳ χωρὶς Χριστοῦ, ἀπηλλοτριωμένοι τῆς πολιτείας τοῦ Ἰσραὴλ καὶ ξένοι τῶν διαθηκῶν τῆς ἐπαγγελίας).

Furthermore, Turner has to make a very unlikely division of the material by ending his first chiasmus with νυνὶ δὲ ἐν Χριστῷ Ἰησοῦ, the first words of the sentence that continues into the second chiasmus. This clearly breaks the flow of syntax, and is a particularly acute problem if one of the functions of chiastic patterning is as a structuring device.[22]

In the second pattern (2.13-17) it is difficult to see the justification, for example, for paralleling ἔχθραν in E with εἰρήνην in E', rather than with ἔχθραν in A'. This may be another instance of choosing parallels in a passage where there is repeated usage of certain terms in such a way as to produce a pattern, rather than the pattern emerging from the flow of syntax.

While Turner has sensed a regularity of movement in the passage, his analysis does not help our understanding of it, fragmenting rather than enhancing its impact, and possibly obscuring the author's purpose.

3.2.2. *The Suggestions of Giavini, Kirby and Bailey*

All these patterns are more akin to each other than to Turner's. Giavini's suggestion is of a scheme with the form ABCDC'B'A',[23] with the central element D capable of subdivision into abcdea'b'c'd'. He balances a long element A (2.11, 12), highlighting τῆς πολιτείας and

---

21. The result of this can be seen in my earlier thesis, *Chiasmus*, pp. 136-38.
22. See 1.5.1 above.
23. Using a standard notation, rather than Giavini's.

ξένοι, with a slightly longer A´ (2.19-22), drawing attention to συμπολῖται and ξένοι. In B (2.13) and B´ (2.17b, 18) he highlights the concepts of being 'far' and 'near', while C (2.14a) and C´ (2.17a) share the concept of peace.

He resolves his central element D thus:

a   2.14b ὁ ποιήσας **τὰ ἀμφότερα ἕν**
b   καὶ τὸ μεσότοιχον τοῦ φραγμοῦ λύσας,
c   **τὴν ἔχθραν,**
d   ἐν τῇ σαρκὶ αὐτοῦ,
e   15 τὸν νόμον τῶν ἐντολῶν ἐν δόγμασιν καταργήσας,
a´   ἵνα **τοὺς δύο** κτίσῃ ἐν αὐτῷ **εἰς ἕνα** καινὸν ἄνθρωπον
    ποιῶν εἰρήνην
b´   16 καὶ ἀποκαταλλάξῃ τοὺς ἀμφοτέρους ἐν ἑνὶ σώματι
    τῷ θεῷ διὰ τοῦ σταυροῦ,
c´   ἀποκτείνας **τὴν ἔχθραν**
d´   ἐν αὐτῷ.

Giavini finds that the correspondences are sometimes verbal and some-times in the contents of the elements.[24] Without offering any detailed exegesis to defend his structure, he suggests that some insights may be gained through it, feeling that it lends order to the different ideas in the passage, and that it confirms Schlier's 'excellent suggestion' that the little passage corresponding to elements ea´b´c´d´ could be a Pauline rein-terpretation demythologizing the Judaeo-gnostic conception of redemp-tion expressed in abcd.[25] The chiastic pattern underlines the central idea of the whole passage—that Christ has reconciled us with God, getting rid of the law and replacing it with his 'corps-sang-chair-esprit-croix'.[26] His analysis of D is not convincing, although he is right to see here the crux of the chiasmus. There is certainly some degree of direct parallelism

24. Giavini, 'Structure', p. 210.
25. Schlier, *Epheser*, pp. 123ff.
26. Giavini's subdivided central panel D with its nine elements is not, of course, chiastic since there is no reversal of the order of the elements within it. This is quite legitimate in terms of the theory of chiasmus. He also makes a tentative suggestion that the presence of this structure and a similiar one that he has identified in Col. 1.12-20 ('La struttura letteraria dell'inno cristologico di Col.1', *RivBib* 15 [1967], pp. 317-20) may have implications for the authorship of Ephesians. No detail is given, other than the speculation that the Ephesian chiasmus may be a Pauline elaboration of earlier material (thus explaining the 'strange language' of 2.14, 15). I do not want to make any judgment on this aspect of his article, although I do feel that it would be a subject worth pursuing.

here that may be present alongside the chiasmus, but a more satisfactory account can be given of it in the pattern proposed by either Kirby or, more likely, by Bailey.

Kirby's and Bailey's patterns adopt an intermediate position between Turner's atomistic proposal and Giavini's (which also misses a number of significant balances, especially in A and A′), and are the most attractive of the four. They both follow the general flow of syntax, dividing the passage into recognizable sense units, without creating any serious imbalances in length between given pairs of elements, and throughout rely on a combination of contrasting words and ideas. Kirby's suggestion is that, in this passage, the author is giving us a Christian midrash on Isa. 57.19, although he does not use the chiasmus in his exegesis.[27] Bailey offers his pattern as an example of one of the types of literary structure he proposes, calling it 'one of the most remarkable poetic structures in all of the New Testament'.[28] Kirby's[29] pattern (using the Greek text) is as follows:

A 2.11 Διὸ μνημονεύετε ὅτι ποτὲ ὑμεῖς **τὰ ἔθνη ἐν σαρκί**,
  B οἱ λεγόμενοι ἀκροβυστία ὑπὸ τῆς λεγομένης περιτομῆς **ἐν σαρκὶ** χειροποιήτου,
    C 12 ὅτι ἦτε τῷ καιρῷ ἐκείνῳ **χωρὶς Χριστοῦ**,
      D **ἀπηλλοτριωμένοι τῆς πολιτείας** τοῦ Ἰσραὴλ
        E καὶ **ξένοι** τῶν διαθηκῶν τῆς ἐπαγγελίας,
          F ἐλπίδα μὴ ἔχοντες καὶ **ἄθεοι** ἐν τῷ κόσμῳ.
            G 13 νυνὶ δὲ ἐν Χριστῷ Ἰησοῦ ὑμεῖς οἵ ποτε ὄντες **μακρὰν**
              H **ἐγενήθητε ἐγγὺς** ἐν τῷ αἵματι τοῦ Χριστοῦ.
                I 14 **Αὐτὸς γάρ ἐστιν ἡ εἰρήνη ἡμῶν**, ὁ ποιήσας τὰ ἀμφότερα ἕν
                  J καὶ τὸ μεσότοιχον τοῦ φραγμοῦ λύσας, **τὴν ἔχθραν**,
                    K (**ἐν τῇ σαρκὶ αὐτοῦ**) 15 τὸν νόμον τῶν ἐντολῶν ἐν δόγμασιν **καταργήσας**,
                    K′ ἵνα τοὺς δύο **κτίσῃ ἐν αὐτῷ** εἰς ἕνα καινὸν ἄνθρωπον
                  J′ ποιῶν **εἰρήνην**, 16 καὶ **ἀποκαταλλάξῃ** τοὺς ἀμφοτέρους ἐν ἑνὶ σώματι τῷ θεῷ διὰ τοῦ σταυροῦ,
                I′ ἀποκτείνας **τὴν ἔχθραν** ἐν αὐτῷ
              H′ 17 καὶ ἐλθὼν εὐηγγελίσατο εἰρήνην ὑμῖν **τοῖς μακρὰν**
            G′ καὶ εἰρήνην **τοῖς ἐγγύς**·
          F′ 18 ὅτι δι' **αὐτοῦ** ἔχομεν τὴν προσαγωγὴν οἱ ἀμφότεροι ἐν ἑνὶ **πνεύματι** πρὸς τὸν πατέρα.

27. Kirby, _Ephesians_, pp. 156-57.
28. Bailey, _Poet_, p. 63.
29. Kirby, _Ephesians_, p. 156.

Ε΄ 19 Ἄρα οὖν **οὐκέτι ἐστὲ ξένοι καὶ πάροικοι**,
Δ΄ ἀλλὰ ἐστὲ **συμπολῖται τῶν ἁγίων** καὶ **οἰκεῖοι τοῦ θεοῦ**,
Γ΄ 20 ἐποικοδομηθέντες ἐπὶ τῷ θεμελίῳ τῶν ἀποστόλων καὶ προφητῶν,
ὄντος ἀκρογωνιαίου αὐτοῦ Χριστοῦ Ἰησοῦ,
Β΄ 21 ἐν ᾧ πᾶσα οἰκοδομὴ συναρμολογουμένη αὔξει εἰς **ναὸν**
ἅγιον ἐν κυρίῳ,
Α΄ 22 ἐν ᾧ καὶ ὑμεῖς συνοικοδομεῖσθε εἰς κατοικητήριον τοῦ
θεοῦ **ἐν πνεύματι**.[30]

Lincoln comments specifically on Kirby's pattern, finding it somewhat
contrived, since some of the parallels, to him, are not convincing. He
sees a contrast *schema* here, and suggests, therefore, that a chiastic pattern is not tenable. The element of truth he finds in the chiastic theory is
that some words are used more than once, but this is explicable in other
ways in a passage that 'at very best is only loosely chiastic'.[31] This
argument is flawed, however, in that it is based on the false premise that
it is necessary to choose between the contrast *schema* and the chiasmus,
when the former may be present in, or superimposed on, the latter. His
other points are dealt with at the appropriate stage in exegesis.

Bailey's[32] pattern shows many similarities to Kirby's:

2.11 Διὸ μνημονεύετε
1 ὅτι ποτὲ ὑμεῖς τὰ ἔθνη **ἐν σαρκί**,
οἱ λεγόμενοι ἀκροβυστία

2 ὑπὸ τῆς λεγομένης περιτομῆς
ἐν σαρκὶ χειροποιήτου,

3 12 ὅτι ἦτε τῷ καιρῷ ἐκείνῳ χωρὶς Χριστοῦ,
ἀπηλλοτριωμένοι τῆς πολιτείας τοῦ Ἰσραὴλ
καὶ ξένοι τῶν διαθηκῶν τῆς ἐπαγγελίας,
4 ἐλπίδα μὴ ἔχοντες
καὶ ἄθεοι **ἐν τῷ κόσμῳ**.

5 13 νυνὶ δὲ ἐν Χριστῷ Ἰησοῦ ὑμεῖς οἵ ποτε ὄντες μακρὰν
ἐγενήθητε ἐγγὺς ἐν τῷ αἵματι τοῦ Χριστοῦ.

30. Kirby, *Ephesians*, pp. 156-57. The emphasis is Kirby's. He maintains that
the parallelism between B and B΄ lies in the fact that 'made in the flesh by hands' is
contrasted with the 'holy temple in the Lord', which is the temple made without
hands. Even if this parallel is rejected as being weak, it need not mean that the whole
structure falls.
31. Lincoln, *Ephesians*, p. 126.
32. Bailey, *Poet*, p. 63. I have reproduced Bailey's notation and emphasized
words, but have used the Greek text. The underlined words represent his use of
italics.

6   14 Αὐτὸς γάρ ἐστιν ἡ εἰρήνη ἡμῶν,
ὁ ποιήσας **τὰ ἀμφότερα ἓν**
καὶ τὸ μεσότοιχον τοῦ φραγμοῦ λύσας,
τὴν ἔχθραν, ἐν τῇ σαρκὶ αὐτοῦ

7   15 τὸν νόμον τῶν ἐντολῶν ἐν δόγμασιν καταργήσας,
ἵνα τοὺς δύο κτίσῃ ἐν αὐτῷ εἰς **ἕνα**
καινὸν ἄνθρωπον

6′ ποιῶν εἰρήνην,
16 καὶ ἀποκαταλλάξῃ **τοὺς ἀμφοτέρους ἐν ἑνὶ
σώματι** τῷ θεῷ διὰ τοῦ σταυροῦ,
ἀποκτείνας τὴν ἔχθραν ἐν αὐτῷ.

5′ 17 καὶ ἐλθὼν εὐηγγελίσατο εἰρήνην ὑμῖν τοῖς μακρὰν
καὶ εἰρήνην τοῖς ἐγγύς·

4′ 18 ὅτι δι᾽ αὐτοῦ ἔχομεν τὴν προσαγωγὴν οἱ ἀμφότεροι
ἐν ἑνὶ πνεύματι πρὸς τὸν πατέρα

3′ 19 Ἄρα οὖν οὐκέτι ἐστὲ ξένοι καὶ πάροικοι,
ἀλλὰ ἐστὲ συμπολῖται τῶν ἁγίων
καὶ οἰκεῖοι τοῦ θεοῦ,

2′ 20 ἐποικοδομηθέντες ἐπὶ τῷ θεμελίῳ τῶν ἀποστόλων καὶ προφητῶν,
(ὄντος ἀκρογωνιαίου αὐτοῦ Χριστοῦ Ἰησοῦ, 21 ἐν ᾧ πᾶσα
οἰκοδομὴ συναρμολογουμένη)
αὔξει εἰς ναὸν ἅγιον **ἐν κυρίῳ**,

1′ 22 ἐν ᾧ καὶ ὑμεῖς συνοικοδομεῖσθε
εἰς κατοικητήριον τοῦ θεοῦ **ἐν πνεύματι**.[33]

3.3. *Further Investigation of the Chiasmus in Ephesians 2.11-22*

3.3.1. *A Proposed Chiastic Pattern for Ephesians 2.11-22*
The structure proposed in this study is very similar to Bailey's.[34] The
main purpose of the current investigation, therefore, should not be seen
as the analysis of a new chiasmus, but as an attempt to show that

33. Bailey, *Poet*, p. 63 n. 45 points out that 3 and 3′ could be read as three separate units, rather than as one. He keeps them together because he suggests that
throughout the author is working with two or three line units. Note, too, his use of
brackets in 2′, where he suggests that this is an additional comment to bring the passage into line with 1 Cor. 3.11.

34. Historically, I have been aware of Kirby's pattern for a number of years. I
felt that it was capable of some refinement and produced the chiasmus laid out in this
study. My attention was drawn to Bailey's work in this field only after I had arrived
at my own conclusions.

Bailey's pattern, slightly modified, is exegetically well-founded.

A   2.11 Διὸ μνημονεύετε ὅτι ποτὲ ὑμεῖς τὰ ἔθνη ἐν σαρκί,
B   οἱ λεγόμενοι ἀκροβυστία ὑπὸ τῆς λεγομένης περιτομῆς
        ἐν σαρκὶ χειροποιήτου,
C   12 ὅτι ἦτε τῷ καιρῷ ἐκείνῳ χωρὶς Χριστοῦ,
D   ἀπηλλοτριωμένοι τῆς πολιτείας τοῦ Ἰσραὴλ
E   καὶ ξένοι τῶν διαθηκῶν τῆς ἐπαγγελίας,
F   ἐλπίδα μὴ ἔχοντες καὶ ἄθεοι ἐν τῷ κόσμῳ.
    {G₁   13 νυνὶ δὲ ἐν Χριστῷ Ἰησοῦ ὑμεῖς οἵ ποτε ὄντες μακρὰν
G {
    {G₂   ἐγενήθητε ἐγγὺς ἐν τῷ αἵματι τοῦ Χριστοῦ.
    {H₁   14 Αὐτὸς γάρ ἐστιν ἡ εἰρήνη ἡμῶν, ὁ ποιήσας τὰ
H {   ἀμφότερα ἓν
    {H₂   καὶ τὸ μεσότοιχον τοῦ φραγμοῦ λύσας, τὴν ἔχθραν, ἐν τῇ
        σαρκὶ αὐτοῦ,
I   15 τὸν νόμον τῶν ἐντολῶν ἐν δόγμασιν καταργήσας,
Ι´   ἵνα τοὺς δύο κτίσῃ ἐν αὐτῷ εἰς ἕνα καινὸν ἄνθρωπον
    {H₁´   ποιῶν εἰρήνην, 16 καὶ ἀποκαταλλάξῃ τοὺς
H´ {   ἀμφοτέρους ἐν ἑνὶ σώματι τῷ θεῷ διὰ τοῦ σταυροῦ,
    {H₂´   ἀποκτείνας τὴν ἔχθραν ἐν αὐτῷ.
    {G₁´   17 καὶ ἐλθὼν εὐηγγελίσατο εἰρήνην ὑμῖν τοῖς μακρὰν
G´ {
    {G₂´   καὶ εἰρήνην τοῖς ἐγγύς·
F´   18 ὅτι δι' αὐτοῦ ἔχομεν τὴν προσαγωγὴν οἱ ἀμφότεροι ἐν
        ἑνὶ πνεύματι πρὸς τὸν πατέρα.
E´   19 Ἄρα οὖν οὐκέτι ἐστὲ ξένοι καὶ πάροικοι,
D´   ἀλλὰ ἐστὲ συμπολῖται τῶν ἁγίων καὶ οἰκεῖοι τοῦ θεοῦ,
C´   20 ἐποικοδομηθέντες ἐπὶ τῷ θεμελίῳ τῶν ἀποστόλων καὶ
        προφητῶν, ὄντος ἀκρογωνιαίου αὐτοῦ Χριστοῦ Ἰησοῦ,
B´   21 ἐν ᾧ πᾶσα οἰκοδομὴ συναρμολογουμένη αὔξει εἰς
        ναὸν ἅγιον ἐν κυρίῳ,
A´   22 ἐν ᾧ καὶ ὑμεῖς συνοικοδομεῖσθε εἰς κατοικητήριον
        τοῦ θεοῦ ἐν πνεύματι.[35]

This is an instance where it is important to suspend judgment about the probability of this being a good example of chiasmus until *all* the evidence is presented and weighed because the parallels are not all equally clear, especially some of those on the perimeter. They are, however, a feature of which a reasonable account can be given. In one or two instances, too, it is possible to construe the Greek differently. This shall be dealt with in the course of exegesis.

---

35. For convenience, a copy of this chiasmus can be found in the Appendix.

3.3.2. *Six Loosely Paralleled Elements: ABCC′B′A′*

The parallelism between A (2.11a), B (2.11b), C (2.12a) and A′ (2.22), B′ (2.21) and C′ (2.20) is not close, or even immediately apparent. The reason for this, developed below, is the emergence in the author's mind of a particular metaphor that is introduced at the expense of maintaining the strong parallelism of the central panel of the passage.[36] Later in this chapter the hypothesis that the author intended the whole to be seen as a chiasmus will be justified. At this stage some conceptual parallels are noted: the chiasmus begins in the realm of the flesh and ends in the realm of the Spirit; it begins with an outward, physical action that divides humankind into two groups and ends with a new, unified, spiritual structure into which 'you also' are built; it begins with a group 'apart from Christ', and ends with a community in which Christ is the 'corner-' or 'key-stone'.

The first occurrence of the term τὰ ἔθνη in Ephesians is in 2.11. The idea of 'Gentiles in the flesh'[37] may be intentionally contrasted with the final phrase of the chiasmus, ἐν πνεύματι. In both A and A′ the use of ὑμεῖς appears to be deliberate, thereby distinguishing the writer from those addressed. Because of this, it may be that ἐν πνεύματι in 2.22 forms a better contrast with ἐν σαρκί in 2.11 than ἐν πνεύματι in 2.18, where the complete phrase is ἐν ἑνὶ πνεύματι, the *one Spirit* being involved in the access of οἱ ἀμφότεροι to God.[38]

The idea of the flesh is emphasized by its repetition in B,[39] in the phrase περιτομῆς ἐν σαρκὶ χειροποιήτου.[40] Although the use in B of λεγόμενοι and λεγομένης are not in themselves disparaging, the overall effect is to highlight the outward nature of circumcision and the

---

36. The introduction of this metaphor, and the fact that it weakens otherwise clear symmetry, may also give a reasonable account of the fact that C′ is somewhat longer than C.

37. 'In the realm of the flesh'—so Barth, *Ephesians*, p. 254.

38. It should be remembered, too, that there are other allusions within the passage that fall outside the chiastic pattern; thus, the 'once' or 'then' reference of 2.11 is picked up again in the 'now'/'then' contrast of 2.13, the whole thrust of 2.11, 12 being summarized in ὑμεῖς οἵ ποτε ὄντες μακράν.

39. I can see no advantage in following Bailey's pattern at this point by assigning οἱ λεγόμενοι ἀκροβυστία to A. Indeed, it might be better to keep the concepts of circumcision and uncircumcision together in the one element, especially as this is more in keeping with the flow of syntax of the section.

40. It may be that Rom. 2.28-29; Phil. 3.2-3 and perhaps also Col. 2.11 are in the background here.

gulf that its presence or absence fixes between Jew and Gentile. In a similar way, the use of χειροποίητος underscores the transient nature of the distinction.[41]

The term χειροποίητος is worth exploring in the context of the chiasmus. This is its only use in the Pauline letters; in its five other New Testament occurrences[42] it is associated with *temples*, as is its opposite, ἀχειροποίητος, on two occasions.[43] Jesus' words reported in Mk 14.58 appear to refer not just to the destruction of a building, but to the destruction of the old order of which it is the symbol and centre.[44] One of the other most striking symbols of that old order was physical circumcision itself. In this hypothetical pattern there may, therefore, be a link between χειροποίητος and ναὸς ἅγιος in B′, although such parallelism is weak.[45] It is difficult, however, to be sure that this usage and, by implication, this vague parallel would have meant anything to the original readers/hearers.[46] Three possible courses of action can now be followed: it can be recognized that this is an example of an otherwise well-founded example of chiasmus with one pair of elements that have no parallels of substance; B and B′ can be combined in some way with the elements immediately preceding or following; they can be accepted as a consciously introduced imbalance that, because of its very presence, draws attention to the point that the author is making (the two groups once separated because of circumcision are now united in a holy temple in the Lord).[47]

41. Robinson, *Ephesians*, p. 158.

42. Mk 14.58; Acts 7.48; 17.24; Heb. 9.11, 24.

43. Mk 14.58; 2 Cor. 5.1; its third appearance is in Col. 2.11.

44. V. Taylor, *The Gospel according to Saint Mark* (London, 2nd edn, 1966), p. 566.

45. Cf. Kirby, *Ephesians*, p. 157, who suggests this link, but without discussing the wider usage of the terms in detail. Bailey, *Poet*, p. 63, apparently sees the balance as being 'in the flesh' in B with 'in the Lord' in B′. Again, however, this is hardly a strong parallel.

46. Having said that, however, it begs the question as to which is the more important—the parallels as conceived in the writer's own mind, or the parallels perceived by the readers. Not every subtlety of structure is necessarily grasped by an audience of very mixed educational background. It seems to be rather patronizing to suggest that a writer would deliberately tailor every allusion so that it might be appreciated by those who may be said to be at 'the lowest common denominator' of educational ability.

47. There is, however, more that can be said about this, and a final decision about the flow of thought of the section is best delayed until later. See further the

In C there are different ways of construing the Greek. The overall syntax of 2.11, 12 is somewhat clumsy. In the first place, it is preferable, with the majority, to take ὅτι in 2.12 as resuming ὅτι in 2.11, rather than being causative.[48] Secondly, χωρὶς Χριστοῦ may be treated as the first predicate of ἦτε, with further predicates in D and E,[49] or be regarded (along with τῷ καιρῷ ἐκείνῳ) as a restatement of their condition[50] that may look back to A. The latter view which sees C as a resumption of A is preferable; otherwise the order of the ensuing catalogue of disadvantage seems a little surprising.[51] Thus, τῷ καιρῷ ἐκείνῳ looks back to ποτέ; χωρὶς Χριστοῦ resumes τὰ ἔθνη ἐν σαρκί, leading to a translation like: 'Remember that you, then Gentiles in the flesh, called...by hands, that you, at that time apart from Christ, were separated...' The effect of this is to draw attention to the long phrase οἱ λεγόμενοι...χειροποιήτου, with its point that the author specifically wishes to make, even at the expense of creating a rather awkward construction.

In C′ the primary point of contrast is to be found in the fact that, far from being without, or apart from, Christ, he has now assumed key importance for the former Gentiles in their changed status. There is more to be said about C′ below.[52]

It should be noted that, in these outside elements, the parallels that have been highlighted have been parallels of *content*, rather than those of *form*. While it is preferable to be able to highlight *formal* parallels first, the nature of this present example, with elements A, B and C only loosely paralleled with their counterparts, means that parallels of content have assumed more significance than those of form.

discussion of the central elements, I and I′ below.

48. See Barth, *Ephesians*, pp. 225-26; Lincoln, *Ephesians*, p. 136.

49. Westcott, *Ephesians*, p. 35; Schnackenburg, *Epheser*, p. 105; Barth, *Ephesians*, p. 253; Lincoln, *Ephesians*, p. 136.

50. Robinson, *Ephesians*, pp. 157-58.

51. Cf. Mitton, *Ephesians*, pp. 102-103, although I am not sure that he is correct in suggesting that 'Christ' is used in the general sense of 'Jewish messiah', or the messiah of Jewish hopes.

52. See 3.4.4 below. It does not matter for my purposes whether ἀκρογωνιαίος is taken to refer to a foundational cornerstone or a crowning keystone. A recent survey of the evidence for both these possibilities and a good discussion of it is found in Lincoln, *Ephesians*, pp. 154-56, whose view is that it should be taken as the keystone. I find his view persuasive.

3.3.3. *The Catalogue of Disadvantage and its Transformation: DEFF′E′D′*

In terms of the chiastic pattern, the striking parallels begin with D (2.12b) and D′ (2.19b). If the above interpretation of C is correct, then D displays the first great disadvantage of those who have been described as Gentiles, or χωρὶς Χριστοῦ—they have been 'alienated from the commonwealth of Israel' or 'excluded from the citizenship of Israel'.[53] They had no part in the community. This is the basic statement of their condition, leading inevitably to their exclusion from all the other privileges (to be detailed in E [2.12c] and F [2.12d]). Although the language and contexts are different, Paul's list in Rom. 9.4-5 is brought to mind, with its opening phrase οἵτινές εἰσιν Ἰσραηλῖται.

In D′ one of the effects of Christ's actions results in those previously excluded from the πολιτεία now being reckoned to be συμπολῖται. However, there may well be another, rather less obvious allusion in D′ to D. This rests on the relationship between οἰκεῖος and ἀλλότριος. These are formal opposites, 'one's own' in contrast to 'another's'.[54] In this passage of many contrasts the use of ἀπαλλοτριόω in D and οἰκεῖος in D′ may be more than just coincidence. Having said this, the fact should not be overlooked that there is also a strong link between οὐκέτι...ξένοι καὶ πάροικοι in E′ (2.19a) with συμπολῖται...καὶ οἰκεῖοι in D′. It will be suggested below that the use of οἰκεῖος (together with πάροικος) may also have been the trigger for the development of the building metaphor in C′, B′, A′.[55]

Alienation or exclusion from the πολιτεία has another inevitable consequence that is described in E by ξένος: they are strangers, or foreigners, to the covenants of promise.[56] These 'covenants' govern the life of the πολιτεία. It is ξένος that is now specifically highlighted in E′ by the statement 'no longer...strangers'.

In E′, however, πάροικος (the first occurrence in the chiasmus of a term derived from οἶκος) is added to ξένος. While the latter has the general sense of foreigner or alien, the former appears to have a more

---

53. Barth, *Ephesians*, p. 257.
54. Robinson, *Ephesians*, p. 163.
55. Robinson, *Ephesians*, p. 163. See below.
56. Both διαθῆκαι (unusually in the New Testament, here and in Rom. 9.4 in the plural) and ἐπαγγελία figure in the list of privileges in Rom. 9.4.

specific connotation of 'resident alien'.[57] Barth is probably right that it is unlikely that the author wishes to distinguish two groups, and that this is simply a hendiadys. However, as has already been noted, the use of πάροικος is neatly contrasted with οἰκεῖος in D'.

The description of the Gentiles' situation is completed in F by the two assertions that they are without hope and without God in the world. The idea of being without hope would appear to be a technical usage,[58] insofar as it is unlikely that the author would claim that those belonging to Israel had a monopoly on this particular emotion. It is possible that what is meant is hope in a life beyond death,[59] or even the hope of sharing the glory of God, as in Rom. 5.2. That hope, of course, is centred in Christ[60] and, to that extent, there may also be an allusion here to their situation without the 'hope of Israel'. When they are said to be ἄθεοι, it appears that this is intended as the climactic statement of their lostness.[61] Barth calls ἐν τῷ κόσμῳ 'a seemingly redundant addition',[62] but this misses the point. To be without God is to be without true hope even in the present world, to say nothing of the one to come.[63]

By F' (2.18), however, a radically changed situation is reflected. The sense of abandonment has gone, to be replaced by access to the Father. While the detail of how this has been accomplished will be divulged in the central elements of the pattern, the access is δι' αὐτοῦ and is open to 'both of us' in one Spirit. Barth[64] draws attention to the 'possessive' nature of the statement in F', with its use of ἔχω—the same verb, of course, the participle of which is used negatively in F as 'not possessing'.[65]

---

57. So Abbott, *Ephesians*, p. 68; Bruce, *Ephesians*, p. 302; Barth, *Ephesians*, p. 269; *et al.*

58. *Contra* Lincoln, *Ephesians*, pp. 137-38 who suggests that any future hope of the Gentiles could be seen as no hope because they were not true hopes.

59. Cf 1 Thess. 4.13 (μὴ ἔχοντες ἐλπίδα); Acts 24.15; Mitton, *Ephesians*, p. 103.

60. Rom. 5.2; Col. 1.27; Acts 28.20.

61. Robinson, *Ephesians*, p. 159; Barth, *Ephesians*, p. 260; *et al.*

62. Barth, *Ephesians*, p. 258.

63. Bruce, *Ephesians*, p. 294.

64. Barth, *Ephesians*, p. 268.

65. 'Hope' (as in F) and 'access' (as in F') are linked elswhere in the Pauline letters, notably in Rom. 5.2.

3.3.4. *The Central Panel*

The display of the chiasmus suggested that G (2.13) and G′ (2.17) can each be subdivided into two elements that keep the same order in the two halves of the chiasmus in an analagous fashion to that seen in the earlier chiastic pattern in Eph. 1.3-10. My chiasmus (like Bailey's) is different from Kirby's at this point, because he contrasts the first μακράν with the second ἐγγύς and the first ἐγγύς with the second μακράν. His pattern may be less satisfactory in light of the influence of Isa. 57.19, where the order of the terms is μακράν...ἐγγυς, a feature that my pattern recognizes and retains. Further resolution like this can be accepted or rejected without affecting the validity of the whole pattern.

Clearly a new situation is envisaged with νυνὶ δέ. A contrast appears to be intended with something that has gone before. The most attractive suggestion[66] may be to see the whole phrase νυνὶ δὲ ἐν Χριστῷ as being contrasted with τῷ καιρῷ ἐκείνῳ χωρὶς Χριστοῦ, although obviously there is also a sense of its being balanced by ποτέ in its own clause.[67] The use of μακράν...ἐγγύς is very understandable in line with the imagery evoked by ἀπηλλοτριωμένοι, and so forth. It may well be this that now prompts in the author's mind the references to 'peace' in the following verses, the whole being tied together in G′ which contains the most explicit allusion to Isa. 57.19. The blood of Christ may be described as the 'agent' of this new status of οἵ ποτε ὄντες μακράν.[68] The 'blood' is also the means of making peace in Col. 1.20, where the ideas of εἰρήνη, αἷμα and σταυρός are all closely linked.

In the light of this, it does not seem surprising that G′ brings together the concepts of 'peace', 'far' and 'near'. There appears to be widespread agreement that Isa. 57.19 lies in the background, although it is not an exact quotation[69]

One new feature that this element introduces is that of public proclamation. This may well be an allusion to Isa. 52.7.[70]

Another new feature of G′ is the way that μακράν and ἐγγύς are used. In G the 'far' are brought 'near', and in context 'near' appears to be an equivalent expression for incorporation into the new people of

---

66. Cf. Abbott, *Ephesians*, p. 59.

67. A timely reminder that there are often more parallels and contrasts in a chiastic pattern than those revealed by the bare outline.

68. Mitton, *Ephesians*, p. 105.

69. Isa. 57.19 (LXX) εἰρήνην ἐπ᾽ εἰρήνην τοῖς μακρὰν καὶ τοῖς ἐγγὺς οὖσιν

70. So Robinson, *Ephesians*, p. 162; Bruce, *Ephesians*, p. 301; *et al.*

God.[71] However, in G´ two different groups are in mind, both of whom need to have peace proclaimed to them as part of God's new people. This raises the question of their identity.[72] The simplest solution, perhaps, is to identify the 'far' with Christians from a Gentile background, and the 'near' with those from a Jewish background,[73] and this, as such, produces a powerful reminder to Jewish Christians that there was a gulf that had to be bridged by Christ before they too could be incorporated into the people of God. This is a good example of the exegetical dividend that can ensue from an asymmetry of content linked to symmetry of form.

The use of ἐλθών gives rise to much pedantic discussion about what precisely is meant by the reference to Christ's coming and preaching (his incarnation, or resurrection appearances, etc?).[74] The occurrence of ἐλθών need have no function other than to prepare for the introduction of the allusions to Isa. 52.7 and 57.19, the author reminding the recipients that the message and mission of Christ are firmly rooted in his historical ministry. The proclamation of peace is not a proclamation from *heaven* as in Isa. 57.19, but one that finds its focus διὰ τοῦ σταυροῦ (2.16), ἐν τῇ σαρκὶ αὐτοῦ (2.14), ἐν τῷ αἵματι τοῦ Χριστοῦ (2.13).

It may also be that H (2.14) and H´ (2.15c, 16) can be subdivided into H_1 and H_2, and so on, because of the linking of εἰρήνη and ἔχθρα in both H and H´ in the same order, although it is theoretically possible that the balance is between the first use of 'peace' with the second use of 'hostility', and so on, as Kirby suggests. However, there is a better balance achieved in my pattern (and again in Bailey's), because in H_2 and $H_2´$ the hostility is said to be destroyed; furthermore, in both H_1 and $H_1´$ the idea of two being made one is present, a point missed in Kirby's pattern.

As has already been noted, the great majority of those who find a 'hymn' within this passage see it beginning at 2.14. Apart from all the problems associated with its 'recovery', 2.14 is, in fact, closely linked to what precedes it, inasmuch as the 'far...near' metaphor may recall Isa. 57.19 to the author's mind, provoking the next statement Αὐτος

71. But see the discussion on H and H´ below.

72. And whether the peace is one between the two groups themselves or between each of them and God—but, again, see the discussion of H and H´.

73. So Abbott, *Ephesians*, p. 67.

74. See, e.g., Mitton, *Ephesians*, p. 109; and the summary in Lincoln, *Ephesians*, pp. 148-49, in which he calls much of the discussion 'redundant'.

γάρ...εἰρήνη ἡμῶν. Indeed, the introduction of the idea of 'peace' is somewhat unexpected in terms of the flow of thought in the passage *up to this point*. Elements A to G have graphically described the position of the Gentiles, but there has been no statement of the existence of any state of hostility, and, in fact, immediately after the assertion that Christ is 'our' peace, his role is defined in terms of his making τὰ ἀμφότερα ἓν, which seems to pick up the idea of the clear and sharp distinction between Jews and Gentiles that has been the dominant theme of the passage so far.

The two neuter genders in the phrase τὰ ἀμφότερα ἓν are best discussed by Barth,[75] who concludes that the idea of two things made one most likely refers to Jews and Gentiles created into 'a single new man' (I', 2.15b).[76]

In the chiastic pattern H₁ is balanced with H₁'. These have in common the ideas of 'making' (although with different objects), 'peace', and 'both' (neuter in one and masculine in the other) becoming 'one' (undefined in the first, and linked with 'body' in the second). At first sight this appears to be a good balance, but closer inspection reveals a recurring problem in passages where similar ideas are used a number of times, viz., why *this* balance should be preferred to that of balancing H₁ with I', with their shared idea of two becoming one, especially if ποιῶν εἰρήνην were removed from H₁' and incorporated in I'.

It is not necessary, however, to choose between one as 'right' and the other as 'wrong'. The phrase itself may have been consciously placed so as to look back to I' as well as introducing H' as a parallel not fully accommodated by the chiastic pattern. There is no compelling reason for balancing H₁ with a modified I' rather than with H₁'. Undoubtedly, I' in part echoes the thought of H₁, but it will be suggested that the principle balance with I' lies in the contrast of 'abolishing' or 'abrogating' in I (2.15a) and 'creating' in I'. The arrangement of the elements in my pattern allows for the display of the strong parallels between D, E, F, G and their counterparts, with the idea of 'two' becoming 'one' running like a connecting thread through the central panel of the chiasmus from H to H'.

The contents of H₂ have provoked much discussion. The term

---

75. Barth, *Ephesians*, pp. 262-63.
76. Westcott, *Ephesians*, pp. 36-37 suggests 'the two systems'—also attractive. However, I find difficult Lincoln's idea that it is best explained as a remnant of the traditional material that originally referred to heaven and earth (*Ephesians*, p. 140).

μεσότοιχον (a dividing wall, partition) occurs only here in the New Testament. φραγμός seems to carry with it the implication of a fence erected for protection or enclosure.[77] In the present phrase τοῦ φραγμοῦ is probably best taken as a genitive of apposition ('the dividing wall, that is, the fence').[78] The question now arises as to whether or not the author had a literal wall in mind, or whether this is metaphorical. Some identify it with the wall in the Temple that separated the Temple proper from the Court of the Gentiles.[79] It may be argued that if Ephesians is pre-70, the wall still stood, making this reference unlikely. My problem with this is to ask if such a cryptic allusion would have any meaning for the readers, especially if they were from a Gentile background, regardless of the date of writing. Schlier's theory that it is the Gnostic barrier that separates this world from the upper world of the πλήρωμα is not attractive, primarily because of the lateness of the evidence.[80] Others suggest a metaphorical usage.[81]

The various options are explored at some length by Schnackenburg and Barth.[82] Barth discusses five: the wall in the Temple, a strange description of the curtain in front of the Holy of Holies, the rabbinical fence around the law, a highly cryptic allusion to sins or the 'flesh' and, lastly, the Gnostic barrier. In this instance Barth's conclusion is helpful that the context suggests that it should not be interpreted in too rigid a fashion:

> It is the fact of the separation between Israel and the nations; it has to do with the law and its statutes and interpretations; it is experienced in the enmity between the Jews and Gentiles; it also consists of the enmity of both Jews and Gentiles against God.[83]

It is important, however, to note that Barth's analysis depends on reading back into the meaning of the wall ideas and concepts that have not yet surfaced in the line-by-line exegesis of the passage. Schnackenburg thinks that the picture is that of the Torah with all its regulations as the

77. Barth, *Ephesians*, p. 263; Abbott, *Ephesians*, p. 61.

78. Cf. Lincoln, *Ephesians*, p. 141.

79. Westcott, *Ephesians*, p. 37; Abbott, *Ephesians*, p. 61; Robinson, *Ephesians*, p. 160; Kirby, *Ephesians*, p. 158.

80. Schlier, *Epheser*, pp. 123-40.

81. Mitton, *Ephesians*, p. 105; Bruce, *Ephesians*, p. 296.

82. Schnackenburg, *Epheser*, pp. 113-14; Barth, *Ephesians*, pp. 283-86.

83. Barth, *Ephesians*, p. 286; he discusses its wider implications in his aptly titled book, *The Broken Wall* (London, 1960).

fence or dividing partition between Jews and non-Jews.[84] A significant consequence of this was that the law came to be identified by the Gentiles with Jewish particularism, and hence became itself a cause of alienation and hostility.[85]

It must now be asked how τὴν ἔχθραν is to be understood, and whether ἐν τῇ σαρκὶ αὐτοῦ belongs in this element or the next. The main options are to take τὴν ἔχθραν as a second object of λύσας, in apposition with μεσότοιχον, in which case, ἐν τῇ σαρκὶ αὐτοῦ can be dependent on λύσας[86] or dependent on καταργήσας[87] or, to take τὴν ἔχθραν as the first stated object of καταργήσας, in apposition with τὸν νόμον,[88] in which case ἐν τῇ σαρκὶ αὐτοῦ, and indeed λύσας itself, would be taken as part of I rather than H. There is no consensus on this.

While it might be possible to follow Bruce[89] and suggest that, since 'wall', 'hostility' and 'law' are so closely associated, the sense is not materially affected by the construction, this seems like a counsel of despair, and certainly sheds no light on the author's thought processes. Those who find that καταργήσας is not particularly appropriate with ἔχθραν make a valid point.[90] Equally, it may be possible to argue that the use of νόμον in the long phrase τὸν νόμον τῶν ἐντολῶν ἐν δόγμασιν has caused it to be chosen 'as an afterthought',[91] but this is not persuasive either since the phrase ἐν τῇ σαρκὶ αὐτοῦ is left occurring between two accusatives in apposition, and materially relating to neither.

The view to be preferred is that τὴν ἔχθραν is a second object of λύσας, to which it is adjacent, and epexegetic of the first. While Barth calls the sudden reference to 'enmity' a 'surprise',[92] this misses the point because the 'surprise', if such a term can be used, is the sudden reference to 'peace' in H_1. As has been seen, up to now the author has well emphasized the differences between Jew and Gentile, but this has

---

84. Cf. the second-century BC *Epistle of Aristeas* 139ff.
85. So Lincoln, *Ephesians*, p. 141.
86. So Barth, *Ephesians*, pp. 253, 263-64.
87. So Schnackenburg, *Epheser*, pp. 113ff.; Mitton, *Ephesians*, p. 105.
88. So Westcott, *Ephesians*, pp. 36-37; Robinson, *Ephesians*, p. 161; Bruce, *Ephesians*, p. 298.
89. Bruce, *Ephesians*, p. 298.
90. Abbott, *Ephesians*, p. 62; *et al.*
91. So Robinson, *Ephesians*, p. 161.
92. Barth, *Ephesians*, p. 264.

been in terms of exclusion and lostness with no hint that a state of hostility existed. Why does peace then have to be made? It has already been suggested that the allusion to peace may be prompted by the influence of Isa. 57.19. It is only *after* the readers are told that the separation has been ended ('the two made one') and the barrier destroyed, that they discover that the dividing wall has been associated with enmity, and consequently why the introduction of the concept of Christ as their peace has been particularly appropriate.

It is more difficult to decide whether to assign ἐν τῇ σαρκὶ αὐτοῦ to H or I. The phrase itself is probably little more than a variant of 'in his blood' or 'through his cross', although it is just possible that it might refer to Jesus' earthly ministry, and could then be paraphrased 'in what he said and did'.[93] It may be that little hangs on this, since it is equally appropriate to refer it to either of the participles. However, 'the blood of Christ', coming at the end of G, is involved in bringing the 'far' 'near'. Element H expands on this, telling us that the two are in fact made one, with the abolition of the dividing wall and the hostility. It is appropriate to end this by reiterating the fact that it is accomplished 'in his flesh'. In addition, element H completes the first half of the chiasmus which now moves to the central elements I and I'. By ending H with the phrase ἐν τῇ σαρκὶ αὐτοῦ, the author may be deliberately echoing the final phrase of A, τὰ ἔθνη ἐν σαρκί; as those outside of Christ are called 'Gentiles in the flesh', so the enmity between them and the Jews is abolished by Jesus 'in his flesh'.[94]

In I and I' the basic balance is the contrast provided by καταργήσας and κτίσῃ, with the abrogation of the law being followed by the creation of the new order. Since the chiastic analysis suggests that I and I' are at the centre of the pattern, it is possible that they are of particular significance for understanding the author's purpose.

There is a striking accumulation of three words related in meaning in the phrase τὸν νόμον τῶν ἐντολῶν ἐν δόγμασιν. This could be a way of emphasizing by repetition, or the author may intend the readers to differentiate between them: 'the law, consisting of commandments, expressed in rigid rules or ordinances'.[95] Even if this is the case, a

---

93. So, e.g., Mitton, *Ephesians*, p. 107.

94. At this point I differ with Kirby and agree with Bailey. Neither of them offer any explanation of why they assign the phrase as they do.

95. So Mitton, *Ephesians*, p. 106; Abbott, *Ephesians*, p. 63; *et al.*

noticeably emphatic statement is still made. Lincoln[96] suggests that some commentators[97] shrink away from interpreting the phrase as a forthright statement of the abolition of the law,[98] motivated, perhaps, by a desire to 'harmonize' the attitude of the present author to the law with that in the undisputed Paulines.[99] While the analysis of what is precisely meant by 'law', and so on, is beyond the scope of this study, Robinson puts it well: 'It is as a code of manifold precepts, expressed in definite ordinances, that he declares it to have been annulled'.[100]

The abrogation of the law is the first part of the essential pivotal statement of the 'new deal' for the Gentile.[101] It was the very existence of the rules and regulations that drove the wedge between Jew and Gentile, supremely illustrated in circumcision. Once these have been rendered inoperative, the way is cleared for the new order, graphically described in Ι′ by the creating of the two εἰς ἕνα καινὸν ἄνθρωπον. This has overtones of the later 'third race' concept. Up to this point the reader could be forgiven for thinking that God's purpose would be satisifed in bringing the 'far' 'near', and that once the barriers associated with the old hostilities had been removed, all would be well between Jew and Gentile. This is now clearly shown to be insufficient. Jew and Gentile alike must be created into one new man in Christ.[102]

In Η′ (2.15b-16) ποιῶν εἰρήνην picks up and explains the opening phrase of Η.[103] In the context, the peace is that between Jew and Gentile. However, Η′ complements Η as the author's argument is pro-

96. As does Abbott, *Ephesians*, p. 64, before him.

97. E.g., Barth, *Ephesians*, pp. 287ff. who argues that it is the divisive aspects of the law that are abandoned; or Schlier, *Epheser*, p. 126, who thinks that it is the casuistry associated with the law.

98. Lincoln, *Ephesians*, p. 142.

99. I am not persuaded by C.J. Roetzel's argument in 'Jewish Christian–Gentile Christian Relations: A Discussion of Eph. 2.15a', *ZNW* 74 (1983), pp. 81-89, that ἐν δόγμασιν is a scribal gloss, despite its omission in 𝔓[46], vg[ms], nor that it should be rendered 'By his statutes, he has abolished the law of commandments' (noted and rejected by Barth, *Ephesians*, p. 264).

100. Robinson, *Ephesians*, p. 161.

101. Although it is not, of course, the first *suggestion* of a new deal: see 2.13-14.

102. Cf. 2 Cor. 5.17. It should be noted that there is a trivial 'shift and reversion' at the centre of this chiasmus in what Westcott, *Ephesians*, p. 38, calls 'the abrupt, unprepared transition from τὰ ἀμφότερα to τοὺς δύο'. In this case, it is of little interest or significance, and the latter immediately gives way to the former again for the remainder of the pattern.

103. So Abbott, *Ephesians*, p. 65.

gressed. It is not enough for peace to exist between Jew and Gentile: there is a more fundamental reconciliation that has to take place, as the two (now described by a masculine, rather than by a neuter as in H) are reconciled to God ἐν ἑνὶ σώματι. This phrase can be interpreted in different ways,[104] the main options being in terms of the physical body of Christ,[105] or Christ's body understood as the church,[106] or both the physical and so-called 'mystical' body,[107] or, indeed, it may be identified with the 'one new man' of I'.[108]

Whether διὰ τοῦ σταυροῦ should be taken with ἀποκαταλλάξῃ or ἀποκτείνας cannot be decided with certainty. Taking it with the former emphasizes the fact that the cross is the means of reconciliation. Taking it with the latter, with which it is juxtaposed, highlights the irony in the idea that the notorious instrument of death, the cross, should itself be the means of killing the hostility that existed between Jew and Gentile in the first instance, and more fundamentally, between humankind and God.

This is linked with the correct interpretation of ἐν αὐτῷ at the end of H₂'. If διὰ τοῦ σταυροῦ is taken with ἀποκαταλλάξῃ, then the obvious interpretation would be to take ἐν αὐτῷ as 'in it' or 'by it', referring to the cross. On the other hand, if διὰ τοῦ σταυροῦ is taken with ἀποκτείνας, the phrase becomes more (and, for me, excessively) convoluted, enmity being killed both in the cross and through the cross: it is both the instrument and the vehicle of Christ's activity.[109] Although any conclusion drawn from hypothesis built upon hypothesis must be treated with very great caution, if, as has been argued here, ἐν τῇ σαρκὶ αὐτοῦ belongs to H₂, then it is possible that, in line with the chiastic pattern, ἐν αὐτῷ actually looks back to this phrase: he kills the enmity in 'himself', in an analogous way to his abolishing the enmity ἐν τῇ σαρκὶ αὐτοῦ.[110] However we choose to interpret H' in detail, it does seem clear that the argument has been advanced from the position in H, as a new strand of thought is added, namely that both Jew and Gentile need to be reconciled to God as well as to each other, and that this reconciliation, described in terms of making peace, is effected through the cross.

---

104. Pursued by, e.g., Barth, *Ephesians*, pp. 297-98.
105. Barth, *Ephesians*, p. 298.
106. So Schnackenburg, *Epheser*, p. 117; Lincoln, *Ephesians*, p. 144; *et al.*
107. Schlier, *Epheser*, p. 135.
108. Abbott, *Ephesians*, p. 66.
109. Westcott, *Ephesians*, p. 39.
110. The reflexive ἑαυτῷ is actually found in F G *pc* lat.

This development is hinted at in I′ where the readers discover for the first time that there is more than just the reconciliation of Jew to Gentile in mind: there is a 'third race' in view. H′ makes this explicit.

The issues raised by G′ (2.17) have already been dealt with, but it should be noted how G′ further reinforces this new strand. Both former groupings of Gentile and Jew need to hear the same message: it is 'peace to the far and peace to the near', the repetition of εἰρήνη serving to underscore this fact.

3.3.5. *The Emergence of the Building Metaphor*
F′ (2.18), E′ (2.19a) and D′ (2.19b) need no further comment at this stage, but some attention has to be given to the final three elements of the pattern, in view of the weaker parallels with their counterparts in the first half. The key to understanding the author's flow of thought is to be found in the use of οἰκεῖος. Robinson is right (except perhaps in relation to authorship) that

> The word οἶκος underlying οἰκεῖοι at once suggests to the Apostle one of his favourite metaphors. From the οἶκος, playing on its double meaning, he passes to the οἰκοδομή. Apart from this suggestion the abruptness of the introduction of the metaphor, which is considerably elaborated, would be very strange.[111]

This may have been further reinforced by the conjunction of ideas in Zech. 6.15.[112]

So strong is the influence of this metaphor that it now tends to obscure the chiastic pattern. Indeed, there may be a case for suggesting that the chiasmus breaks down at this point and should be restricted to D to D′. The advantage of this approach is that it would then produce a pattern of clearly paralleled elements. However, by so doing, one problem is exchanged for another, notably a pattern that would begin in the middle of a clause, thus clearly interrupting the flow of syntax. It is preferable, on this basis, to argue that the writer intended to use a chiastic pattern that began with 2.11, but, by 2.20, the attractiveness of the building metaphor is now in competition with the need to conclude the pattern. Of the two, the usefulness of the building metaphor predominates, and the final three elements merely look back to the first three in a rather vague way. It may be said that the carefully patterned chiasmus

---

111. Robinson, *Ephesians*, p. 163.
112. Zech. 6.15 (LXX): καὶ οἱ μακρὰν ἀπ' αὐτῶν ἥξουσιν καὶ οἰκοδομήσουσιν ἐν τῷ οἴκῳ κυρίου.

that extends to D′ becomes, for the final three elements, a passage that
exhibits chiastic tendencies.

There is a very considerable literature on the variations in, and use of,
building metaphors in the Pauline corpus.[113] Discussion of this falls
largely outside the scope of this study, as do the implications for authorship of the ideas of building on the foundations of the apostles and
prophets, if this is the correct interpretation of the text. In terms of such
chiastic balance as exists with C, this is found in the final phrase of C′,
ὄντος ἀκρογωνιαίου αὐτοῦ Χριστοῦ Ἰησοῦ. While the meaning of
ἀκρογωνιαῖος is much disputed (the 'keystone' in an arch, or the
'cornerstone' in a foundation, etc.),[114] it seems beyond question that the
author intends to convey the fact that, in this new building into which
the former Gentiles are now to be incorporated, Christ plays a vital and
unique role. In C the fact of the former Gentiles' not belonging is
emphasized in the phrase χωρὶς Χριστοῦ; in C′ their new relationship is
cemented in the concept of Christ the ἀκρογωνιαῖος. In this way some
reasonable account can be given of the phrase ὄντος ἀκρογωνιαίου
αὐτοῦ Χριστοῦ Ἰησοῦ that Bailey regards as being included because
of the influence of 1 Cor. 3.11 (and, by implication, not properly part of
the chiasmus).

That the influence of the building metaphor continues to be very
strong is further shown in B and B′, where Kirby's effort to tie the two
together by looking at the occurrence of χειροποίητος in the remainder of the New Testament, and its link with temples has already been
noted. This should not be written off too quickly as a despairing attempt
to maintain a chiastic balancing where none may be intended. What is
clear is that the building metaphor develops in B′ in an unexpected way.
The absence of the article in πᾶσα οἰκοδομή suggests that this should
be translated as 'each building' rather than as 'the whole building'.[115]
Even if it is translated as 'the whole building', on the strength of other
anarthrous uses of πᾶς,[116] the strange conception of a completed build-

113. Useful bibliographies are provided by Barth, *Ephesians*, p. 270 n. 73;
Schnackenburg, *Epheser*, p. 103.

114. See Barth, *Ephesians*, pp. 317ff.; Lincoln, *Ephesians*, pp. 154-56; *et al.*

115. Although there is MSS evidence for the variant πᾶσα ἡ οἰκοδομή, the article
perhaps being added later to clarify the sense; so B.M. Metzger, *A Textual
Commentary on the Greek New Testament* (London, 1975), p. 603.

116. Barth, *Ephesians*, p. 272 n. 76, claims Rom. 3.20, 11.26, Acts 17.26
among others as parallels; Lincoln suggests a Hebraism for 'the whole building'
(*Ephesians*, p. 156).

ing spoken of as being fitted or framed together remains, with the even stranger idea of the whole edifice 'growing' into a temple.[117] The building metaphor appears to make way temporarily for a biological one, in order to make the point about the growth into a holy temple in the Lord. It may be, however, that this is to expect more logical precision from the metaphor than the author intended.

There is, however, another approach—but, it must be admitted, one that many dismiss[118]—that keeps the more literal translation 'each building', and refers them in some way to Jews and Gentiles.[119] Westcott reminds us that the council chambers, treasuries, cloisters, and so on, all became part of the temple.[120] Typical, however, is Abbott's comment that 'Paul' has 'just used a forcible figure to express the unity of the whole Church, and it would be strange if he now weakened it by speaking of several buildings'. This can be countered by pointing out that the author still speaks of 'you Gentiles' in 3.1, has to remind them again in 3.6 that they are fellow-heirs and members of the same body, and, indeed, ends this present passage by focusing attention emphatically on the former Gentiles (καὶ ὑμεῖς, 2.22). Abbott is looking at this passage from a conventional modern viewpoint, where the argument is expected to reach its climax at the end rather than to turn back on itself, its focal point having been reached at the central element. In fact, it is an elegant extension of the author's argument to suggest that 'each structure', the once far Gentiles, the once near Jews, have now been fitted together and are growing into the holy temple in the Lord.

Thus, in B (2.11b) the author describes two groups, the circumcised and the uncircumcised, separated by something done in the flesh by hands, now in B' (both having been created into one new man and reconciled in one body to God), joined together and growing into a new temple in the Lord. The 'separateness' of B is replaced by the 'togetherness' of B'. The human, fleshly basis of B (ἐν σαρκὶ χειροποιήτου) is replaced by the Christ-centred (ἐν ᾧ) focus of B'. A hesitation about pressing this argument is that the author does not use ἀμφότεροι again, perhaps in a phrase like ἀμφότεραι αἱ οἰκοδομαί.[121] Of course, this

117. Abbott, *Ephesians*, pp. 73-74; *et al.*
118. E.g., Robinson, *Ephesians*, p. 165; Abbott, *Ephesians*, pp. 74-75; Barth, *Ephesians*, p. 272.
119. As did Jerome, Ambrosiaster, for example.
120. Westcott, *Ephesians*, p. 41; cf. Mk 13.1, 2.
121. Robinson, *Ephesians*, p. 165.

may simply be stylistic variation (as in I') or because ἀμφότεροι is used elsewhere in the passage only in an absolute sense.

In A' (2.22) the building metaphor continues to dominate with the incorporation of the former Gentiles (ποτὲ ὑμεῖς τὰ ἔθνη, A) again being stressed, both by means of καὶ ὑμεῖς, and συνοικοδομεῖσθε, a συν-compound that occurs only here in the New Testament. The final ἐν πνεύματι may stand in contrast to ἐν σαρκί in A.

Thus, while we have moved away from the clearly paralleled elements that characterized the central elements of the chiasmus, there are still some allusions in 2.20-22 to 2.11, 12a. The emergence of the building metaphor gives a reasonable account of why the parallels are weaker in an otherwise striking chiastic pattern, although the interpretation suggested here, especially of B', appears to make good sense in view of the literal meaning of the text, and is in line with what might be expected from chiastic ordering of the passage.

3.4. *The Chiasms of 1.3-10 and 2.11-22 in their Wider Context in Ephesians*

3.4.1. *Ephesians 2.11-22 in its Context in the Letter*

In the previous chapter[122] reference was made to the key role of Eph. 1.3-14 for the understanding of Ephesians. It was suggested that one of the themes present therein was the first statement of the idea of the uniting of τὰ πάντα in Christ. It was argued that the author carefully distinguished 'we Jews' from 'you Gentiles', particularly in 1.11-14. The present passage continues the author's fuller development of that theme.

For many, the dominant feature of Ephesians is its ecclesiology, and, especially, the relationship between that ecclesiology and its Christology. The theme of unity in the church runs like a thread almost from beginning to end, but it is a unity that is firmly based and centred on Christ. As an adjunct to this, a greater, cosmic unity comes into view on occasion. In some ways it is difficult to separate ecclesiology from Christology in Ephesians, Lincoln putting it succinctly by suggesting that the ecclesiology is thoroughly christological. However, he is mistaken to dismiss the place of Christ's death to 'a few brief references'.[123] While it may be granted that they are neither many nor long, such references as there are occur in the first two chapters at very important points in

122. See 2.6 above.
123. Lincoln, *Ephesians*, pp. xci and xc respectively.

terms of the chiasms, with the central reference in 1.7 and the threefold references (2.13, 14, 16) in the central panel of 2.11-22.

It was suggested in the previous chapter that τὰ πάντα in 1.10 should not be interpreted in the first instance in the light of the later development of the concept in the epistle, with the implication that the emphasis in that verse is on 'uniting'. 'We' are chosen to be holy and blameless (1.4), and are destined for adoption (1.5), thus beginning, as it were, the process of uniting τὰ πάντα. Throughout, the events described are 'in Christ', with both cosmic and eternal overtones, inasmuch as the chiasmus encompasses not only eternity past to eternity future, but also heaven and earth. However, the whole process is rooted in the crucial historical death of Christ (1.7). As the readers learn in 1.11-14 that they have not always necessarily been part of that plan, they are assured that they too have been sealed with the promised Holy Spirit, whom 'we' and 'you' have in common as the guarantor of inheritance (1.13-14).

In the prayer of 1.15-23 the author asks that they might understand the implications of this particularly in relation to their inheritance and the power of God (themes from 1.11-14) in language that is again strikingly reminiscent of the earlier chiasmus—ὁ θεὸς τοῦ κυρίου ἡμῶν Ἰησοῦ Χριστοῦ (cf. 1.3), δόξα, σοφία, ἐπίγνωσις (1.17, cf. γνωρίσας, 1.9), πλοῦτος, ἅγιος, ἐν τοῖς ἐπουρανίοις, πᾶς, κεφαλή, πλήρωμα—and, to a lesser extent, reminiscent of the author's summary and first development of the chiasmus in 1.11-14. There is now, however, quite clearly a larger, cosmic dimension in view (1.21-22), and for the first time, too, the church as an entity appears (1.22).

Eph. 2.1-10 constitutes a discrete unit with the *inclusio* formed by the repetition of περιπατέω, and with 2.5 as its pivotal verse.[124] The assertion χάριτί ἐστε σεσῳσμένοι well summarizes its theme as the contrast is drawn between the Gentile believers' former and present condition. It begins with καὶ ὑμᾶς, although the presence of καί clearly does not connect 2.1 directly with 1.23. The writer is picking up a strand of thought begun in 1.13, and 'interrupted' to some extent by the focus on the cosmic Christ with which the thanksgiving ends. Beginning again, with the readers' previous state being emphasized (2.1, 2), it is the first indication in the epistle of the nature of their lostness (a lostness that was shared by the author's group, too, 2.3). The sovereign actions of God, however, transformed 'our' situation (2.4-7), using language that once

124. Lincoln, *Ephesians*, p. 85.

more has connections with both the vocabulary and themes of 1.3-10. God's dealing with those dead in trespasses is reminiscent of the forgiveness of trespasses in 1.7. The phrase τὸ πλοῦτος τῆς χάριτος αὐτοῦ is clearly echoed in 2.7, but with the addition of ὑπερβάλλον. Eph. 2.6 recalls the language of 1.3, and the idea of God's having prepared good works for believers to live out may be related to the thought of 1.4b.[125]

It is interesting that the writer has returned to the idea of grace, so important in the original chiasmus (and developed exclusively in relation to 'us'), but pointedly absent from 1.11-14. Just as 1.11-14 was concerned primarily with the first statement of the theme of the unity of believers from different backgrounds in Christ, so the author is now concerned to make clear that God's grace was operative in transforming *their* lostness too (2.5, 8). The description of the richness of grace in 2.7, now applied to 'us' (i.e., to both Jewish Christians and Gentile Christians), as τὸ ὑπερβάλλον πλοῦτος τῆς χάριτος αὐτοῦ is apt indeed!

In 2.1-10 there is an implicit ποτέ...νῦν contrast drawn. In fact, the ποτέ of 2.2 is never specifically balanced by νῦν. It may however, have served as the trigger for the more fully developed *schema* of 2.11-22. Having established in 2.1-10 that grace is the basis of salvation (2.4, 5, 7, 8), 2.11-22 begins with the reminder that humankind was formerly divided into two groups, the author's goal being to show how the basis on which this division was made, and the cause of the division, the 'law', has been abrogated, and how subsequently, from the two, one new man has been created in Christ, along with some of the attendant consequences.

In more detail, having reminded the readers (identifying them specifically as 'you Gentiles') of their former status (A), and pointedly digressing to make reference to their lack of circumcision that is the principal outward symbol of the division (B), summing up their status again as being 'apart from Christ' (C), their condition is catalogued in a series of statements that seems to call to mind many of the blessings that Jews held most dear (D, E, F). Now, however, the 'far' Gentiles have been brought 'near', apparently to enjoy the same status as the Jews, the means of this transformation being the blood of Christ (G). However, the reference to 'far' and 'near' brings to mind Isa. 57.19, leading the author to make more of this particular metaphor in describing Jesus

125. So Lincoln, *Ephesians*, p. 86.

as 'our peace'. Once more, Christ's task is described in terms of making two into one, abolishing the 'wall' and the hostility that formerly existed between Jew and Gentile in his flesh (H). This, in turn, results in the key statement of the abrogating of the rigid system of commandments and ordinances, with the consequence that one new man is created in Christ (I).

After the central point of the chiasmus, the theme of peace-making is picked up again, and what we have learned so far is amplified in that reconciliation is seen as involving not only Jew to Gentile, but, more importantly, both Jew and Gentile to God, so that the hostility is killed, with the cross as the means (H'). As if to remove any possible doubt that it is both Jew and Gentile that require reconciliation to God as the new man is created, the significant ideas of Isa. 57.19 are reiterated, although in such a way as to emphasize the preaching of peace both to the 'far' and to the 'near'. The path is now clear for the author to pick up the key points that underscored the Gentiles' separation from God already listed in D, E and F, and to go through the list in reverse order in F', E' and D', this time emphasizing the former Gentiles' sharing in the blessings in a distinctly specific way.

At this stage, however, the use of πάροικος in E' and οἰκεῖος in D' become the trigger for the author to develop a building metaphor—obviously a suitable one for the new situation thus far described in terms of 'two' becoming 'one'. This development obscures the chiastic patterning, and the parallels between C', B' and A' with their counterparts in the first half are not strong, although there are still some allusions, even if only to a limited extent. The Gentiles have come from the situation of having been apart from Christ to one where he has now become the key- or cornerstone (C') in their incorporation. There is no longer a division made in the flesh by hands and highlighted by that circumcision, but a joining together into a holy temple in the Lord (B'), resulting in a suitable dwelling place of God, the whole being accomplished in the Spirit (A'), and no longer in the flesh as in A.

3.4.2. *The Wider Influence of Ephesians 1.3-10 in the Letter*
In Eph. 3.2 it is clearly significant that 'Paul's' ministry is described as the οἰκονομία τῆς χάριτος τοῦ θεοῦ.[126] As has already been pointed

---

126. Note the use of οἰκονομία from the chiasmus of 1.3-10, but in a different sense.

out,[127] the ensuing verses are full of terminological allusions to the chiasmus of 1.3-10, leading up to the author's understanding of the mystery of Christ (τὴν σύνεσίν μου ἐν τῷ μυστηρίῳ τοῦ Χριστοῦ, 3.4), which is described as the incorporation of the Gentiles as fellow-heirs. Again this has cosmic implications (3.10), the whole being rounded off with another plea that the readers might understand the scope of the love of Christ and be filled with the fullness of God (3.17-19).

In ch. 4 the letter moves into paraenesis, by way of the veiled allusion in 4.1 to 1.4b, with an appeal for conduct characterized by harmony and unity (4.1-3). Unity is not a metaphysical state reserved for future eternity, but has practical implications for the life of the church in the present. Diversity of giftedness must still maintain unity (4.13) and result in the maturity of the whole body, as the combination of building and biological metaphors first seen in the chiasmus in 2.11-22 again reappears (4.15, 16). In 4.17 the readers are strongly urged to live no longer as the Gentiles do. Since the writer has made his case for the plan of God and for the revelation of the mystery of Christ, a wedge can now be driven between the former Gentiles now incorporated into the body of Christ and those as yet outside of Christ by writing disparagingly of the current lifestyle of 'the Gentiles' (4.17-19), thus distinguishing 'the Gentiles' as a group distinct from the believers.

The practical exhortations of 4.17–5.20, with their ethical overtones, are followed by the *Haustafel* of 5.21–6.9, in turn followed by the final appeal of 6.10-20. In one sense this last section may take the reader unawares,[128] although some of the terminology has already occurred earlier in the letter. It has only a distant allusion to 1.3-10 in ἐν τοῖς ἐπουρανίοις (6.12). While it may be legitimate to infer that the new unity in Christ has to be guarded in the context of ongoing spiritual warfare, it might be suggested that the author has introduced here a new metaphor that is seen as a fitting way of concluding the letter, but one that is not directly derived from the theme of the chiasmus of 1.3-10. Although it has been maintained that the first chiasmus and its development in 1.11-14 provides the key to understanding the author's purpose, the hypothesis should not be pushed too far, with the suggestion that it unlocks every door in the letter.

127. See 2.4.3 above.
128. So Mitton, *Ephesians*, p. 218.

3.5. *Conclusion*

A number of chiastic analyses have been proposed for Eph. 2.11-22. That suggested in this chapter unifies and enhances the impact of the author's thought, in contrast to Turner's patterns that serve only to fragment it. This analysis is to be preferred to Giavini's, which, while sensing the general direction of thought, has failed to take account of a number of balances that seem to be very obviously present. It has been suggested that Kirby's chiasmus is to be preferred to that of Giavini, but Bailey's pattern is the most satisfying. With one or two alterations, a slightly modified chiasmus has emerged that has highlighted the parallels and the contrasts more clearly.

Furthermore, the suggestion that the principal focus of 2.11-22 is the abrogation of the law and the creation of one new man with the resulting new status of former Jews and Gentiles in Christ fits in well with the theme of 1.3-14, and is an important part of the writer's purpose in the whole letter.

Chapter 4

GALATIANS 5.13–6.2: WARNING OR APPEAL?

4.1. *Introduction*

Betz's landmark rhetorical analysis of Galatians as an instance of the judicial species of rhetoric and as an example of the 'apologetic letter' genre is now well known,[1] and was quickly used in other subsequent studies in Galatians.[2] More recently, however, it has come in for some considerable criticism on two fronts: that of the species of rhetoric with which it best accords,[3] and that of its relationship to the so-called 'apologetic letter' genre.[4] His analysis is, perhaps, least helpful for paraenesis,[5] as he himself acknowledges that paraenesis has only a

---

1. Betz, *Galatians*, pp. 14-25.
2. E.g., B.H. Brinsmead, *Galatians: Dialogical Response to Opponents* (SBLDS, 65; Chico, CA, 1982).
3. On the first, attention may be drawn to D. Aune, Review of Betz, *Galatians*, *RSR* 7 (1981), pp. 323-28, 325, where he suggests that Gal. 1–2 is forensic (or judicial) rhetoric, but Gal. 3–4 is deliberative; Kennedy's criticisms (*Interpretation*, pp. 144-52) include his suggestion that Galatians best accords with deliberative rhetoric (*Interpretation*, p. 145); G.W. Hansen, *Abraham in Galatians: Epistolary and Rhetorical Contexts* (JSNTS, 29; Sheffield, 1989), p. 59, too, finds it to be a mixture of the forensic and deliberative.
4. Hansen, *Galatians*, pp. 26-27, and R.N. Longenecker, *Galatians* (WBC, 41; Waco, TX, 1990), pp. civ-cv, both criticize Betz severely on the basis of his examples of alleged 'apologetic letters', suggesting that they do not serve as precedents for Galatians. It may be, therefore, that Meeks was right when he said of Betz's analysis, 'He does not offer us a single instance of the apologetic letter with which we can compare Galatians. We are therefore asked to interpret Galatians as an example of a genre for which no other example can apparently be cited.' (W. Meeks, Review of Betz, *Galatians*, *JBL* 100 [1981], pp. 304-306, 306.)
5. R.B. Hays, 'Christology and Ethics in Galatians: The Law of Christ', *CBQ* 49 (1987), pp. 268-90, 270, is right that the bridge that Betz constructs between theology and ethics is tenuous.

marginal role in the ancient rhetorical handbooks, with its formal character and function still having been little investigated.[6] The hypothesis of a chiasmus developed in this chapter will display the formal character of part of the paraenetic teaching of Galatians, and will suggest, in the context of the epistle as a whole, that it has a function far removed from that of being a 'mere appendage'.[7] The chiastic pattern extends from 5.13 to 6.2, with 6.3-10 closely related to it, and will reveal how carefully Paul makes and builds his points throughout.

4.2. A Possible Chiasmus in Galatians 5.13–6.2

The first hint of a chiasmus in this section is furnished by the presence of two lists, those in 5.19-21a and 5.22-23a, separated by a strongly worded warning (5.21b). It is, therefore, worth testing to see if this is only an ABA pattern, or if, in fact, symmetry is extended on either side.

Thus, an initial hypothesis would be of a chiasmus centred upon Gal. 5.21b, as a unique element, G.

G   21b ἃ προλέγω ὑμῖν καθὼς προεῖπον ὅτι οἱ τὰ τοιαῦτα
      πράσσοντες βασιλείαν θεοῦ οὐ κληρονομήσουσιν.

The function of this as a central element is discussed later. There is a sudden change to first person singular in προλέγω and προεῖπον in the middle of a passage that is otherwise in the third person (5.19-24), thus possibly providing a 'shift and reversion' at the centre. This, however, may be less significant when it is noted that the first person singular is also suddenly introduced at 5.16 (Λέγω δέ...), although, in this instance, it may be more as an emphasizing rhetorical device 'not strictly necessary to the expression of the thought'.[8] In 5.21b the personal 'warnings', however, are an integral part of Paul's flow of thought.

In the next two elements the basic balancing of the ideas of the works of the flesh and the fruit of the Spirit, with their attendant catalogues, is sufficiently obvious as to need no further comment at this stage.

---

6.   Betz, *Galatians*, pp. 253ff. For Betz, the paraenetic section of Galatians consists of 5.1–6.10, and is equated with the *exhortatio* in his analysis.

7.   *Pace* H. Boers, 'The Form Critical Study of Paul's Letters. 1 Thessalonians as a Case Study', *NTS* 22 (1976), pp. 140-58, whose description this is, p. 153 n. 2.

8.   E. De W. Burton, *A Critical and Exegetical Commentary on the Epistle to the Galatians* (ICC; Edinburgh, 1920), p. 297.

F 19 φανερὰ δέ ἐστιν **τὰ ἔργα τῆς σαρκός**, ἅτινά ἐστιν
πορνεία, ἀκαθαρσία, ἀσέλγεια, 20 εἰδωλολατρία,
φαρμακεία, ἔχθραι, ἔρις, ζῆλος, θυμοί, ἐριθεῖαι,
διχοστασίαι, αἱρέσεις, 21 φθόνοι, μέθαι, κῶμοι, καὶ τὰ
ὅμοια τούτοις,

F′ 22 ὁ **δὲ καρπὸς τοῦ πνεύματός** ἐστιν ἀγάπη χαρά
εἰρήνη, μακροθυμία χρηστότης ἀγαθωσύνη, πίστις
23 πραΰτης ἐγκράτεια·

Moving outwards from the centre, the next pair might be:

E 18 εἰ δὲ πνεύματι ἄγεσθε, **οὐκ ἐστὲ ὑπὸ νόμον.**

E′ 23b κατὰ τῶν τοιούτων **οὐκ ἔστιν νόμος.**

In both E and E′ there are said to be spheres in which the law is denied influence. These two spheres share the feature of the Spirit's activity in them, explicitly stated in E, speaking of those led by the Spirit, and implicitly in E′, because κατὰ τῶν τοιούτων looks back to the catalogue of 'virtues' (or, possibly, to those practising them) that compose the fruit of the Spirit.

Continuing to move out, elements D and D′ become:

D 17 ἡ γὰρ **σὰρξ ἐπιθυμεῖ** κατὰ τοῦ πνεύματος, τὸ δὲ
πνεῦμα κατὰ τῆς σαρκός, ταῦτα γὰρ ἀλλήλοις
ἀντίκειται, ἵνα μὴ ἃ ἐὰν θέλητε ταῦτα ποιῆτε.

D′ 24 οἱ δὲ τοῦ Χριστοῦ Ἰησοῦ **τὴν σάρκα** ἐσταύρωσαν
σὺν τοῖς παθήμασιν καὶ ταῖς **ἐπιθυμίαις.**

It might be sufficient here to point out the occurrence of σάρξ in conjunction with ἐπιθυμέω in D and with ἐπιθυμία in D′. In D the desires of the flesh are opposed to those of the Spirit; in D′ the flesh with its desires is crucified. The relationship between the two elements will be further developed later.

There is, however, another conjunction of σάρξ and ἐπιθυμία—that found in 5.16. The question therefore arises as to why the choice has been made to balance 5.17 and 5.24, rather than 5.16 with either of the other two. To balance 5.16 with 5.17 would clearly destroy the chiastic pattern, but there may be no real balance intended here anyway. The concept ἐπιθυμία σαρκός is introduced in 5.16 and picked up immediately in the analogous clause ἡ γὰρ σὰρξ ἐπιθυμεῖ... in 5.17, enlarging its meaning. More difficult is why 5.16 could not be balanced with 5.24. After all, not gratifying the desires of the flesh (5.16) has a clear affinity with crucifying the flesh with its desires (5.24). This possibility cannot be ruled out, but may be an instance of the situation where not all parallels can be accommodated by a chiastic pattern, especially since there is another important balance, that of 5.16 with 5.25. Thus:

C   16 Λέγω δέ, **πνεύματι περιπατεῖτε** καὶ ἐπιθυμίαν σαρκὸς οὐ μὴ τελέσητε.

C′ 25 Εἰ **ζῶμεν πνεύματι**, πνεύματι καὶ στοιχῶμεν.

The idea of walking by the Spirit is balanced by the virtually identical one of living by the Spirit. When there is an obviously possible correspondence between 5.17 and 5.24, and a clear balance between 5.16 and 5.25, this would seem as reasonable a course to follow as any other at this stage.[9]

It should be noted in passing that 5.16-25 forms a well-defined unit with a clear beginning and end.[10] However, there may be further symmetry beyond these limits. Thus, B and B′ may be:

B   15 εἰ δὲ **ἀλλήλους** δάκνετε καὶ κατεσθίετε, βλέπετε μὴ ὑπ᾽ **ἀλλήλων** ἀναλωθῆτε.

B′ 26 μὴ γινώμεθα κενόδοξοι, **ἀλλήλους** προκαλούμενοι, **ἀλλήλοις** φθονοῦντες.

These are both concerned with relationships within the fellowship, the first dealing with the consequences of wrong relationships, and the second an exhortation to right relationships by describing bad behaviour.

The question of relationships also forms one of the themes of the longer elements A and A′. They may be capable of further resolution, but this discussion is best delayed until later. At this stage a possible structure is laid out for them, and attention (by highlighting) is drawn to some features which they share. Whether B, B′, A and A′ are truly part of the chiastic pattern will be considered when the hypothesis that 5.16-25 is a chiasmus has been better established.

A   5.13 Ὑμεῖς γὰρ ἐπ᾽ ἐλευθερίᾳ ἐκλήθητε, **ἀδελφοί**· μόνον μὴ τὴν ἐλευθερίαν εἰς ἀφορμὴν τῇ σαρκί, ἀλλὰ διὰ τῆς ἀγάπης **δουλεύετε ἀλλήλοις**. 14 ὁ γὰρ πᾶς **νόμος** ἐν ἑνὶ λόγῳ **πεπλήρωται**, ἐν τῷ· ἀγαπήσεις τὸν πλησίον σου ὡς σεαυτόν.

9.   The possibility of combining D and E, and D′ and E′ is discussed below in relation to Bligh's chiastic pattern.

10.   Gal. 5.25 itself is also a good example of the rhetorical figure, *regressio*—see 1.1.1 above.

A′   6.1 'Αδελφοί, ἐὰν καὶ προλημφθῇ ἄνθρωπος ἔν τινι
      παραπτώματι, ὑμεῖς οἱ πνευματικοὶ καταρτίζετε τὸν
      τοιοῦτον ἐν πνεύματι πραΰτητος, σκοπῶν σεαυτὸν μὴ
      καὶ σὺ πειρασθῇς. 2 **Ἀλλήλων τὰ βάρη βαστάζετε**, καὶ
      οὕτως**ἀναπληρώσετε** τὸν νόμον τοῦ Χριστοῦ.

Beyond this point any chiastic patterning breaks down. The complete
chiasmus is, therefore, as follows:

A   5.13 Ὑμεῖς γὰρ ἐπ' ἐλευθερίᾳ ἐκλήθητε, ἀδελφοί· μόνον μὴ
      τὴν ἐλευθερίαν εἰς ἀφορμὴν τῇ σαρκί, ἀλλὰ διὰ τῆς ἀγάπης
      δουλεύετε ἀλλήλοις. 14 ὁ γὰρ πᾶς νόμος ἐν ἑνὶ λόγῳ
      πεπλήρωται, ἐν τῷ· ἀγαπήσεις τὸν πλησίον σου ὡς σεαυτόν.

B   15 εἰ δὲ ἀλλήλους δάκνετε καὶ κατεσθίετε, βλέπετε μὴ ὑπ'
      ἀλλήλων ἀναλωθῆτε.

C   16 Λέγω δέ, πνεύματι περιπατεῖτε καὶ ἐπιθυμίαν σαρκὸς οὐ
      μὴ τελέσητε.

D   17 ἡ γὰρ σὰρξ ἐπιθυμεῖ κατὰ τοῦ πνεύματος, τὸ δὲ πνεῦμα
      κατὰ τῆς σαρκός· ταῦτα γὰρ ἀλλήλοις ἀντίκειται, ἵνα μὴ ἃ
      ἐὰν θέλητε ταῦτα ποιῆτε.

E   18 εἰ δὲ πνεύματι ἄγεσθε, οὐκ ἐστὲ ὑπὸ νόμον.

F   19 φανερὰ δέ ἐστιν τὰ ἔργα τῆς σαρκός, ἅτινά ἐστιν
      πορνεία, ἀκαθαρσία, ἀσέλγεια, 20 εἰδωλολατρία,
      φαρμακεία, ἔχθραι, ἔρις, ζῆλος, θυμοί ἐριθεῖαι,
      διχοστασίαι, αἱρέσεις, 21 φθόνοι, μέθαι, κῶμοι, καὶ τὰ ὅμοια
      τούτοις,

G   21b ἃ προλέγω ὑμῖν, καθὼς προεῖπον ὅτι οἱ τὰ τοιαῦτα
      πράσσοντες βασιλείαν θεοῦ οὐ κληρονομήσουσιν.

F′   22 ὁ δὲ καρπὸς τοῦ πνεύματός ἐστιν ἀγάπη χαρὰ εἰρήνη,
      μακροθυμία χρηστότης ἀγαθωσύνη, πίστις 23 πραΰτης
      ἐγκράτεια·

E′   23b κατὰ τῶν τοιούτων οὐκ ἔστιν νόμος.

D′   24 οἱ δὲ τοῦ Χριστοῦ Ἰησοῦ τὴν σάρκα ἐσταύρωσαν σὺν
      τοῖς παθήμασιν καὶ ταῖς ἐπιθυμίαις.

C′   25 Εἰ ζῶμεν πνεύματι, πνεύματι καὶ στοιχῶμεν.

B′   26 μὴ γινώμεθα κενόδοξοι, ἀλλήλους προκαλούμενοι,
      ἀλλήλοις φθονοῦντες.

A′   6.1 'Αδελφοί, ἐὰν καὶ προλημφθῇ ἄνθρωπος ἔν τινι
      παραπτώματι, ὑμεῖς οἱ πνευματικοὶ καταρτίζετε τὸν
      τοιοῦτον ἐν πνεύματι πραΰτητος, σκοπῶν σεαυτὸν, μὴ καὶ
      σὺ πειρασθῇς. 2 Ἀλλήλων τὰ βάρη βαστάζετε, καὶ οὕτως
      ἀναπληρώσετε τὸν νόμον τοῦ Χριστοῦ.[11]

11. For ease of reference, this chiasmus is reproduced in the Appendix at the
end of this study. The majority of scholars have been rightly sceptical of 'the strange

4.3. *Exegesis of the Suggested Chiasmus*

4.3.1. *A (5.13, 14) and A' (6.1, 2)*

It is now necessary to embark upon a step-by-step exegesis of the passage, in the course of which other points of contact between suggested chiastic partners will be noted. Care will be exercised in differentiating exegetical insights that strengthen the chiastic pattern from those that may emerge from such a pattern, as Paul's motives are sought for his writing in this way. In many respects, the ground is well trodden. Of particular interest, therefore, will be some of the unresolved issues relating to this passage, where possibly fresh or further light might be shed by the chiasmus. There is also one new issue to address, created by the chiastic pattern: the relationship of 6.3-10 to 5.13–6.2, since, traditionally, no structural division is recognized between 6.2 and 6.3.

As yet, no evidence has been offered as to why Gal. 5.13, 14 should balance 6.1, 2. This is because it is not immediately apparent whether

jig-saw puzzle' (so H.D. Betz, Review of Bligh, *Galatians in Greek*, *JBL* 89 [1970], pp. 126-27) of chiastic patterns that Bligh finds at every conceivable point in Galatians, but, among his many unconvincing suggestions, his so-called 'Eighth Tertiary Chiasm', Gal. 5.13b–6.2 (Bligh, *Galatians in Greek*, pp. 60-61) is akin to the chiasmus presented in this chapter, although differing from it at several strategic points. Bligh's pattern has a wholly unlikely beginning that clearly interrupts the flow of syntax in 5.13, starting with ἀλλὰ διὰ τῆς ἀγάπης in 5.13b. This occurs because he assigns 5.13a to the final element of his previous chiasmus, 5.1-13a (Bligh, *Galatians in Greek*, pp. 56-57), a completely improbable example. Having done this, in order to produce the parallel between his first and last elements (5.13b and 6.2 respectively), he has to incorporate 6.1 into his second last element (5.26–6.1) which he then balances with 5.15, and thus misses the significant correspondences in A and A' in my pattern. He also coalesces 5.16 and 17 (my elements C and D), and 5.24 and 25 (my elements D' and C'), although his analysis becomes most confusing at this point because of typographical errors and an English 'chiasmus-by-heading' version that does not correspond with his Greek text version. In principle, coalescing of neighbouring elements is always possible, and means only that one pattern is more highly resolved than another. Here, however, Bligh's longer elements fail to highlight some clear parallels. C (5.16) and C' (5.25) deal with walking or living by the Spirit, and while C moves on into a discussion of the desires of the flesh in D (5.17), its chiastic partner D' (5.24) begins with such a discussion. Bligh does not use his chiastic pattern at all in his subsequent exegetical notes on the passage (Bligh, *Galatians in Greek*, pp. 198-207), and, indeed, makes very little use of any of his chiasms in his subsequent commentary, *Galatians: A Discussion of St Paul's Epistle* (Householder Commentaries; London, 1969).

that balance should be painted with broad brush-strokes or in finer detail. Three instances of potentially balancing words or phrases were highlighted, these occurring in the same order in both elements. It is possible, therefore, that the two longer elements A and A′ can be further resolved, perhaps into A(a_1, a_2, a_3) and A′(a_1', a_2', a_3'). In this case, while the objective evidence may point in this direction, it is not by itself conclusive, and careful exegesis is necessary before such a suggestion can be supported.

A reasonable case can be made for suggesting that γάρ links 5.13 to more than just 5.12.[12] Duncan puts it well: 'It is the summing up on a position already established, which in turn becomes the text for a practical appeal'.[13] Whether linked with 5.1 or 5.12 alone, with 5.1-12 as a whole, or indeed with the broader sweep of Paul's argument to date, the clause acts as a bridge, leading into another phase of his letter.[14] Paul addresses his readers emphatically using ὑμεῖς as the first word in its clause, and juxtaposed with ὑμᾶς in the previous verse. At the end of the clause, too, ἀδελφοί becomes prominent, giving rise to a translation such as 'For you, my brothers...'[15]

Paul's indicative in 5.13 is followed by an implicit imperative. He makes his new point in the elliptical phrase μόνον μὴ τὴν ἐλευθερίαν εἰς ἀφορμὴν τῇ σαρκί. Among the most important of a number of questions raised by this phrase is the matter of its relationship to the actual Galatian situation. The many points of view on this include the ideas that 5.13–6.10 is a later interpolation or contains unrelated materials, which might be in the nature of an apologetic appendix, or indeed may be directed against a second, perhaps libertine, front, or even the suggestion that Paul was countering Gnostic-type teaching. Others have

12. So, for example, H. Schlier, *Der Brief an die Galater* (KEK, 7; Göttingen, 14th edn, 1971), p. 241; Betz, *Galatians*, p. 272; F. Mussner, *Der Galaterbrief* (HTKNT, 9; Freiburg, 1974), p. 366.

13. G.S. Duncan, *The Epistle of Paul to the Galatians* (London, 1934), p. 162; cf., too, M.J. Lagrange, *Saint Paul, épitre aux Galates* (EBib; Paris, 1950), p. 145; Burton, *Galatians*, p. 291.

14. O'Neill's position (J.C. O'Neill, *The Recovery of Paul's Letter to the Galatians* [London, 1972], p. 67), that the section beginning with 5.13 'has nothing in particular to do with the urgent problem Paul was trying to meet in his original letter', has not found support. (See Longenecker, *Galatians*, p. 270.) Unless there are compelling reasons to the contrary, it is better to assume that the text as we have it is as Paul intended it.

15. So Betz, *Galatians*, p. 271; Bruce, *Galatians*, p. 239.

seen the passage as an attempt to dispel the Galatians' moral confusion, or suggest that it may simply be a continuation of Paul's polemic against the law.[16] The view to be developed in this study is that it is a much more closely argued section than many would recognize, in which there is a powerful combination of polemical and paraenetic material that functions as a logical and necessary conclusion to Paul's letter. Thus Paul's exhortation 'develops out of and concludes his earlier arguments', necessitated by the fact that 'a major ingredient in the Galatian dispute is the question of how the members of God's people should live', with the attendant problems caused, not by two separate groups (that might be described as nomist and libertine) but by 'moral confusion together with a loss of confidence in Paul's prescription for ethics'.[17]

Betz makes the valid point that we should not read the use of σάρξ in Romans 7–8 into Galatians. In the former the 'flesh' is a more complex idea.[18] The most intriguing question, however, is that posed by Guthrie who asks, 'But why think of "flesh" as the main opponent of freedom? Why not "law", or even "sin" as in Romans 7.8?'[19] Barclay may have the answer, seeing the use of 'flesh' as stemming from the earlier discussion of Galatians 2 where Paul has argued that, while it was 'sin' to eat with Gentiles from the point of view of the law, these standards did not apply to those who had died to the law. If Paul had continued to use such vocabulary as ἁμαρτία, his Galatian audience 'would all too readily hear in it its standard association with disobedience to the law'.[20] The source of the Spirit/flesh dualism may well be Gal. 3.2, 3 as Paul puts the crucial questions to the Galatians: 'Did you receive the Spirit by works of the law, or by hearing with faith?... Having begun with the Spirit, are you now ending with the flesh?' Here, σάρξ can apparently include what he has just called ἔργα νόμου.[21] This broader

---

16. Summarized, e.g., in J.M.G. Barclay, *Obeying the Truth: A Study of Paul's Ethics in Galatians* (SNTW; Edinburgh, 1988), pp. 9-23.

17. Barclay, *Obeying*, pp. 216-18. He gives each of the quotations above special prominence by italicizing them. See further 4.4 below.

18. Betz, *Galatians*, p. 272 n. 16.

19. D. Guthrie, *Galatians* (The Century Bible NS; London, rev. edn, 1974), p. 133.

20. Barclay, *Obeying*, p. 110.

21. Barclay, *Obeying*, pp. 85-86.

understanding of σάρξ in 3.3 is to be preferred,[22] to that which makes it refer more narrowly to circumcision only.[23] The word σάρξ, thus, appears to be, in effect, an umbrella term for Paul in Galatians.[24]

What, then, does Paul mean by ἀφορμή τῇ σαρκί? The military overtones of ἀφορμή, noted by a number of commentators,[25] are seen in its original meaning of a 'starting point' or 'base of operations', and then more generally 'opportunity', 'pretext'. Presumably, therefore, Paul has in mind some course of action upon which the Christian embarks believing that he is using his new-found freedom, only to find that he has fallen into the trap of the 'flesh'. However, does Paul have some specific situation in mind? It seems just possible that the exhortation could look back to the question of circumcision, discussed in 5.1-12. This would be a total travesty of the concept of freedom, if the Christian were freely to submit to the yoke of slavery (5.1), because by so doing he would of necessity be seeking justification by the law (5.4). This would be 'an opportunity for the flesh' with the most far-reaching consequences! It is difficult to imagine that the recipient of 5.1-12 (and indeed of much of the earlier material) would not see some kind of association between 'opportunity for the flesh' and 'works of the law'.

However, Paul may also have another situation in mind. Two different suggestions are made that tie the warning to subsequent verses: the first is that of Bruce, who links it to quarrelsomeness in the sequentially close v. 15,[26] which might be seen as the first subsequent reference to a work of the flesh. However, despite the vigour and forcefulness of the language, v. 15 may well be the symptom rather than the disease itself, the 'biting' and 'devouring' of one another stemming from a further set of problems.

The second suggestion is that of Betz who finds a concrete *Sitz im Leben* in 6.1, seeing there a reference to 'flagrant misconduct',[27] although he does not discuss what this might be. The terminology he

---

22. Cf. F.F. Bruce, *The Epistle to the Galatians: A Commentary on the Greek Text* (NIGTC; Exeter, 1982), p. 149; Schlier, *Galater*, p. 123.

23. So Betz, *Galatians*, pp. 133-34; Burton, *Galatians*, p. 148.

24. This is basically Barclay's conclusion in a long, detailed discussion of flesh and Spirit, which is mostly devoted to a study of the concept of σάρξ (*Obeying*, pp. 178-215).

25. Betz, *Galatians*, p. 272; *et al.*

26. Bruce, *Galatians*, p. 240.

27. Betz, *Galatians*, p. 273.

uses may not be the best to describe a situation of which we know so little, and may be an instance of over-enthusiastic mirror-reading.[28] At this point Longenecker's description of the situation as 'loveless strife' might be more apposite.[29] However, Betz makes the link that the chiasmus suggests.

If Barclay's conclusions are taken seriously about the function of the paraenetic material, and if it is accepted, as he suggests, that there is a moral confusion in the Galatian churches, occasioned in part at least by Paul's insistence on ethical conduct that does not rest upon keeping the law, there should not be great surprise that, when οἱ πνευματικοί try to correct the transgressors, they may do so in an unhelpful way, unwittingly or unintentionally, thus providing the very 'opportunity for the flesh' that Paul so clearly warns against in 5.13.[30] Picking up 5.16 and 5.25, this is Paul's pointed reminder that those who possess the Spirit must live by the Spirit's standards. The community must live in a disciplined and loving manner.[31] Gal. 6.1 also ends very appositely (σκοπῶν σεαυτόν, μὴ καὶ σὺ πειρασθῇς), if Paul intended it to balance 5.13a. The transgressor and those responsible for correction must each guard against giving opportunity to the flesh. The process of correction can degenerate into biting and devouring (5.15) on the one hand, and into the self-conceit and provocation of 5.26 on the other.

Thus, when Paul warns against freedom becoming an opportunity for the flesh, he has more in mind than just the immediate circumstances of 6.1 as is evident from 5.15, 17, 19-21a and so on. The appeal of 6.1 illustrates the case of a theme that occurs at the beginning of a chiasmus being repeated (and in this case developed) at its end. It will also be suggested that there is a link between these elements and the central element, G.[32] The verses between the warning of 5.13 and the specific instance of 6.1, among other things, furnish both explanation and examples of the concept of works of the flesh and their consequences, and the role of the Spirit and its fruit in relation to limits to freedom. By

---

28. Further discussed in 4.5.3 below.

29. Longenecker, *Galatians*, p. 238; the other phrase that Longenecker uses 'loveless libertinism' (e.g. *Galatians*, p. 247) may go beyond the evidence.

30. *Pace* Schlier, *Galater*, p. 270, who finds the term οἱ πνευματικοί to be ironical.

31. So R.B. Hays, *The Faith of Jesus Christ: An Investigation of the Narrative Substructure of Galatians 3:1–4:11* (SBLDS, 56; Chico, CA, 1983), p. 260.

32. See 1.4.2 d above.

the time Paul comes to the specific instance he has in mind, the Galatians should be well on the way to knowing how to deal with the situation for themselves. As shown below, Paul further strengthens the links between the beginning and end of the chiasmus by paralleling 6.2 and 5.13b, 14. The advice about the right treatment of the transgressor deliberately looks back to, and picks up terminology from, 5.22-23a in the phrase ἐν πνεύματι πραΰτητος.

Paul concludes 5.13 with the call to the one form of slavery that is acceptable to the 'free' Christian—the slavery of love. The juxtaposition of ἐνευθερία and δουλεύω in 5.13 throws the two terms into sharp relief, perhaps intentionally heightening the paradox, but love and its practice begins to set the boundaries to any 'freedom'. Love, of course, at its best is spontaneous and quite voluntary, yet ἀγάπη carries with it commitments that require it to be sustained even in situations of strain and tension. It is the commitment to one another that is an intrinsic part of the exercise of love that makes the idea of mutual enslavement in love both an acceptable and an appropriate one.[33] Keck's statement of the relationship is memorable: 'In Paul's understanding of freedom...the self is always in a sphere of power in which one has a Lord and a brother and sister'.[34]

Paul makes more of this mutual obligation of service in love in 6.2a ('Αλλήλων τὰ βάρη βαστάζετε), the close connections of which to 5.13-14 are widely acknowledged. 'Indeed the theme of mutual obligation is in each case, more specifically, mutual *service*, since the bearing of burdens is a slave's task.'[35] Certainly, Betz makes the connection between 5.13, 14 and 6.2a by noting that Paul finds 6.2a 'useful because it sums up his teaching in 5.13-14, and is also related to 6.1'.[36] Barclay and Betz are correct in seeing such a parallel, which is one of ideas rather than of words.

A considerable range of opinion is found on the link between 6.1 and

33. Betz, *Galatians*, pp. 273-74 *et al.*, and a more helpful approach than that of Schlier (*Galater*, p. 244) who interprets the idea of δουλεύω in terms of one's sur-rendering of freedom in order to be at the disposal of God and other people, linking it with Mk 10.41-45.

34. L.E. Keck, *Paul and his Letters* (Proclamation Commentaries; Philadelphia, 2nd edn, 1988), p. 88.

35. Barclay, *Obeying*, p. 131.

36. Betz, *Galatians*, p. 299.

6.2a that extends from those who see no connection between them,[37] to those who see 6.2a as an injunction consequential upon the need to deal with another's failure,[38] and to those who see the injunction of 6.2a as a general statement of which 6.1 furnishes a specific kind of example.[39] However, no one who sees a link between 6.1 and 6.2 has commented on the fact that the appeal of 6.2a does not seem to follow logically from the immediately preceding warning (σκοπῶν σεαυτὸν...πειρασθῇς), but is separated by this warning from the exhortation to restore gently the transgressor.[40]

It appears, therefore, that the connection between 6.1 and 6.2a is not particularly clear or strong, either grammatically[41] or exegetically. A more satisfactory explanation of the function of 6.2a may be found on the basis of the chiastic patterning of the passage. If the proposal of chiastically balanced elements A and A′ is correct, with directly paralleled internal sub-elements, a_1 and a_1' (correction in the wrong spirit in 6.1 providing just such an opportunity for the flesh that Paul is keen to deny to it in 5.13), then it may be worth considering that the direct parallelism between the two elements is extended and that the mutual service motif of 5.13b is picked up again in 6.2a (these two forming a_2 and a_2').

When Barclay writes of the 'close' connection of 6.2 and 5.13.14,[42] he suggested two parallel references, the first of which has been discussed, turning on the echoing of mutual service (5.13) in mutual

37. Lagrange, *Galates*, pp. 156-57; J.G. Strelan, 'Burden-Bearing and the Law of Christ: A Re-examination of Galatians 6:2', *JBL* 94 (1975), pp. 266-76, whose view that βάρη implies financial burdens that have to be shared is rightly rejected by Bruce, *Galatians*, p. 261, and Barclay, *Obeying*, p. 132.

38. J.B. Lightfoot, *Saint Paul's Epistle to the Galatians* (London, 2nd edn, 1866), p. 216 (who suggests that the spiritual must bear their neighbour's errors—but, surely, neighbour's *errors* must be corrected. It is their *weaknesses* [Rom. 15.1] that are borne); Mussner, *Galater*, p. 399.

39. Burton, *Galatians*, p. 329; Duncan, *Galatians*, p. 181; Schlier, *Galater*, p. 271; Guthrie, *Galatians*, p. 143 ('A Christian falls to a surprise temptation and immediately other Christians are to seek ways and means of restoring the fallen brother. His burden has become theirs.'); Betz, *Galatians*, p. 299.

40. However, D.W. Kuck, 'Each Will Bear his Own Burden: Paul's Creative Use of an Apocalyptic Motif', *NTS* 40 (1994), pp. 289-97, 292, does see 6.2 as 'a slight interruption in the flow of thought' and refers it back to 5.14.

41. Mussner, *Galater*, p. 398, notes that it is an asyndeton.

42. Barclay, *Obeying*, p. 131.

burden-bearing (6.2). The second is the repetition of verbs from the root πληρόω: πεπλήρωται in 5.14 and ἀναπληρώσετε in 6.2. However, in his description of the parallelism, he makes what may be an unwarranted assumption. Having noted the link between mutual service and burden-bearing, he continues,

> Thus whether Paul has in mind the specific βάρη of moral failure (6.1) or, more generally, the manifold spiritual and physical burdens of everyday life, what he enjoins in this verse is 'serving one another through love' (5.13). Thus the following phrase 'and so you will fulfil the law of Christ' *must* be interpreted with reference to the statement in 5.14 about the fulfilment of the whole law through the love command.[43]

There is, however, no *a priori* reason why there is a necessary connection between the two phrases involving the idea of fulfilment. While it may be argued that the idea of love is *implicit* in 6.2a, it is certainly not *explicit*. However, it *is* explicit in 5.13b (διὰ τῆς ἀγάπης) and it is *this* which is picked up in 5.14 (ἀγαπήσεις...) Of course, it fits the purpose of this study well for Barclay to be right, and, although a similar conclusion to his is reached, it is arrived at by travelling a rather different road. There are in 5.13b and 6.2a balancing concepts of mutual obligation, each followed by a clause relating to law and its fulfilment, without, at the initial stage, assuming that the one has to be interpreted in the light of the other.

The use of 'law' in 5.14, and more so in the phrase 'the law of Christ' in 6.2b, is surprising in view of 3.6-14 and 3.23–4.7. The phrase 'the law of Christ' may be understood in four different ways:[44]

a. The phrase reflects a rabbinic notion of the 'law of the messiah', viz. a messianic re-interpretation of the old law.

b. The phrase indicates that Paul thought of Jesus' teaching as a Christian law.

c. The phrase was actually one in vogue with Paul's opponents, taken up by him and turned against these opponents.

d. The phrase employs νόμος in its extended sense of 'norm' or 'principle', and may thus also involve conscious wordplay with the more traditional meaning.

43. Barclay, *Obeying*, pp. 131-32. Italics mine. This connection is widely recognized. See, e.g., V.P. Furnish, *Theology and Ethics in Paul* (Nashville, 1968), pp. 64-65.
44. So Barclay, *Obeying*, pp. 125-31.

Barclay rightly criticizes (a) and (b) on the grounds of lack of evidence, and points out the improbability of Paul regarding Jesus as a 'second Moses' and thus the unlikelihood of his using a phrase like 'the law of Christ' to imply a code of precepts. His own conclusion to this problem revolves around the range of possible meanings of the Greek genitive.[45] He quotes Moule[46] with approval: 'A genitive like "of Christ" must often be interpreted largely by the context and the probabilities', and concludes that here the context (especially the link with 5.13-14) suggests that Paul is referring to fulfilling the (Mosaic) law τοῦ Χριστοῦ, implying 'the law in its relationship to Christ', that is, 'the law as redefined and fulfilled by Christ in love'. This is certainly possible.

In Gal. 6.2b it is intriguing that Paul chose such a loaded term as 'law' at all,[47] when he could have written 'the teaching of Christ' or even 'the gospel'. However, it may be that the use of this difficult word from the earlier discussion in the epistle is primarily rhetorically rather than theologically motivated in this instance, as Paul deliberately picks up this term from its chiastic partner and sets it in a phrase that again helps to tie together the beginning and ending of the pattern. Certainly, the phrase is not part of his stock-in-trade, since he uses it nowhere else. Somewhat similar phrases, however, are employed, as in 1 Cor. 9.20, 21, where he is discussing his strategies for winning individuals for the gospel, becoming as a Jew in order to win Jews, to those ὑπὸ νόμον ὡς ὑπὸ νόμον...τοῖς ἀνόμοις ὡς ἄνομος—a striking statement that he has to qualify immediately—μὴ ὢν ἄνομος θεοῦ ἀλλ' ἔννομος Χριστοῦ. Here, the phrase ἔννομος Χριστοῦ has been used as a balancing contrast to ἄνομος θεοῦ. In other words, the phrase ἔννομος Χριστοῦ is one which is rhetorically motivated and constructed. It keeps the balance of his syntax and avoids the embarrassment of his being charged with being ὡς ἄνομος![48] The immediate context of

45. Barclay, *Obeying*, p. 134 n. 92, lists five other instances where a genitive is associated with νόμος, these giving rise to a range of meanings.

46. C.F.D. Moule, '"Fulness" and "Fill" in the New Testament', *SJT* 4 (1951), pp. 79-86, 82.

47. Hays, 'Christology', p. 276 rightly calls it 'a breathtaking paradox' in the context of Galatians.

48. See further C.K. Barrett, *The First Epistle to the Corinthians* (BNTC; London, 2nd edn, 1971), pp. 212-13. It is possible that there are other passages where the use of 'law' is sometimes rhetorically motivated—notably Rom. 7.21-23. See further the discussions in Dunn, *Romans*, p. 393, who finds a 'note of irony' in Rom. 7.21, and J. Ziesler, *Paul's Letter to the Romans* (TPINTC; London, 1989),

Gal. 6.2b suggests no such rhetorical motivation, but an excellent one is furnished by referring it to its chiastic partner. Thus, in translation, 6.2b might be rendered 'and so you will fulfil the "law" of Christ', verging on the ironical. Indeed, Hays thinks that it is 'apparent' that the phrase 'the law of Christ' functions as 'an ironic rhetorical formulation', with Christ being seen as 'an ethical exemplar'.[49]

One more matter must be briefly addressed in relation to A and A': that of the possible relationship between the 'law' of Christ and the quotation of Lev. 19.18b. This can be approached from two starting points. The first would be on the assumption that sufficient evidence has already been adduced to make it reasonable to consider 5.13, 14 and 6.1, 2 as balancing elements of a chiasmus. On this basis, because an unfolding parallelism in content has been observed between these verses, it is certainly possible to equate 'the "law" of Christ' with the Levitical love-command if the two balancing elements are taken as mutually explanatory. On the other hand, if it were considered that there were a significant degree of doubt in the parallels adduced so far, then the overwhelming weight of exegetical tradition ties these two verses together. The link is strongly suggested by Sanders who concludes that 'Bear one another's burdens' is probably not to be distinguished from 'love your neighbour as yourself'.[50]

As a result of this extended discussion, it is reasonable to portray 5.13, 14 and 6.1, 2 as chiastically balanced elements, either as two unresolved elements A and A' respectively or as the more finely resolved structure suggested below:

A a₁ 5.13 Ὑμεῖς γὰρ ἐπ' ἐλευθερίᾳ ἐκλήθητε, **ἀδελφοί**· μόνον
μὴ τὴν ἐλευθερίαν εἰς ἀφορμὴν τῇ σαρκί,

a₂ ἀλλὰ διὰ τῆς ἀγάπης **δουλεύετε ἀλλήλοις**.

a₃ 14 ὁ γὰρ πᾶς **νόμος** ἐν ἑνὶ λόγῳ **πεπλήρωται**, ἐν τῷ·
ἀγαπήσεις τὸν πλησίον σου ὡς σεαυτόν.

p. 197, suggesting 'a play on words' in 'law' in the same verse.

49. Hays, 'Christology', pp. 275 (citing 1 Cor. 9.21 as an important parallel) and 287 respectively.

50. E.P. Sanders, *Paul, the Law and the Jewish People* (Philadelphia, 1983), p. 98. Cf. too Burton, *Galatians*, p. 329 implicitly; Lagrange, *Galates*, p. 156; Duncan, *Galatians*, p. 181; Betz, *Galatians*, p. 301; Mussner, *Galater*, p. 399; U. Borse, *Der Brief an die Galater* (RNT; Regensburg, 1984), p. 210; Barclay, *Obeying*, p. 142.

Α' α₁'   6.1 **Ἀδελφοί**, ἐὰν καὶ προλημφθῇ ἄνθρωπος ἔν τινι
παραπτώματι, ὑμεῖς οἱ πνευματικοὶ καταρτίζετε τὸν
τοιοῦτον ἐν πνεύματι πραΰτητος, σκοπῶν σεαυτόν, μὴ
καὶ σὺ πειρασθῇς.
α₂'   2 **Ἀλλήλων τὰ βάρη βαστάζετε,**
α₃'   **καὶ οὕτως ἀναπληρώσετε τὸν νόμον** τοῦ Χριστοῦ.

4.3.2. B (5.15) and B' (5.26)

The form of the conditional in B suggests a condition of fact. It reads as
a vivid description of community dissension and the possible consequences of such bad behaviour,[51] the colourful language bringing to
mind the ferocious fighting of wild animals. The problem is whether this
is merely a sarcastic[52] or parenthetic warning,[53] or whether Paul has a
concrete instance in mind. Undoubtedly there is a sharp contrast to 5.14,
but why should the contrasting statement of 5.15 be so much more
powerfully vivid than the original statement of 5.14, especially if it is
merely hypothetical? It may be far more plausible to suggest that he
includes this striking warning precisely because of some significant discord within the fellowship, thus earthing his ethical appeal to the realities
of the Galatian situation. Although the details of that situation may not
be recoverable with any degree of certainty, with the result that the
precise cause of the dispute must remain a matter of some speculation,
few would deny its reality. What is reflected in 5.15 may be, in fact, the
kind of ἀφορμή τῇ σαρκί that Paul cautions against in 5.13, and may
be linked to the problem of the correction of transgressors alluded to in
6.1. The biting and devouring of 5.15 is the very opposite of the
πνεῦμα πραΰτητος of Α'.

Barclay's approach to the exegesis of 5.13–6.10 is thematic rather
than sequential, and thus he deals with 5.15 apparently as one of Paul's
collection of maxims, linking it with 5.26, and the emphasis on social
sins, seeing them as a clear indication of the social disharmony and
breakdown of community life threatening the Galatian churches.[54] The
main strength of this approach is that it underlines some of the intercon-
nections within the passage (as has already been seen in his discussion of

51. *Pace* Schlier, *Galater*, p. 246, who sees it with reference to a lack of inner
freedom.
52. So Betz, *Galatians*, p. 277; Mussner, *Galater*, p. 373; Longenecker,
Galatians, p. 244.
53. Lightfoot, *Galatians*, p. 309.
54. Barclay, *Obeying*, p. 156; cf also, *Obeying*, p. 152.

mutual obligation and the 'law' of Christ), but more traditional, sequential exegesis also has a part to play in showing how Paul builds his argument. The 'maxim' (if that is its best description) of 5.15 is an integral part of the building of that argument, and is more than just one among many maxims.

Betz does not directly link 5.15 and 26, but his analysis of the latter does seem to underline a similarity in metaphor between the two, especially in the second part ἀλλήλους προκαλούμενοι, ἀλλήλοις φθονοῦτες. He suggests that

> the comparison presupposes two contestants engaged in hostilities by 'provoking one another' (26b) and by 'envying one another' (26c). While the first describes the hostile turning against each other, the latter implies the turning away from one another.[55]

Thus B is perhaps best described as a warning concerned with the consequences of a breakdown of relationships within the fellowship, and B′ as a warning against the empty pretentiousness of κενοδοξία with the attendant provocation and envy of one another.

Finally it is worth noting that, just as B stands in contrast to A and provides the first real illustration (or indication) of what Paul means by the misuse of freedom εἰς ἀφορμὴν τῇ σαρκί, so B′, picking up φθόνοι from the list of works of the flesh (5.21), leads into the concrete situation of A′, with the problem of the right approach and attitude to the correction of a transgressor, using πραΰτης from the list of the fruit of the Spirit (5.23).

4.3.3. *C (5.16) and C′ (5.25)*

Paul's use of λέγω δέ as the opening words of C appears to herald the fact that he is moving on to the next important step in his argument. He employs some kind of construction with λέγω four other times in Galatians as a means of emphasis: 1.9; 3.17; 4.1; 5.2.[56] The new idea that he is about to develop is that of walking by the Spirit, as the second half of 5.16 picks up the idea of σάρξ again. If the flesh were wrongly or unwittingly given 'opportunity' (as in 5.13), then the danger is that one would end up fulfilling the desires of the flesh. Walking by the Spirit, Paul confidently asserts, prevents this. The grounds for such confidence,

55. Betz, *Galatians*, p. 294.

56. Of these four, only Gal. 4.1 is formally identical to 5.16, and in this instance, too, it indicates the start of the next step in his argument.

however, are not discussed until later.

In both C and C′ πνεῦμα occurs in phrases that have very similar meanings and it would be difficult to find any substantive difference in περιπατέω (5.16) and στοιχέω (5.25)—or, indeed, with ζάω. C falls into two parts, the imperative to walk by the Spirit and the emphatically negative future statement 'and you will not fulfil the desires of the flesh'.[57] There is, in fact, an implicit conditionality between the two halves of C, so that hypotaxis might be substituted for parataxis.[58] Such implicit conditionality makes the link in form with the explicitly conditional C′ even more obvious, although the person of the verb has changed from second to first person plural, and the idea of walking by the Spirit is replaced by the albeit clearly related one of living by the Spirit. By C′ Paul is back where he started in C, having made his case to his own satisfaction, with the emphatic assurance about what the Galatians will *not* do, replaced by a positive appeal for what they should do in the life lived in the Spirit.

. In some ways, C′ is a little more problematical, not in terms of its content, but in that some[59] place it at the beginning of a new section in Paul's argument, and therefore see it more as a forward-looking verse. In fact, it may be better described as the *end* of a stage (i.e. 5.16-25) in Paul's argument that does, nevertheless, lead the believer to expect something new to be said. Thus, 5.16 heralds the beginning of a generalized discussion of the catalogues that encompass what Paul calls 'the works of the flesh' and 'the fruit of the Spirit'. That section ends with the appeal of 5.25, while 5.26 deals again with the particularities of the Galatian situation, last referred to in 5.15. Such a theory, of course, does not affect the legitimacy of the chiasmus as a whole, but the chiastic pattern does make 5.16-25 stand out as a unit that is different in tone from the rest of the chiasmus. More will be said about 5.25 when the contents of 5.17-24 are considered.

---

57. Such a translation is supported by Lightfoot, *Galatians*, p. 209; Betz, *Galatians*, p. 278; Bruce, *Galatians*, p. 243; Burton, *Galatians*, p. 297; Lagrange, *Galates*, p. 147; *et al.*; see further BDF, §365 for οὐ μή with the future subjunctive as a strong form of negation.

58. This would produce a translation such as, 'If you walk by the Spirit, you will not fulfil the desires of the flesh'; cf. Bruce, *Galatians*, p. 243; Burton, *Galatians*, p. 297, takes a similar line.

59. See 4.4.1 below.

4.3.4. *D (5.17) and D′ (5.24)*

In 5.17 Paul begins to unpack the implications of the Spirit's role in preventing the fulfilment of the desires of the flesh. He does this, using a little chiasmus to highlight the ethical dualism:[60]

ἡ γὰρ σάρξ ἐπιθυμεῖ	κατὰ τοῦ πνεύματος
τὸ δὲ πνεῦμα	κατὰ τῆς σαρκός·

This ABBA structure seems to have little exegetical significance, except perhaps lending a marginal emphasis to the centrality of the Spirit. It seems best to regard it as a simple rhetorical feature which heightens the contrast between σάρξ and πνεῦμα.

Having categorically stated in C that the Galatians will not gratify the desires of the flesh, Paul now has to embark on the explanation of his grounds for such confidence. This begins with 5.17a, which sets out the relationship between flesh and Spirit by means of the somewhat obscure construction with ἐπιθυμέω κατά (used uniquely here in the New Testament). The NIV perhaps best captures the spirit of Paul's intention (although the more traditional translation of σάρξ as 'flesh' rather than 'sinful nature' is to be preferred): 'For the sinful nature desires what is contrary to the Spirit, and the Spirit what is contrary to the sinful nature'. At this point Paul is not so much describing the *conflict*[61] between flesh and Spirit, as the *relationship* between them. It is true that ἐπιθυμέω suggests that there could be such a conflict, but that it is actually so is the point of the next phrase: ταῦτα γὰρ ἀλλήλοις ἀντίκειται. It is not just a situation where two 'forces' or 'principles' have incompatible desires; they are actually set against one another (ἀντίκειται). At this point Barclay concludes, 'Such mutual opposition clearly implies mutual exclusion and thus satisfactorily explains why the Galatians' walk in the Spirit will not fulfil the desires of the flesh (5.16)'. This, however, may be too simple. Such a mutual exclusion may well be *implied*, but how is it known that the Spirit will overcome the flesh, and that the flesh will not overwhelm the Spirit? Paul's answer to this is not completed until the chiastic partner of 5.17, that is 5.24, is taken into account.[62]

---

60. Noted by Jeremias, 'Chiasmus', p. 147; Betz, *Galatians*, p. 278; *et al.* See, too, Longenecker, *Galatians*, p. 245.

61. *Pace* Barclay, *Obeying*, p. 111.

62. It is not enough to point to 5.16 as the answer to this question. In this verse Paul merely makes the *unsupported assertion* that the Galatians will not fulfil the desires of the flesh.

The last clause of 5.17 is complex: ἵνα μὴ ἃ ἐὰν θέλητε ταῦτα ποιῆτε. There are two related conundra in this: (a) whether this clause contains a telic ἵνα (i.e. of purpose) or an ecbatic ἵνα (i.e. of result) and (b) the identity of the wants (ἃ ἐὰν θέλητε) which are being forestalled. There are three approaches to these inter-related problems:

a.   5.17 expresses the conflict of flesh and Spirit which results in the flesh frustrating the Spirit-inspired wishes of the believer. (This can be rejected as inconsistent with what Paul is saying in the passage.)

b.   5.17 expresses the conflict of flesh and Spirit as two forces which equally frustrate each other (ecbatic ἵνα) or attempt to do so (telic ἵνα). This can be criticized on the grounds that a stalemate between flesh and Spirit does not sit well with the confidence expressed in the previous verse.

c.   5.17 expresses the conflict of flesh and Spirit as having the purpose (or result) of frustrating the fleshly desires. This fits the context well, both supporting and illustrating the confident statement of 5.16. 'Its problems lie in accommodating the central clause ("these are opposed *to each other*"), and in explaining why "whatever you want" should be taken as "what the flesh desires".'[63]

Barclay's own conclusion to this conundrum is both simple and elegant. Because flesh and Spirit are in conflict, those who are seeking to walk by the Spirit are inevitably drawn into that conflict—they are not free to do whatever they want (i.e. ἵνα μὴ ἃ ἐὰν θέλητε ταῦτα ποιῆτε)! In fact, they must be led or directed by the Spirit (5.18). There is *not* an even balance or a stalemate between flesh and Spirit, but a state of warfare which inevitably puts restrictions upon those who would walk by the Spirit. This is a most attractive explanation which gives due weight to each part of 5.17 and ties it in well to both 5.16 and 5.18.

The effect of Barclay's interpretation is to highlight Paul's step-by-step examination of the place and role of the Spirit. But the fate of the flesh is the as yet unanswered part of this situation. That answer is found in 5.24, the chiastic partner of 5.17. Those who belong to Christ Jesus have crucified the flesh with its passions and desires! It may be that Paul deliberately uses ἐπιθυμία in 5.24 giving it prominence as the last word

---

63. Barclay, *Obeying*, p. 114, on whose analysis this whole paragraph rests.

of the sentence, and consciously picking up the language last used in 5.17. It is interesting that Barclay too (without, of course, any reference to a chiastic pattern) links 5.24 with 5.17.[64] His analysis of it, however, may suggest that it is somewhat in the nature of an appendage, whereas it is better seen as an integral part of the answer to the question of why Paul can have such unequivocal grounds for confidence in the outcome of the Galatians' walk (5.16). It is noteworthy, too, that it is to the same theme that Paul immediately returns in 5.25. Thus, establishing the chiastic nature of the passage helps us to see the close relationship in Paul's thought between verses that are sequentially separated. Reading 5.16, 17 and 5.24, 25 together produces a powerfully coherent argument for Paul.

4.3.5. *E (5.18) and E′ (5.23b)*
With 5.18 Paul changes one element of the contrast he has been drawing. For the moment, the contrast between Spirit and flesh gives way to one between Spirit and law. The ongoing association between flesh and law in Galatians is an intriguing aspect of Paul's thought. That Paul does relate the two is perhaps most obvious in Gal. 3.3, where, as a neat contrast to πνεῦμα, Paul seizes on σάρξ, apparently including within that term what he has just called ἔργα νόμου.[65] For the purpose of this study, the precise relationship of σάρξ and νόμος, and the degree to which Galatians should or should not be read in conjunction with Romans (especially Rom. 7 and 8), while important issues in themselves, need to be left to one side as more appropriate to an in-depth study of Paul's use of these terms.[66]

It has already been suggested that, because of the opposition of, and conflict between, flesh and Spirit, a Christian does not have unbounded freedom, but a freedom necessarily circumscribed by that conflict and by the fact that believers are caught up in it, 'so that you may not do

---

64. Barclay, *Obeying*, p. 118, sees 5.24 as supporting and securing Paul's earlier remarks in 5.16-18.

65. Barclay, *Obeying*, pp. 85-86.

66. A passing impression is that great caution should be exercised in elucidating the use of these terms in Galatians by their use in Romans because of the clearly different situations they reflect, the different purposes for which they were written, and the different times of writing in Paul's career. I can see no *a priori* reason for Paul to use even such important concepts as the relationship between Spirit, law and flesh in precisely the same way in the different contexts.

whatever you want'. The matter of what sets those boundaries still remains. Gal. 5.18 starts to address the issue. It is tied up with the nature of the Spirit's role in the believers' lives. The protasis (εἰ δὲ πνεύματι ἄγεσθε) introduces a new, much more active dimension in the Spirit's relationship with the believer when compared with the vaguer and more bland expression of 5.16 (πνεύματι περιπατεῖτε).[67] Betz likens it to being carried away or driven by the Spirit.[68] Perhaps he overstates it a little, and it may be better to liken the Spirit to a guide who directs.[69] Already Paul has made plain that it is the Spirit's role in the believers' lives that is going to provide the boundaries to freedom. The apodosis takes him to the next stage (οὐκ ἐστὲ ὑπὸ νόμον): the law is not needed.

In Galatians the law's influence has often been described by Paul essentially in negative terms: 3.23, 'confined under law, kept under restraint'; 3.24, the law as the believer's child-minder; 5.1, the law likened implicitly to a yoke of slavery.[70] In the new situation of the Christians called to freedom, and led or directed by the Spirit, Paul can state simply οὐκ ἐστὲ ὑπὸ νόμον. It is a statement, however, that in a sense is not complete without an explanation. What are going to be the results of being led by the Spirit, and, in particular, how can it be true that there is no need for law? The answer is in the chiastic partner of 5.18, which is 5.23b.

This deceptively simple statement (i.e. 5.23b) has been said to have three inter-related puzzles associated with it: (a) the force of κατά; (b) the gender of τοιούτων; (c) the reason for Paul including it at all. However, these puzzles appear to stem from the comments of a number of German scholars. Schlier agrees with Hoffmann's comment on it as being 'more than unnecessary' and Oepke calls it 'a trite phrase'.[71]

On the other hand, it has to be said that by no means all commentators seem to see any significant problem. Indeed, some or all of the difficulties associated with it disappear if the passage is recognized as

67. Hence a possible further reason for paralleling 5.16 with 5.25 which is also a less forceful protasis than 5.18.

68. Betz, *Galatians*, p. 281.

69. Guthrie, *Galatians*, p. 136; Barclay, *Obeying*, p. 116, respectively.

70. Despite this essentially negative influence, Paul can still see that some law can be positively fulfilled by the love-command of 5.14.

71. Schlier, *Galater*, p. 262; A. Oepke, *Der Brief des Paulus an die Galater* (THKNT, 9; Berlin, 5th edn, 1984), p. 183 (cited in Barclay, *Obeying*, p. 122).

chiastic. In this respect, Lightfoot's simple approach to 5.23b may provide all the explanation needed (although he has nothing to say about
any chiastic ordering), suggesting that this statement 'substantiates the
proposition in verse 18'.[72] Of course, in this analysis, 5.18 is the chiastic
partner of 5.23b.

Barclay feels that Lightfoot[73] has 'to stretch the meaning of κατά
here considerably',[74] in order to arrive at the meaning 'there is no law
(required) to restrain such people'. But both Lightfoot and Duncan
render κατά simply as 'against'. If the law 'restrains' (Lightfoot's term)
or 'regulates' (Duncan's term) then the clause can still be translated
quite simply as 'against such things (or people) there is no law'.[75] On
the other hand, Barclay notes that there are those who give κατά a
force, unusual in the New Testament, translating it as 'concerning'.[76]
This certainly would appear to be the case when κατά is used with the
genitive. Compelling evidence would be needed to show that κατά had
to be given this meaning when the much more common one of 'against'
seems to fit.

The second puzzle that is said to be present in this clause is the gender
of τοιούτων. The two feasible options are masculine and neuter, the
consensus being for the neuter, with τοιούτων referring back to the
individual elements that comprise the fruit of the Spirit. There would
then perhaps be some sort of analogy with τὰ τοιαῦτα in 5.21b.[77] This
repeated generic use of τοιαῦτα is an example of a parallel that exists
alongside a chiastic pattern, but is not accommodated by that pattern. In
this discussion Barclay's point is well made that, since such qualities as
comprise the fruit of the Spirit can be displayed only in the lives of individuals, there is ultimately little difference in either position.[78]

The charge that 5.23b is trivial does not stand up to close examination. Recapitulating what Paul has already said, because flesh and Spirit

72. Lightfoot, *Galatians*, p. 213.

73. And Duncan, *Galatians*, pp. 175-76 who adopts a position similar to
Lightfoot's.

74. Barclay, *Obeying*, p. 122 n. 50.

75. Duncan, *Galatians*, p. 175.

76. Barclay, *Obeying*, p. 123.

77. This suggestion is widely made by, for example, Betz, *Galatians*, p. 288;
Schlier, *Galater*, p. 262; Burton, *Galatians*, p. 219; *et al.*, although the closeness of
the analogy should not be overstated.

78. Barclay, *Obeying*, p. 123.

are in conflict, the believer's freedom is not unbounded (5.17). This, in turn, gives rise to the statement about the relationship of the Spirit-led to the law (5.18), viz., that it is not law that sets the bounds to freedom. Two explanatory statements follow that contrast τὰ ἔργα τῆς σαρκός (5.19-21a) and ὁ καρπὸς τοῦ πνεύματος (5.22-23c). Paul then moves back to his case that the Spirit-led are not under law with the statement of 5.23b: there is no law against such things as comprise the fruit of the Spirit. The law has nothing to say about the fruit of the Spirit, or to those who are led by that Spirit. Note that in this instance, too, there is ultimately little difference in whether κατά in 5.23b is rendered as 'against' or 'concerning'. It is *not* that κατά has both these meanings, but, in the context of the passage, to say that there is no law 'against these things' (or 'people') carries the clear implication that the law does not legislate for 'these things' at all. This is his argument! The boundaries of the Spirit-led life are not set by law at all. In this sense Lightfoot is quite right in suggesting that 5.23b (E′) is the substantiation of the proposition of 5.18 (E), and thus is an integral step in Paul's argument, and neither trivial nor superfluous.

4.3.6. *F (5.19-21a) and F′ (5.22-23a)*
In 5.19 it is again interesting to observe how Paul's thought moves with apparent ease between νόμος and τὰ ἔργα τῆς σαρκός. The classical and Jewish background to such catalogues of vices (and virtues) are extensively discussed by Longenecker[79] who concludes that those in Galatians are modelled on a Hellenistic catalogue genre rather than a Jewish 'Two Ways' pattern. Some of the older commentators suggest that the catalogue of vices can be grouped in some way. Thus, Burton proposes four groups: the first of the first three terms 'in which sensuality in the narrower sense is present'; the next two 'are associated with heathen religions'; the following eight constitute a group 'in which the element of conflict with others is present'; the final two consist of 'drunkenness and its natural accompaniments'.[80] Many of the more recent scholars see them only as a random collection of terms.[81]

Certainly, the catalogue appears to bear no detailed relationship to the

79. Longenecker, *Galatians*, pp. 249-52.
80. Burton, *Galatians*, p. 304; Lightfoot, *Galatians*, p. 210, divides the 15 in the same general fashion.
81. So Betz, *Galatians*, p. 283; Schlier, *Galater*, p. 251; Mussner, *Galater*, p. 381; Longenecker, *Galatians*, p. 253.

nine components of the fruit of the Spirit, which Betz suggests should be seen as 'three sets of three concepts...the most important of which are placed at the beginning and the end'.[82] In this he apparently followed Lightfoot who found that

> The catalogue falls into three groups of three each. The first of these comprises Christian habits of mind in their more general aspect, 'love, joy, peace'; the second gives special qualities affecting a man's intercourse with his neighbours, 'long-suffering, kindness, beneficence'; while the third, again general in character like the first, exhibits the principles which guide a Christian's conduct, 'honesty, gentleness, temperance'.[83]

A number of scholars find it striking that there is a group of eight nouns in the centre of the list of vices (beginning with ἔχθραι and ending with φθόνοι), all of which refer to disturbances within the community structure,[84] leading to community dissension or disturbances within the Galatian churches. Barclay concludes that Paul has deliberately emphasized these features of fleshly conduct, and that this, together with the warnings of 5.15 and 5.26, points to a situation of discord in the Galatian churches. To this might be added the evidence of 6.1 also. Regarding the 'catalogue of vices', however, no certainty can be reached as to what extent Paul may be relying on traditional lists.[85] Account must be taken of the fact that in 2 Cor. 12.20 Paul repeats four of these 'social vices' in a verbatim parallel (ἔρις, ζῆλος, θυμοί, ἐριθεῖαι), including the very unusual use of the plurals θυμοί and ἐριθεῖαι.[86] Indeed these are the only two occurences of these two words in the plural anywhere in the New Testament. It may therefore be that, at least in this grouping of four, Paul is relying on a traditional list. This does not imply, however, that these four vices were not part of the Galatian problem.

That this is partly preformed material may be underscored by 5.21b, where Paul specifically says that he is repeating something he has

---

82. Betz, *Galatians*, p. 286.

83. Lightfoot, *Galatians*, p. 212. This has the characteristics of an ABA ordering. Note, too, the Nestle-Aland punctuation of the Greek text.

84. So G. Ebeling, *The Truth of the Gospel: An Exposition of Galatians* (trans. D. Green; Philadelphia, 1985), p. 258; cf., too, Burton, *Galatians*, p. 304; Barclay, *Obeying*, p. 153; *et al.*

85. See, e.g., Betz, *Galatians*, pp. 281-82.

86. θυμός occurs elsewhere in the Pauline corpus in Rom. 2.8; Col. 3.8; Eph. 4.31—all in the singular. ἐριθεία is used in Rom. 2.8, Phil. 1.17, 2.3, again all in the singular.

already told the Galatians, using the 'somewhat archaic language'[87] of the phrase οἱ τὰ τοιαῦτα πράσσοντες βασιλείαν θεοῦ οὐ κληρονομήσουσιν. Betz shows the relative rarity of the phrase βασιλεία θεοῦ in Paul, the use of κληρονομέω in a rather different way from elsewhere in Galatians, and points to a 'traditional', rather than Pauline, use of πράσσω. He suggests that 'Form-critically, v. 21b is an eschatological warning and in this sense a statement of eschatological law. It is related to the catalogues of vices and virtues because they contain the condition for entering into the Kingdom of God.'

4.3.7. *The Central Element, G (5.21b)*

Gal. 5.21b lies at the mid-point of the chiastic pattern, forming its unique centre. Before deciding its function in this particular chiasmus, it is necessary to examine its opening clause (ἃ προλέγω ὑμῖν καθὼς προεῖπον) more closely. Betz calls this a 'puzzling remark' and offers a literal translation: 'in respect to which I predict to you as I have predicted [sc., in the past]'. He finds parallels to this in Gal. 1.15, 2 Cor. 13.2 and 1 Thess. 4.6, which lead him to conclude that this phrase is a 'quotation formula indicating a set style of quoting what the individual himself has stated previously'. He suggests that, in this instance, his remark includes the material in vv. 19-21, 22-23a which can be related to primitive Christian catechetical instruction.[88] Others are less inclined to translate προλέγω this way. Guthrie is happy to follow the RSV: 'I warn you as I warned you before', although he recognizes that προλέγω has the literal meaning 'to say beforehand', with a derived meaning 'to declare'.[89]

The sense and implications of what Paul is saying is not much altered by these different translations of προλέγω. That Paul is conveying a serious warning about the fate of those who 'do the works of the flesh' seems beyond doubt. I am persuaded by those like Betz who argue that the material in 5.19-23a may well belong together as material partly, at least, preformed in the catechetical tradition. It cannot be proven if, or how, Paul has altered or adapted the material for his own purposes, other than to interject his personal warning ἃ προλέγω ὑμῖν καθὼς

---

87. Betz, *Galatians*, p. 285.

88. Betz, *Galatians*, p. 284. Betz is not alone in wishing to give προλέγω its full weight as 'I predict': Burton also is 'quite certain' that this is its meaning here (Burton, *Galatians*, p. 311).

89. Guthrie, *Galatians*, p. 138.

προεῖπον at its centre. Even if such a line of argument is not fully convincing, we still have two clearly contrasted catalogues of 'vices' and
'virtues', with 5.21b standing between, forming the central element of
the chiasmus.

I would suggest that the chiastic patterning of 5.13–6.2 has now been
established by exegesis as a reasonable hypothesis, primarily on a linguistic basis in the balancing of words and phrases. It is further strengthened by the balancing of ideas in complementary or contrasting pairs of
elements. Considerable care has been taken not to impose a pattern on
the text that it does not clearly support. It is recognized, however, that
more prominence has been given to the link between the idea of the
correction of an erring brother in the wrong spirit and that of allowing
freedom to be used as an opportunity for the flesh than the objective
evidence may suggest, and this will need further substantiation later.
Throughout, it has been maintained that 5.16-24 is different in tone from
the remainder of the passage (except in the personal warning of 5.21b),
and that it may be seen as the teaching that lies behind, and supports,
Paul's practical concerns in showing how, in the absence of law, the
Spirit guides the freedom of the Galatians' lives, allowing them to
triumph over the 'works of the flesh'.

4.4. *Paul's Purpose in Writing Galatians 5.13–6.2:* *Warning or Appeal?*

With so much rich material for exegete and theologian alike in this chiasmus, it is difficult to decide if 5.21b describes the focus of Paul's
thought: in other words, can Gal. 5.13–6.2 be fairly or adequately portrayed as being a warning to the Galatians about the consequences of
the way they live, or is its purpose to be sought elsewhere? Some preliminary 'negative conclusions' may be accepted: 'Paul did *not* write this
exhortation to give a generalised description of Christian ethics, *nor* was
he concerned to counter antinomian licence, *nor* was his purpose solely
defensive'.[90]

The chiasmus begins with a warning (5.13): μόνον μὴ τὴν
ἐλευθερίαν εἰς ἀφορμὴν τῇ σαρκί. It continues with the vivid
warning of 5.15, and then has the personal warning of 5.21b. There is

---

90. Barclay, *Obeying*, p. 219. He considers 5.13–6.10 as a unit, but these conclusions are largely determined by the section under consideration here, viz. 5.13–
6.2.

warning again in 5.26, and the pattern ends with the warning of 6.1. It appears that all of these have the same basic thread running through them, as they are all related to the consequences of giving opportunity to the flesh. There is no intention to imply that this is Paul's *sole aim*, but it might well be his primary purpose.

He does, however, have a powerful secondary purpose. So far, by describing the repeated warning note, the negative elements (in the sense of warnings *against* the misuse of freedom etc.) which occur throughout have been accentuated. Paul, however, appears deliberately and consistently to balance these by positive injunctions to what may be called a Spirit-led life. This, too, is highlighted by the chiastic patterning of the passage. Thus each negative warning is associated with a positive injunction (i.e. an appeal towards doing or being something).

Laying this out schematically, gives:

A	negative warning	against misuse of freedom
	positive injunction	to mutual service
B	negative warning	against community dissension
C	positive injunction	to walk by the Spirit
G	negative warning	against the results of doing the works of the flesh
C′	positive injunction	to walk by the Spirit
B′	negative warning	against community dissension
A′	negative warning?	against the spiritual being tempted?[91]
	positive injunction	to mutual burden bearing

Not too much emphasis should be placed on such a scheme. Obviously, there are a number of elements which contain neither warning or appeal, and in some of these in the above diagram, 'warning' or 'appeal' describes their function only partially. It does suggest, however, that 'warning' elements in the first half are balanced by 'warning' elements in the second; likewise elements containing an appeal are similarly balanced. However, in this scheme G stands out as a single, unparalleled 'warning' element. Barclay's analysis, while noting the element of warning,[92] does not take enough account of it as a feature recurring throughout the passage, whereas the chiastic pattern suggests that Paul's primary concern was, in fact, to warn against the flesh, closely allied to a

---

91. This also contains the positive appeal for the recipients to look to themselves.
92. As in Barclay, *Obeying*, p. 219.

secondary purpose of appealing for the Spirit-led life, in the assurance
that the Spirit can provide adequate moral constraint.

4.5. *The Integrity of the Chiasmus and its Setting in the Wider Context of Galatians*

4.5.1. *The Integrity of the Chiasmus*

A number of commentators begin a new section at Gal. 5.25,[93] others at
5.26.[94] Others, again, find the break at 6.1.[95]

The suggestion made in this study is that 5.25 is an integral part of the
chiastic pattern, and ends that part of the chiasmus which begins at 5.16.
It has already been indicated that there may be a change of tone in
Paul's writing after the sharply pointed warning of 5.15, which rings
with knowledge of a specific situation in the Galatian churches, with the
discussion becoming much more general in nature from 5.16 on. It is
almost as though Paul has no specific problem in mind (other, perhaps,
than the problems which he may be highlighting by the grouping of the
eight central terms of the catalogue of vices) until he comes to the
warning couched in the first person singular in 5.21b. Again the discussion becomes more general until 5.26 is reached with its specific warning μὴ γινώμεθα κενόδοξοι. Thus, as the specific warning of 5.15
leads to the more general appeal of 5.16, so the general appeal of 5.25 is
followed by the specific warning of 5.26. This is part of the elegant and,
perhaps, conscious pattern of warning and appeal that Paul weaves into
this structure. It is not suggested, however, that the sole function of 5.25
is to look back to 5.16. It does look forward, not just to 5.26, but to 6.1-
10 also. Its appeal πνεύματι καὶ στοιχῶμεν leads the Galatians to look
for some examples of what a spirit-led life entails.

It may not be safe to assume, therefore, that Paul intended to begin a
new section at 5.25 and it may be reasonable to regard 5.13–6.2 as a

---

93. Including Duncan, *Galatians*, p. 177; Schlier, *Galater*, p. 268; Betz,
Galatians, p. 291; Barclay, *Obeying*, p. 155.

94. Mussner, *Galater*, p. 374, although he appears to be inconsistent, referring to
5.16-26 as comprising one section, while in the text (p. 391) he stops that section at
5.25, and begins the next with 5.26 (p. 395). There is further inconsistency in his
analysis of the remainder of the passage to 6.10—cf. pp. 395 and 402. Lagrange,
Galater, p. 153, does not offer a traditional 'structure', but says of 5.25, 'Ce rattache
étroitement à ce qui précède, comme la conclusion pratique'.

95. E.g., Burton, *Galatians*, p. 324; Bruce, *Galatians*, p. 259; Guthrie,
Galatians, p. 142 (with reservations); Longenecker, *Galatians*, p. 268.

broadly unified entity, in which the recipients constantly look backwards and forwards over the two halves of the chiastic pattern.

4.5.2. *The Relationship of the Chiasmus to Gal. 6.3-10*

This matter arises directly as a result of the identification of the chiasmus. Traditionally, Gal. 6.3 has not been seen as the start of a new section,[96] but a close connection between 6.2 and 6.3 should not be tacitly assumed. The use of γάρ should be given its full force.[97] Longenecker suggests that it is explanatory, in support of 6.2,[98] but the logical connection appears to be rather tenuous. Indeed, it may be much more satisfactory to see γάρ as introducing the first comment on the whole chiasmus, with its fiasco of community dissension, its loveless back-biting providing opportunity for the flesh, and with the so-called 'spiritual' people[99] correcting transgressors in an unhelpful way. Barrett insists that 6.3 must have a specific reference, since otherwise it is 'so obvious and trite as to be ridiculous'.[100] Likewise, Barclay's comment on 6.3 is interesting: 'To reckon yourself to be something when you are nothing...is precisely the error of vanity which Paul had warned about in the introduction (κενόδοξοι, 5.26; cf. δοκεῖ, 6.3)'.[101] Thus, there is a link in substance between 6.3 and B′, but one, too, that is clearly at the heart of the repeated warnings of the whole chiasmus.

Part of the difficulty of dealing with the *sententiae* of 6.3-10 is that there is no general agreement as to their structure. Indeed, some do not attempt any analysis at all,[102] while at the other end of the scale Betz

---

96. This is not suggested here either: it will be argued that 6.3-10 is comment on, and reinforcement of, the focus of the chiasmus.

97. The NIV translators omit it altogether!

98. Longenecker, *Galatians*, p. 276.

99. Schlier, *Galater*, p. 270, sees this as ironical; *pace* Betz, *Galatians*, pp. 296-97, who thinks that the Galatians would have approved of it as a self-designation. The two views are not necessarily exclusive, since Paul may be using their self-designation in an ironical fashion.

100. He sees it as a reintroduction at the end of the epistle of the irony of 2.6, 9 (C.K. Barrett, *Freedom and Obligation: A Study of the Epistle to the Galatians* [London, 1985], pp. 80-81). Betz, *Galatians*, p. 301, and Longenecker, *Galatians*, p. 276, both find links between this statement and traditional forms known from the Graeco-Roman world.

101. Barclay, *Obeying*, p. 159.

102. E.g., Duncan, *Galatians*, p. 117; Bruce, *Galatians*, p. 58; Schlier, *Galater*, p. 269.

divides 5.25–6.10 into no fewer than 11 subsections, one of which is
further divided into two, and another of which is divided into five![103]
This is not helpful in terms of trying to understand Paul's flow of
thought, and serves as little more than a listing of contents.

Barclay has a new approach to the collection of maxims (which he
sees as beginning at 5.25). His structure is:

5.25-26	The Heading—appeal and prohibition.
6.1a	Responsibility to correct a sinning church-member (A).
6.1b	Accountability—'look to yourself' (B).
6.2	Responsibility to bear the burdens of one another (A).
6.3-5	Accountability—'test your own work, bear your own load' (B).
6.6	Responsibility to support those who teach (A).
6.7-8	Accountability—'how you sow will be how you reap' (B).
6.9-10	Responsibility to do good to all men, especially Christians (A).

In this structure those designated (A) 'emphasize the Galatians' corporate responsibilities to one another', while those designated (B) 'concern
the individual's accountability before God.'[104] He immediately recognizes, however, that

> Although it is based on an eight-part division, it should be clear that this
> analysis by no means represents an atomistic understanding of the text.
> Rather it aims to highlight its internal connections in the interweaving of
> the two complementary themes.

Barclay's structure is attractive, but is not beyond criticism. Thus, while
6.2 undoubtedly enjoins the responsibility of mutual burden-bearing, it
may also have an element of accountability before God in the clause
'and so fulfil the law of Christ'. Likewise, it is not immediately apparent
why 6.3 should be included as part of a section that speaks of the individual's accountability before God.

It is possible, too, that there is a further allusion to the chiasmus in 6.4,
for this verse concerns itself with testing ($\delta o\kappa \iota \mu \acute{\alpha} \zeta \omega$), as does A'
($\pi \epsilon \iota \rho \acute{\alpha} \zeta \omega$), these two verbs being listed as virtual synonyms by Abbott-
Smith and Trench.[105] The 'negative' approach to testing in 6.1 is

---

103. Betz, *Galatians*, p. 23. Longenecker, *Galatians*, p. 270, appropriately
describes it as 'atomistic'.

104. Barclay, *Obeying*, pp. 149-50.

105. G. Abbott-Smith, *A Manual Greek Lexicon of the New Testament*
(Edinburgh, 3rd edn, 1937); R.C. Trench, *'The New Testament Synonyms'*
(Cambridge, 1863), pp. 106-11.

warned against, but testing in the right context (as in 6.4) is encouraged. The 'testing' of A´ (πειράζω) may well have had the result of 'entangling the person so tried in sin',[106] while the 'testing' of 6.4 (δοκιμάζω) has within it the implications of 'a coming victoriously out of the trial'.[107]

At a number of points in this section, Barclay's comments are helpful. Because of his conviction that 5.13–6.10 is basically an entity, he tends to interpret the maxims, not in the isolation that some others do, but in the light of the earlier part of the section. Thus the second clause of 6.4 (one which causes some discussion in the commentaries), καὶ τότε εἰς ἑαυτὸν μόνον τὸ καύχημα ἕξει καὶ οὐκ εἰς τὸν ἕτερον, is helpfully integrated within the wider context:

> A strong case can be made for understanding εἰς in terms of 'direction' and translating the phrase 'and then he will direct his boast to himself alone and not to his neighbour.' If this is correct, the point of Paul's injunction is to minimise rivalry (5.26) and to encourage self-control (see again 5.23 ἐγκράτεια)...[108]

With βαστάσει in 6.5 another term is taken from the chiasmus (cf. βαστάζετε in A´). There is no contradiction between the two occurrences, since in 6.5 it is in a section concerned with the individual's accountability before God, while in 6.2 it is in a section emphasizing corporate responsibility.[109] Burton puts it well: 'It is the man who knows he has a burden of his own that is willing to bear his fellow's burden'.[110] Kuck has made a good case for seeing this verse as a reference to the eschatological judgment of God, suggesting that, for Paul, 'the symbolic language of future judgment helps to resolve the tension between the desire for individual status and the need to sublimate that desire for the sake of the unity of the church'.[111] The warning at the heart of the chiasmus in G is equally placed within an eschatological framework.[112]

106. Trench, *Synonyms*, p. 109.
107. Trench, *Synonyms*, p. 107.
108. Barclay, *Obeying*, p. 160.
109. So Barclay, *Obeying*, pp. 160-61.
110. Burton, *Galatians*, p. 334.
111. Kuck, 'Burden', p. 296, although I disagree with him that 6.5 forms the climax of 6.1-5.
112. *Pace* Hays, *Faith*, p. 263, who does not seem to be aware of this framework, either in 6.5 or in 5.21b: 'In Galatians...Paul traces the story...forwards no farther than the immediately controverted future of the Galatian churches'.

Gal. 6.6 seems at first sight not to 'fit' with the premise that 6.3-10 is comment on the chiasmus. Bruce, however, finds it to be 'an instance of the mutual help inculcated in v. 2a' (i.e. in A').[113] Lightfoot takes a similar view, while Barclay sees it as 'a practical application of the fruit of the Spirit; the Galatians are to walk in the Spirit by exercising ἀγαθωσύνη (cf. 5.22)'.[114]

The way that Paul chooses to end this section may well be significant for a correct understanding of Paul's focus of thought. Thus, Gal. 6.7 and 8 are associated with one another as Paul returns for the last time to the antithesis of flesh and Spirit, and to the theme of warning which played such a prominent part in the chiasmus. To sow to one's flesh is to indulge in pride, envy and other 'works of the flesh' which Paul has highlighted, but to sow to the Spirit is to walk in line with the Spirit's direction and to put into practice 'the fruit of the Spirit', with the one agricultural metaphor recalling the other.[115]

The final reference in the section is to the positive injunction of mutual obligation, implied in the phrases τὸ καλὸν ποιοῦντες and ἐργαζώμεθα τὸ ἀγαθόν (6.9, 10),[116] looking back to the theme with which the chiasmus began and ended. It is interesting, too, that these verses have an eschatological dimension, highlighted in the clause καιρῷ γὰρ ἰδίῳ θερίσομεν (6.9) and again possibly in ὡς καιρὸν ἔχομεν (6.10).[117] In the context of the chiastic pattern, there has been an eschatological reference at its centre in G.

This approach to 6.3-10 has illustrated the way in which many of its themes flow from, or look back to, the chiasmus. These involve some of the more important and positive aspects of what Paul is arguing throughout the chiasmus, and certainly reinforce the idea that, in Galatians, there is a situation of dissension in the community. Most of the allusions appear to be to material from the ends or the centre of the chiasmus. Those noted here include 6.3 and B'; 6.4 and A', B'; 6.5 and A', G; 6.6 and A' or F'; 6.7, 8 and A (and possibly F and F'); 6.9, 10 and A, A' and G.

Not all of these are equally certain or specific. What, however, they

---

113. Bruce, *Galatians*, p. 126.

114. Lightfoot, *Galatians*, p. 217, and Barclay, *Obeying*, p. 163, respectively.

115. Barclay, *Obeying*, pp. 164-65. Cf., too, Furnish, *Ethic*, p. 239.

116. Cf. Barclay, *Obeying*, p. 165.

117. See, e.g., Betz, *Galatians*, p. 309; Barclay, *Obeying*, p. 166; Bruce, *Galatians*, p. 265; *et al.*

highlight is both the fact that, and the way in which, Paul uses 6.3-10, beyond the constraints of chiastic patterning, as comment on, and rein-forcement of, his message to the Galatians—warning against the misuse of freedom, balanced by the appeal to the Galatians to live the Spirit-led life. Even such a brief survey surely illustrates that these maxims are not merely a random collection of *sententiae*. Barclay would be the first to admit that the twin themes that he identifies of corporate responsibility and individual accountability do not tell the whole story of the section, although they are undoubtedly present. Ebeling views this section in a way not too dissimilar to Barclay, though he does not identify such a tight organization of the themes. Of it (actually 5.25–6.10) he writes,

> What is crucial is the relationship of one person to another. It is character-istic that the passage repeatedly considers the relationship of individuals to themselves and to others from the perspective of their mutual involve-ment. Those who would truly see and understand others must first truly see and understand themselves.[118]

4.5.3. *The Chiasmus in the Wider Context of Galatians*

The chiastic analysis, as well as suggesting that Paul's focus of thought lies primarily in warning, has also had the effect of putting more atten-tion on 6.1, and the dangers inherent in the correcting of a transgressing brother. It must be asked whether this has any place in a wider under-standing of the Galatian situation.

In this connection the repeated use of the vocative ἀδελφοί through-out the letter is interesting (cf. Gal. 1.11; 3.15; 4.12, 28, 31; 5.11, 13; 6.1, 18—and nominative in 1.2), both because of *why* and *where* it occurs. It may be used to underline the recipients' relationship to Paul, and to remind them of their own interdependence.[119] It would certainly appear to be more than just a casual term of affection in this letter, and may actually be an emphasizing device, used primarily to highlight the content of the statement to which it is attached (except, perhaps, in 6.18, where it emphasizes not so much the content of the statement as the relationship between Paul and the Galatians).[120]

Space precludes any but the briefest acknowledgment of the long and

---

118. Ebeling, *Truth*, pp. 259-60.

119. Cf. Guthrie, *Galatians*, p. 65.

120. *Pace* Longenecker, *Galatians*, p. 239, who sees it in terms of an epistolary convention to identify the beginning of a new section. Longenecker's thesis is weak in 4.28, 31, 5.11, 6.18—and, if the hypothesis of this chapter is accepted, in 6.1.

wide-ranging debate about the details of the situation that Paul is confronting in Galatians. These include Schmithals's thesis that the problem was the presence of Jewish-Christian Gnostics who were libertine in moral conduct, but nonetheless advocated circumcision;[121] Bruce prefers the simple solution that the agitators were from a Jewish background, teaching that the 'full' gospel required circumcision;[122] Betz suggests that the Galatians faced a number of specific moral problems and tried to use the Jewish Torah as a means of dealing with them.[123] Barclay's conclusion (supported in this chapter) is that the problem is a compounding of moral confusion with a loss of confidence in Paul's prescription for ethics.[124]

It may be possible, however, to go beyond this general conclusion to see if there is anything evidenced in 5.13–6.10 that is adding to already existing community dissension. If we set up the hypothesis that the dissension is being exacerbated by Christians 'lording' it over one another as 'superiors', perhaps arrogantly correcting others, then it should be possible to test this hypothesis using Barclay's proposed methodology for mirror-reading polemic.[125] Thus, in 5.13–6.2 there are a considerable number of prohibitions and commands that specifically reflect *community* rather than *individual* life (5.13, 14, 15, 26; 6.1, 2). The tone is urgent and emphatic (5.13, 15, 21b, 26; 6.1), and the frequency and clarity of warning has been adequately demonstrated above. The theme of the unhelpful correction of a transgressing brother is not a familiar motif in the other Pauline letters.[126] Finally, a consistent picture of a problem emerges that is certainly historically plausible. Arrogantly correcting others is the very opposite of what Paul counsels in 5.13b, and is the total denial of the love-command of 5.14b. Such a wrong spirit in dealing with a transgressing brother would fit in well with the metaphors

121. W. Schmithals, 'The Heretics in Galatia', in *Paul and the Gnostics* (trans. J.E. Steely; Nashville, 1972), pp. 13-64.

122. Bruce, *Galatians*, pp. 31-32.

123. Betz, *Galatians*, pp. 8-9.

124. Barclay, *Obeying*, p. 218.

125. J.M.G. Barclay, 'Mirror-Reading a Polemical Letter: Galatians as a Test Case', *JSNT* 31 (1987), pp. 73-93, 84-85. See 5.5 below for a fuller discussion and application of Barclay's criteria and methodology.

126. Although Kuck, 'Burden', p. 297, makes a good case for some basic similarities between Gal. 6.1-5 (his rhetorical unit) and Rom. 14.1-12 and 1 Cor. 3.5–4.5, with community tensions in each passage related to individuals striving for status with resulting judgmental attitudes.

of biting and devouring in 5.15, and could certainly lead to the community dissensions emphasized in the middle of the catalogue of vices (5.19-21). Such actions also represent a denial of the whole catalogue of the fruit of the Spirit (5.22-23a). When Paul returns to the specifics of the Galatian situation in 5.26, it is again in terms that fit well with the scenario of the correction of a transgressing brother, and when he finally reveals the matter that is so troubling him in 6.1, he follows it once more by the warning and appeal of 6.2, the latter clearly recalling 5.13b, 14.

Moreover, the Christian exercising correction is open to the very danger of 6.3, and needs to be reminded to test his own work (6.4), for which he is accountable before God (6.5). Such a wrong approach to correction, too, could lead to a breakdown of relationships between those who teach and those taught, giving rise to the appeal of 6.6. In the same way, the warning of 6.7, 8 that all reap what they sow is particularly apposite, as is the final appeal to mutual responsibility (6.9, 10) in doing good to all people, and especially to those of the household of faith.

This accords well, too, with the main theme of the letter that appropriate patterns of behaviour for new Christians, freed from the law, are not to be found in that law and its works.[127] That the background includes misuse or misapplication of the Jewish law is widely accepted and is further hinted at in the use of 'law' in the chiasmus at 5.14, 18, 23b and in the ironical 6.2. Other hints of loveless strife occur earlier in the letter in (possibly) 2.20 and 5.6.

Such a mirror-reading exercise has been accomplished independently of the chiastic pattern, but its effect is to lend weight to the suggestion thrown up by the chiasmus that the note of warning related to correction in the wrong spirit lies at the centre of Paul's focus of interest in the whole of 5.13–6.10. It is, in fact, the conclusion of his earlier arguments. Debates about ethical issues or the role of the Torah, or Jewish circumcision or whatever are conducted by *people*, and those people need to be able to conduct the debate in a right spirit. There is little point in winning the argument but destroying the community in the process.

---

127. Cf. Betz, *Galatians*, p. 273; Ebeling, *Truth*, p. 251; Barclay, *Obeying*, p. 73.

Chapter 5

COLOSSIANS 2.6-19: A KEY PASSAGE IN A COMPLEX LETTER

5.1. *Introduction*

There is no disagreement about the importance of this passage in Colossians. Syntactically complex, exegetically puzzling, it lies at the heart of the letter. Its analysis as a chiasmus enriches our understanding of the movement of Paul's thought as the chiastic centre suggests that Paul's focus lies, not so much in the combatting of a particular syncretistic heretical system, but in the less specific, although equally important, encouragement of believers to walk aright in the light of Christ's death and resurrection, and their identification with those actions. In recent years there has been considerable debate on both the nature and the reality of the 'heresy' at Colossae.[1]

Detailed examination of the question of authorship lies beyond the scope of this study, although it cannot be entirely divorced from it. There is a divergence of opinion among those who deny Pauline authorship about whether the arguments that clinch their case rest on stylistic features (the number of *hapax legomenoi*, the sentence structure, the paucity of 'Pauline' connective particles, etc.) or on theological differences (its Christology, eschatology and ecclesiology, and the absence of favourite Pauline themes, such as righteousness, law, salvation), although it may be reasonably countered that their strongest case lies in an amalgam of the two.

Recently there have been some impressive defences of Pauline authorship that make it possible to suggest that many (but, admittedly, not all) of the stylistic and theological differences can be accounted for by the hypothesis that Paul used, and was subsequently influenced by,

---

1. Sparked again by Morna Hooker's aptly titled paper 'Were there False Teachers in Colossae?', reproduced in M.D. Hooker, *From Adam to Christ: Essays on Paul* (Cambridge, 1990), pp. 121-36.

traditional material (as, for example, in Col. 1.15-20). Other differences may be explained by the echoing of the language of the 'opposition',[2] the development of Paul's own thinking during his writing career, the fitting of message to situation, and so on.[3]

5.2. *The Chiastic Outline of Colossians 2.6-19*

This section highlights such verbal and exegetical parallels as are needed to produce a hypothetical pattern that can then be tested by more detailed study. Many structural and exegetical questions are inter-related, and, as always, an awareness of the danger of circular reasoning is necessary.[4]

The hypothetical pattern consists of 12 elements, centred on 2.12, 13, giving:

F 2.12 **συνταφέντες** αὐτῷ ἐν τῷ βαπτισμῷ,
   ἐν ᾧ καὶ **συνηγέρθητε** διὰ τῆς πίστεως τῆς ἐνεργείας τοῦ
   θεοῦ τοῦ ἐγείραντος αὐτὸν ἐκ νεκρῶν·

F′ 2.13 καὶ ὑμᾶς **νεκροὺς ὄντας** [ἐν] τοῖς παραπτώμασιν καὶ
   τῇ ἀκροβυστίᾳ τῆς σαρκὸς ὑμῶν,
   συνεζωοποίησεν ὑμᾶς σὺν αὐτῷ, χαρισάμενος ἡμῖν
   πάντα τὰ παραπτώματα.

The variant ἡμᾶς for the second ὑμᾶς in 2.13 (and its omission in some MSS) will be discussed below, but with either reading there is a shift of both subject and object in 2.13. From 2.6 to 2.12 the subject of the verb has been 'you' plural. With συνεζωοποίησεν it becomes third person singular. Likewise, ὑμῖν might have been expected[5] and not ἡμῖν after χαρισάμενος. The use of 'us' is not repeated after 2.14. The concepts

2.   Although such 'mirror-reading' is fraught with difficulties—see 5.5 below.

3.   Among recent defences of Pauline authorship are O'Brien, *Colossians*, pp. xli-xlix; R.P. Martin, *Colossians: The Church's Lord and the Christian's Liberty* (Exeter, 1972), pp. 160-64; Bruce, *Colossians*, pp. 28-33; Wright, *Colossians*, pp. 31-34. Recent writers to argue against Pauline authorship include E. Schweizer, *The Letter to the Colossians* (trans. A. Chester; London, 1982), pp. 15-24; E. Lohse, *Colossians and Philemon* (trans. W.R. Poehlmann and R.J. Karris; Philadelphia, 1971), pp. 84-91, 177-83 (a careful and thorough study); Meeks, *Urban Christians*, pp. 125ff.

4.   See 1.4.4 above.

5.   This is actually present in a few later texts (א[2] K* L P), but is not well attested.

of being buried and raised in F may be deliberately balanced with the ideas of being dead and made to live again in F'.

Moving outwards from the centre, 2.11 and 2.14 are set side by side:

E   2.11 Ἐν ᾧ καὶ περιετμήθητε περιτομῇ ἀχειροποιήτῳ
ἐν τῇ ἀπεκδύσει τοῦ σώματος τῆς σαρκός, ἐν τῇ περιτομῇ
τοῦ Χριστοῦ,

E'   2.14 ἐξαλείψας τὸ καθ' ἡμῶν **χειρόγραφον** τοῖς δόγμασιν ὃ
ἦν ὑπεναντίον ἡμῖν, καὶ αὐτὸ ἦρκεν ἐκ τοῦ μέσου
προσηλώσας αὐτὸ τῷ σταυρῷ.

Leaving the complex exegetical issues to be considered later, note is taken of the fact that 2.11 is concerned with circumcision, the supreme sign for Jews of the covenant that laid upon the bearer of the mark the obligation to keep the law. Here, however, a kind of circumcision described as ἀχειροποίητος is in view. In 2.14 the root χειρ- occurs again, in χειρόγραφον, a handwritten document, commonly suggested to be a document of human guilt, an acknowledgment of breach of the contract to keep the law. There may also be parallelism intended between ἐν τῇ ἀπεκδύσει τοῦ σώματος τῆς σαρκός in E and the implicit reference to Christ's death in E'.

As so often in these patterns, there are other verbal parallels that occur outside the chiastic scheme. Thus ἀπεκδύω occurs in 2.15, and δογματίζω in 2.20—reminders again that chiasmus provides the skeletal framework of a passage, rather than a complete description of all its exegetical nuances and links.

There are clear verbal parallels in the next pair of elements.

D   2.10b ὅς ἐστιν ἡ κεφαλὴ πάσης **ἀρχῆς καὶ ἐξουσίας,**

D'   2.15 ἀπεκδυσάμενος **τὰς ἀρχὰς καὶ τὰς ἐξουσίας**
ἐδειγμάτισεν ἐν παρρησίᾳ, θριαμβεύσας αὐτοὺς ἐν αὐτῷ.

At first sight, the difference of thought may be striking, but the possibility will be discussed that there is conscious linkage in Paul's mind.

There are exegetical complexities in C and C':

C   2.9 ὅτι ἐν αὐτῷ κατοικεῖ πᾶν τὸ πλήρωμα τῆς θεότητος
σωματικῶς, 2.10a καὶ ἐστὲ ἐν αὐτῷ πεπληρωμένοι,

C'   2.16 Μὴ οὖν τις ὑμᾶς κρινέτω ἐν βρώσει καὶ ἐν πόσει ἢ ἐν
μέρει ἑορτῆς ἢ νεομηνίας ἢ σαββάτων· 2.17 ἅ ἐστιν σκιὰ τῶν
μελλόντων, τὸ δὲ **σῶμα** τοῦ Χριστοῦ.

The phrases τῆς θεότητος **σωματικῶς** in C and τὸ δὲ **σῶμα** τοῦ Χριστοῦ in C′ should be noted. C makes clear that the Colossians are to come to fullness of life in Christ. The suggestion will be made that questions of food and drink, relegated to the positions of shadows in C′, have no part in that fullness of life.

In B and B′ two injunctions are connected with the dangers of false doctrine. The 'philosophy and empty deceit' of B is *not according to Christ*. In B′ anyone who would disqualify the Colossian Christians, insisting on strange doctrines, is *not holding fast to the Head*.

B   2.8 Βλέπετε μή τις ὑμᾶς ἔσται ὁ συλαγωγῶν διὰ τῆς
     φιλοσοφίας καὶ κενῆς ἀπάτης κατὰ τὴν παράδοσιν τῶν
     ἀνθρώπων, κατὰ τὰ στοιχεῖα τοῦ κόσμου **καὶ οὐ κατὰ
     Χριστόν**·

B′   2.18 μηδεὶς ὑμᾶς καταβραβευέτω θέλων ἐν ταπεινοφροσύνῃ
     καὶ θρησκείᾳ τῶν ἀγγέλων, ἃ ἑόρακεν ἐμβατεύων, εἰκῇ
     φυσιούμενος ὑπὸ τοῦ νοὸς τῆς σαρκὸς αὐτοῦ, 2.19 **καὶ οὐ
     κρατῶν τὴν κεφαλήν**,

There are other verbal parallels here that do not fit within the chiastic framework—notably στοιχεῖα in B with the same term in 2.20, and κεφαλή in B′ with 2.10.

In A and A′ two different metaphors of Christian growth are present. These elements are:

A   2.7 ἐρριζωμένοι καὶ ἐποικοδομούμενοι ἐν αὐτῷ καὶ
     βεβαιούμενοι τῇ πίστει καθὼς ἐδιδάχθητε, περισσεύοντες ἐν
     εὐχαριστίᾳ.

A′   2.19b ἐξ οὗ πᾶν τὸ σῶμα διὰ τῶν ἁφῶν καὶ συνδέσμων
     ἐπιχορηγούμενον καὶ συμβιβαζόμενον αὔξει τὴν αὔξησιν
     τοῦ θεοῦ.

The chiasmus is prefaced by an introduction, associated with, but not belonging to, the chiastic pattern itself.

2.6 Ὡς οὖν παρελάβετε τὸν Χριστὸν Ἰησοῦν τὸν κύριον, ἐν
     αὐτῷ περιπατεῖτε,

The chiasmus may, therefore, be represented as follows:[6]

6. For convenience, a copy of this chiasmus can be found in the Appendix.

Introduction
    2.6 Ὡς οὖν παρελάβετε τὸν Χριστὸν Ἰησοῦν τὸν κύριον, ἐν αὐτῷ περιπατεῖτε,

A   2.7 ἐρριζωμένοι καὶ ἐποικοδομούμενοι ἐν αὐτῷ καὶ βεβαιούμενοι τῇ πίστει καθὼς ἐδιδάχθητε, περισσεύοντες ἐν εὐχαριστίᾳ.

B   2.8 Βλέπετε μή τις ὑμᾶς ἔσται ὁ συλαγωγῶν διὰ τῆς φιλοσοφίας καὶ κενῆς ἀπάτης κατὰ τὴν παράδοσιν τῶν ἀνθρώπων, κατὰ τὰ στοιχεῖα τοῦ κόσμου καὶ οὐ κατὰ Χριστόν·

C   2.9 ὅτι ἐν αὐτῷ κατοικεῖ πᾶν τὸ πλήρωμα τῆς θεότητος σωματικῶς, 2.10a καὶ ἐστὲ ἐν αὐτῷ πεπληρωμένοι,

D   2.10b ὅς ἐστιν ἡ κεφαλὴ πάσης ἀρχῆς καὶ ἐξουσίας.

E   2.11 Ἐν ᾧ καὶ περιετμήθητε περιτομῇ ἀχειροποιήτῳ ἐν τῇ ἀπεκδύσει τοῦ σώματος τῆς σαρκός, ἐν τῇ περιτομῇ τοῦ Χριστοῦ,

F   2.12 συνταφέντες αὐτῷ ἐν τῷ βαπτισμῷ, ἐν ᾧ καὶ συνηγέρθητε διὰ τῆς πίστεως τῆς ἐνεργείας τοῦ θεοῦ τοῦ ἐγείραντος αὐτὸν ἐκ νεκρῶν·

F′   2.13 καὶ ὑμᾶς νεκροὺς ὄντας [ἐν] τοῖς παραπτώμασιν καὶ τῇ ἀκροβυστίᾳ τῆς σαρκὸς ὑμῶν, συνεζωοποίησεν ὑμᾶς σὺν αὐτῷ, χαρισάμενος ἡμῖν πάντα τὰ παραπτώματα.

E′   2.14 ἐξαλείψας τὸ καθ' ἡμῶν χειρόγραφον τοῖς δόγμασιν ὃ ἦν ὑπεναντίον ἡμῖν, καὶ αὐτὸ ἦρκεν ἐκ τοῦ μέσου προσηλώσας αὐτὸ τῷ σταυρῷ·

D′   2.15 ἀπεκδυσάμενος τὰς ἀρχὰς καὶ τὰς ἐξουσίας ἐδειγμάτισεν ἐν παρρησίᾳ, θριαμβεύσας αὐτοὺς ἐν αὐτῷ.

C′   2.16 Μὴ οὖν τις ὑμᾶς κρινέτω ἐν βρώσει καὶ ἐν πόσει ἢ ἐν μέρει ἑορτῆς ἢ νεομηνίας ἢ σαββάτων· 2.17 ἅ ἐστιν σκιὰ τῶν μελλόντων, τὸ δὲ σῶμα τοῦ Χριστοῦ.

B′   2.18 μηδεὶς ὑμᾶς καταβραβευέτω θέλων ἐν ταπεινοφροσύνῃ καὶ θρησκείᾳ τῶν ἀγγέλων, ἃ ἑόρακεν ἐμβατεύων, εἰκῇ φυσιούμενος ὑπὸ τοῦ νοὸς τῆς σαρκὸς αὐτοῦ, 2.19a καὶ οὐ κρατῶν τὴν κεφαλήν,

A′   2.19b ἐξ οὗ πᾶν τὸ σῶμα διὰ τῶν ἁφῶν καὶ συνδέσμων ἐπιχορηγούμενον καὶ συμβιβαζόμενον αὔξει τὴν αὔξησιν τοῦ θεοῦ.

5.3. *A More Detailed Exegesis of the Chiasmus*

5.3.1. *Towards the Centre*

If παραλαμβάνω describes the passing on of the kerygmatic tradition (which is certainly the majority view), then, however the remaining words in 2.6 may be construed,[7] the Colossians are said to have received 'Christ', a highly elliptical description of the content of the apostolic teaching.[8] This is now qualified by the addition of the name of Jesus and the concept of lordship. In the light of Phil. 2.11, 1 Cor. 12.3 and Rom. 10.9, there is little doubt about the confessional nature of the statement 'Jesus is Lord'. It has been argued that it is a baptismal profession in this context,[9] but it may be best to suggest that this could be an *oblique allusion* to baptism.[10]

It is possible that this expression furnishes Paul with the springboard from which to launch his subsequent thinking. Certainly, the baptismal metaphor does not become explicit until nearer the centre of the pattern, and then disappears to re-emerge in 2.20, first in the rich phrase Εἰ ἀπεθάνετε σὺν Χριστῷ, and then again in 3.1, these two now being seen as complementary, conditional statements linking respectively the negative side of baptism (dying) and its positive counterpart (rising with Christ) to a new lifestyle.

Receiving the apostolic teaching about Christ is a dynamic experience that must inevitably lead to change in the believer's life, highlighted in A (2.7) by the combining of an agricultural allusion (ἐρριζωμένοι) with a building metaphor (ἐποικοδομούμενοι).[11] The same combination of

---

7.   There are at least three possibilities: Christ, as Jesus the Lord; Christ Jesus as (the) Lord; or Christ Jesus the Lord.

8.   So, e.g., Lohse, *Colossians*, p. 93.

9.   See Martin, *Colossians: Church*, p. 72; R.P. Martin, *Colossians and Philemon* (NCB; London, 1974), pp. 77-78; Wright, Colossians, pp. 98-99, concludes that with this phrase Paul has the moment and the significance of baptism in mind. Despite the fact that it might be said to bolster my case, I do not agree with the view that παρελάβετε τὸν Χριστὸν Ἰησοῦν τὸν κύριον is a direct reference to the believer's relationship with Christ, in which he receives him as Lord in baptism—the view of K. Wegenast, *Das Verständnis der Tradition bei Paulus und in den Deuteropaulinen* (WMANT, 8; Neukirchen–Vluyn, 1962), p. 128.

10.   Of course, received tradition need not always be helpful as in 2.8 and the 'regulations' of 2.20-21, specifically described as διδασκαλίας τῶν ἀνθρώπων in 2.22.

11.   Cf. Eph. 3.17 (the only other New Testament occurrence of ῥιζόω).

metaphors is present in 1 Cor. 3. 6-11, although in a different way. In A neither of the metaphors is developed, but a third is immediately introduced with βεβαιούμενοι. Whether this is a legal metaphor[12] or simply continues the idea of the Christian's consolation,[13] it allows Paul to emphasize again the importance of teaching.

In this accumulation of metaphors, however, sight must not be lost of the significance of the growing process that begins with ἐρριζωμένοι. The 'planting' or 'rooting' (aorist) of the Christian in Christ is followed by the ongoing and continual 'building up' implied by the present participle ἐποικοδομούμενοι,[14] the whole process leading to the establishment or consolidation of the Christian. After A this range of metaphors disappears completely from the passage until it is suddenly reintroduced as a growth metaphor in A′, although this time, related to bodily growth.

There may be a tendency among some commentators to exaggerate the force of βλέπετε in B (2.8).[15] Paul used βλέπω to introduce a warning on a number of occasions in which the degree of urgency is very different, ranging from the passion of Phil. 3.2, through Gal. 5.15 and 1 Cor. 8.9 to the call to rational thinking in 1 Cor. 10.18. Usually, too, when βλέπετε is followed by μή, it is with the subjunctive.[16] Here it is with the indicative, with Moulton suggesting that we are dealing with a *cautious* assertion.[17]

Indeed, the warning in B seems to be of a very non-specific nature, especially in the light of Hooker's paper. If the passage ended at 2.8, the thesis of the Colossians falling prey to a specific 'heresy' might never have been raised. It is obvious, too, that this warning is very different in tone from that addressed to the Galatians, with its passion and note of distress. Neither is this like the way that Paul deals with the specific problems of the Corinthian situation, nor is the anger of Phil. 3.2 present.[18] Indeed, Col. 2.8 may simply continue a series of warning or

---

12. So Martin, *Colossians: Church*, p. 73; *et al.*

13. Lohse, *Colossians*, p. 94; *et al.*

14. So Abbott, *Ephesians*, p. 245; Wright, *Colossians*, pp. 99-100.

15. Lohse, *Colossians*, p. 94, typifies this: 'An urgent warning cry is intended to rouse the community to a state of watchful attention...'

16. Cf. 1 Cor. 8.9; 10.12; Gal. 5.15.

17. J.H. Moulton, *A Grammar of New Testament Greek*. I. *Prolegomena* (Edinburgh, 3rd edn, 1908), p. 192.

18. Cf. Hooker, *Adam*, p. 124.

admonitory statements that have already occurred in the letter—notably in Col. 1.23 and 2.4.

While Abbott thinks that the use of τίς in this verse indicates that Paul has some particular person in mind whom he does not wish to name,[19] Paul can equally use it with no apparent point of reference (e.g., five times in 2 Cor. 11.20), and no certainty about it can be reached, especially after the general warning against the possibility of being deluded with beguiling speech (Col. 2.4). It may therefore be that it suits many commentators' presuppositions to propose a specific individual or group in 2.8 as they begin to build their picture of the 'heresy'. The safest course is to keep an open mind.

The rare verb συλαγωγέω is defined as 'to carry off as booty or as a captive, *rob* τινά *someone*'.[20] Wright suggests that it is used because it makes a contemptuous pun with 'synagogue',[21] although the assumption should not be made that it necessarily implies an anti-Jewish polemic.[22]

While this is the only occurrence of φιλοσοφία in the New Testament, it was used very widely in the ancient world to describe many kinds of viewpoints within both the Greek and Jewish worlds.[23] It is very possible that it is employed here as an umbrella term that could even include Hellenistic Judaism, since there is contemporary evidence for it, too, being described as a 'philosophy'.[24] When he adds the phrase καὶ κενῆς ἀπάτης, he is further depicting it as an 'empty deceit', (using an epexegetic καί)[25] that can be dismissed as being κατὰ τὴν παράδοσιν τῶν ἀνθρώπων. Surprisingly and unexpectedly, however, no description of the *content* of the παράδοσις or the φιλοσοφία is given until C'.[26] Instead, Paul sets off immediately in 2.9-15 to describe

19. Abbott, *Colossians*, p. 246; cf. 2 Cor. 11.21.

20. See BAGD. Italics mine.

21. Wright, *Colossians*, p. 100.

22. However, the pun rather loses its point if it would not be understood by the readers/hearers!

23. For its breadth of use, see O. Michel, 'φιλοσοφία', *TDNT*, IX, pp. 172-88.

24. Cf. O'Brien, *Colossians*, p. 109; Wright, *Colossians*, p. 101; *et al.*

25. Bruce, *Colossians*, p. 98; G.B. Caird, *Paul's Letters from Prison* (Oxford, 1976), p. 189; *contra* O'Brien, *Colossians*, p. 109.

26. It will be argued later that what is described is not a single, coherent 'philosophy' infiltrating the Colossian situation, but is a description of errors, typical of many systems. This approach has the great advantage of rendering it completely unnecessary to 'identify' such an eclectic 'heresy' as Jewish, or a combination of

the significance of Christ and our relationship to him in baptism in a positive way. It may need to be suggested that those who read 2.9-15 as Paul's rebuttal of the teachings of a specific philosophy or human tradition are making a not inconsiderable assumption.[27] The ultimate test of such a system has to be whether it is κατὰ Χριστόν or κατὰ τὴν παράδοσιν τῶν ἀνθρώπων.

The observation that Christianity was not born into a spiritual vacuum, but was merely one among many contending 'faiths' or 'philosophies' is a cliché. The pressures on any newly baptized Christian, unsure of what new-found faith allows, or of its relationship to an old religion (especially if that was Hellenistic Judaism), must have been enormous. But Paul congratulates them on their progress so far (1.4, 8, and especially 2.5) and gives this generalized warning in 2.8, which may well arise out of pastoral concern rather than from any specific knowledge of the presence of a dangerous heresy in Colossae.[28]

The phrase κατὰ τὰ στοιχεῖα τοῦ κόσμου is much debated! By Paul's day, στοιχεῖα already had a long history and could carry more than one meaning, depending on author and context.[29] Bandstra develops three lines of interpretation:

a. τὰ στοιχεῖα τοῦ κόσμου are to be identified with elementary principles that may refer to the Mosaic law or to principles common to all humankind, and therefore are conceived more as 'teachings' or 'forces';

b. they are physical and/or astronomical elements regulating the Jewish sacred seasons or denoting pagan objects of worship;

c. they are elemental and/or astral spirits which may be identified with angelic mediators of the law, or as cosmic spirits or even demonic forces.[30]

Bandstra himself argues persuasively for the first line of interpretation, particularly in view of the relative lateness of much of the evidence for

Jewish and Hellenistic elements, or as an early form of mystery religion, or as a gnostic system and so forth.

27. See, too, Schweizer, *Colossians*, pp. 132ff.—although I do not share his conclusion that we are dealing with a Jewish Pythagoreanism.

28. Cf. Hooker, *Adam*, esp. pp. 123-25. See 5.5 below.

29. A.J. Bandstra, *The Law and the Elements of the World: An Exegetical Study in Aspects of Paul's Teaching* (Kampen, 1964), pp. 31-46.

30. Bandstra, *Law*, p. 171.

its use in its other two senses.[31] He suggests that some of the phrases in Col. 2.6-23 'seem to be chosen to cover both Jewish and pagan items'. Thus, 'philosophy' does not exclude Jewish law, in the same way as 'traditions of men' should not be limited to Jewish tradition, but may imply traditions common to humankind.[32]

O'Brien prefers the currently prevailing view, taking στοιχεῖα as 'the elemental spirits of the universe',[33] criticizing Bandstra's position because it was worked out more in relation to Galatians than Colossians, and particularly because, even in Gal. 4.3, 9, 'Paul speaks of them (στοιχεῖα) in a rather personal fashion', while in Col. 2.10, 15 again 'other personal beings or forces are referred to'.[34] The fact that Bandstra works out his position as O'Brien suggests need not necessarily invalidate his conclusion. Obviously, because of uncertainties regarding authorship, there is a danger of importing uncritically *any position* adopted in relation to use in Galatians into use in Colossians, and Bandstra's opinion as to the meaning of στοιχεῖα in Colossians should be able to stand independently of its use elsewhere. In reply to O'Brien's point that Paul speaks of the στοιχεῖα in a rather personal fashion, it may be countered that, on O'Brien's own premise of Pauline authorship, Paul can do the same with a range of other abstract concepts such as sin and law (notably in Rom. 7.7-25), love (1 Cor. 13.4-7), and peace (Col. 3.15 with βραβεύω).

Although not the most popular position today, there is an attractiveness in the view that κατὰ τὰ στοιχεῖα τοῦ κόσμου in 2.8 stands in simple apposition to the immediately preceding κατὰ τὴν παράδοσιν τῶν ἀνθρώπων. Adopting this approach leads to the suggestion that Paul is impressing on his readers that any and all 'philosophy', with its empty deceit that arises from the tradition of humans and the principles or teachings of the world, can make prey on the unwary because it is not κατὰ Χριστόν. The commonly described antithesis between κατὰ τὰ στοιχεῖα and οὐ κατὰ Χριστόν, often used to 'personalize' στοιχεῖα, is not valid in the context of the *whole* of 2.8, since grammatically it is antithetical also to κατὰ τὴν παράδοσιν τῶν ἀνθρώπων, and possibly to the whole of the verse

---

31. The earliest irrefutable evidence for its usage as 'astral spirits' may be as late as third or fourth century AD according to Bandstra, *Law*, p. 44.

32. Bandstra, *Law*, p. 70.

33. O'Brien, *Colossians*, pp. 110 and esp. 129-32.

34. O'Brien, *Colossians*, p. 131.

following συλαγωγῶν.[35] Having said this, however, it would be foolish to assert that τὰ στοιχεῖα τοῦ κόσμου can only have a single, exclusive meaning for Paul, and some caution must be exercised.

On the other hand, recognition must be given to the superficial appeal of the 'personalized-cosmological' view of the στοιχεῖα that sees them contrasted with the fullness of deity belonging to Christ who is the head of all rule and authority.[36] The major problems with this approach remain the lateness of the evidence both for the use of στοιχεῖα in the sense of 'spiritual forces',[37] and for the use of πλήρωμα in C in a technical or Gnostic sense in the mid-first century.[38] Rather than assuming that Paul is borrowing from the vocabulary of the 'heretics', πλήρωμα may be his own term, prompted (as is more of C) by its use in Col. 1.15-20. Although any detailed examination of the form or provenance of Col. 1.15-20 is beyond the scope of this chapter,[39] it may suffice to note that the Old Testament can provide adequate background for its use in Col. 1.19,[40] with πᾶν τὸ πλήρωμα being simply a circumlocution for 'God in all his fullness'.

The phrase πᾶν τὸ πλήρωμα τῆς θεότητος in C has a similar meaning to its allied phrase in 1.19.[41] Thus, there is no need for any other philosophy based on human tradition or worldly principles—the complete answer is in Christ, since the whole fulness of deity dwells in him, and, indeed, does so σωματικῶς. The position of this adverb in its clause lends it particular prominence. Some interpret it in the light of τὸ

---

35. See further T.J. Sappington, *Revelation and Redemption at Colossae* (JSNTSup, 53; Sheffield, 1991), pp. 168-69, although I disagree with his conclusion that a specific heresy linked with the ascetic-mystical piety of Jewish apocalypticism is in view. (*Revelation*, pp. 224-25.).

36. Indeed, the presence of πλήρωμα almost seems to act as a trigger for many of those who want to interpret στοιχεῖα along the lines of 'spiritual forces'.

37. A point well made and discussed by W. Carr, *Angels and Principalities* (Cambridge, 1981), pp. 72-76.

38. So P.D. Overfield, 'Pleroma: a Study in Content and Context', *NTS* 25 (1978–79), pp. 384-96, esp. 392; Carr, *Angels*, p. 78.

39. Recently discussed again by Wright, 'Poetry'; S.E. Fowl, *The Story of Christ in the Ethics of Paul: An Analysis of the Function of the Hymnic Material in the Pauline Corpus* (JSNTSup, 36; Sheffield, 1990), pp. 103-21.

40. O'Brien, *Colossians*, pp. 52-53.

41. Wright's comment on 1.19 is equally apposite here. 'The full divinity of the man Jesus is stated without any implication that there are two Gods. It is the one God, in all his fullness, who dwells in him.' (*Colossians*, pp. 75-76) Cf. Wright, *Colossians*, p. 103; so, too, Carr, *Angels*, pp. 77-78.

δὲ σῶμα τοῦ Χριστοῦ in 2.17 (i.e. C'), leading to a translation such as 'in solid reality'.[42] This may be a possibility, but care has to be taken in reading back into σωματικῶς in C the meaning of σῶμα in C'. As Paul develops his argument, he is insisting in C that God dwells in Christ *in bodily form*. His point is that Christian faith resides in a unique person, not in a pagan pantheon or in any philosophy that is only empty deception.

Element C is completed by a play on the idea of fullness that begins to spell out its implications for the Colossians: it is only through union with Christ (ἐν αὐτῷ) that they can possess this fullness, and in fact possess it already (πεπληρωμένοι is a perfect participle). There is no need to see behind this evidence of the heretical teaching.[43]

Subordinate clauses are frequent in this chiasmus, and D (2.10b) is only loosely joined to C by the relative pronoun ὅς, the antecedent of which is most likely to be Christ. More terms that have earlier occurred in Col. 1.15-20 reappear—ἀρχή, ἐξουσία (1.16) and κεφαλή (1.18)— but are used to convey a different thought. In Col. 1.15-20 the head-body (= church) metaphor is specifically in view, although this is unlikely to be the case here, as Christ is said to be the head over all rule (or 'power', cf. NIV) and authority.[44] The Colossians need submit to no other master. Yet again it is not necessary at this point to presuppose that Paul has in mind evilly-intentioned spirit or cosmic powers.[45] Carr's argument[46] is worth considering, that 'this verse is not a simple statement of fact relating to Christ's supposed conquest of demonic forces. Indeed, if these beings and their defeat were so central, it is difficult to see why the references to them are so oblique.' Carr's case, that the ἀρχαὶ καὶ ἐξουσίαι are at worst neutral, and at best the hosts of God,[47] is carefully made, and allows a consistent interpretation of ἀρχή and ἐξουσία in Col. 1.16, the present passage, and in its more

---

42. Caird, *Letters*, pp. 191-92; also Bruce, *Colossians*, p. 101; C.F.D. Moule, *The Epistles of Paul the Apostle to the Colossians and to Philemon* (Cambridge, 1968), pp. 92-94, discusses five different meanings.

43. *Pace* Dibelius-Greeven, *Kolosser*, p. 29.

44. *Pace* Dibelius-Greeven, *Kolosser*, p. 29, who suggests that the 'powers' were organized as a body against Christ.

45. *Pace* Martin, *Colossians*, p. 81; O'Brien, *Colossians*, p. 114; Bruce, *Colossians*, p. 102; *et al.*

46. Carr, *Angels*, p. 81.

47. Carr, *Angels*, pp. 47-85.

complex partner D′, where Carr's thinking will be more critically examined.

5.3.2. *Around the Centre*

Element E (2.11) is another subordinate clause, which suddenly introduces the concept of circumcision. At one extreme Lohse accounts for it as being part of mystery initiation rites,[48] but, on the other hand, Wright is sure that the prominence given to it is a demonstration of the fact that the 'heresy' has its source in Judaism.[49] However, it is significant that this passage contains no *condemnation* of circumcision such as is found in Galatians or Philippians, but a *reinterpretation* of it in a figurative fashion. It is argued in this study that Paul is urging the Colossians to look out for *any* false teaching that might upset their faith. Some of his other epistles bear ample testimony to the problems caused by the pressures put on new Christians by Judaizers. Therefore, while he does not have a specific system in mind, it is not surprising that Jewish categories will be close to the surface of his thinking.[50]

It seems clear that, whatever is meant by 'circumcision made without hands', it is a work of God. A great deal of discussion revolves around the second half of 2.11 (ἐν τῇ ἀπεκδύσει...τοῦ Χριστοῦ). At the risk of doing injustice to the various views, they may be condensed into two main approaches, with the appearance of a more recent, but rather idiosyncratic, third way. The first sees the introduction of a baptismal metaphor in which the stripping off of the body of flesh becomes a spiritual 'Christian' equivalent of Jewish circumcision, but now accomplished in baptism. The genitive in the phrase ἐν τῇ περιτομῇ τοῦ Χριστοῦ becomes subjective, and is interpreted as 'the circumcision which Christ gave', that is baptism.[51] The second approach sees a

---

48. Lohse, *Colossians*, p. 102—unrestrained mirror-reading? See 5.5 below.

49. Wright, *Colossians*, p. 204.

50. This is true in B, too, if Wright's suggestion about the pun on συλαγωγέω is correct. There is a constant danger of over-subtle interpretation of an author's own vocabulary.

51. With some variations, the view of Lohse, *Colossians*, pp. 101-103; Caird, *Letters*, pp. 192-94; J.L. Houlden, *Paul's Letters from Prison* (Harmondsworth, 1970), pp. 188-89; Bruce, *Colossians*, pp. 103-104; Meeks, *Urban Christians*, pp. 88, 155, sees the language as having its roots in aspects of the Adam legends that spoke of the image of God (Gen. 1.26) as a 'garment of light', lost when the first human sinned, to be replaced by 'garments of skin' (Gen. 3.21), or the human body, with baptism suggesting a restoration of the paradisaic motifs—see, too, W. Meeks,

figurative, but vivid, allusion to the death of Christ, and the believer's sharing in it, and is the one preferred in this study. In this the genitive in the phrase ἐν τῇ περιτομῇ τοῦ Χριστοῦ is objective, and Christ's circumcision is seen, not as 'the stripping off of a small portion of flesh, but the violent removal of the whole body in death'.[52] This is highly unusual and colourful language, and makes the death of Christ seem particularly gruesome.[53] In this interpretation, περιετμήθητε becomes a figurative way of saying 'you died', leading, in fact, to a similar kind of development of thought as in Rom. 6.3-8, the language of circumcision (i.e. you were circumcised in his circumcision) taking the place of the perhaps more familiar idea of sharing in his crucifixion (cf. Rom. 6.6; Gal. 2.19). This interpretation may be reinforced in E'.

The third approach is Wright's, who recognizes the possible allusion to baptism, and points to Caird's arguments for not allowing the metaphor to refer to the death of Christ.[54] Wright suggests that the context requires Paul to say something about what has happened to the Colossians in their becoming Christians. He points out that 'body' can refer to a group of people, and that 'body of flesh' can therefore mean 'family solidarity' (cf. Rom. 11.14). The metaphor thus becomes one of transfer from the old solidarity to the new.[55] Despite his claim that this fits in well with the rest of the section, it seems to force the metaphor and to introduce yet another meaning of 'body', another meaning of 'flesh' (and a very unusual one), and to require that the whole element is seen as being, basically, a baptismal allusion.

All three lines of interpretation have problems associated with them, and the choice among them is finely balanced. Although it is not in any way conclusive, by taking E as an allusion to Christ's death and the believer's identification with it, the order of the apostolic preaching of 1 Cor. 15.3, 4 is preserved: Christ died for our sins, was buried and raised,[56] naturally and directly leading into the idea of burial in the next element.

'The Image of the Androgyne: Some Uses of a Symbol in Earliest Christianity', *HR* 13 (1974), pp. 165-208.

52. O'Brien, *Colossians*, p. 117.

53. Cf. G.R. Beasley-Murray, *Baptism in the New Testament* (London, 1962), p. 152.

54. Caird, *Letters*, pp. 193-94, whose main objection is that stripping off the physical body at death contradicts Paul's theology of resurrection. The 'problem', of course, disappears if the author of Colossians is other than Paul.

55. Wright, *Colossians*, pp. 105-106.

56. So O'Brien, *Colossians*, p. 117.

With F (2.12) the centre of the chiasmus is reached, and the oblique allusion to the baptismal confession 'Jesus is Lord' hinted at in the introductory clause (2.6) becomes explicit. The appearance of the baptismal metaphor at this point is not surprising, since Paul wishes to clarify the believer's relationship to the death of Christ and, equally importantly for his purpose in demonstrating the power of God, the believer's relationship to the resurrection of Christ. The exegesis of F needs little comment, other than to underline the idea of the divine. In this passage faith is not simply faith in Jesus Christ (as in Rom. 3.22 etc.) Likewise, in Rom. 6.4 Christ is raised by the *glory* of the Father. Here it is faith in the *power* (so NIV) of God to raise him from the dead that is in the forefront (cf. Eph. 1.19-20?)

The passage began with the call to live in such a way as accords with the apostolic teaching (παρελάβετε τὸν Χριστὸν Ἰησοῦν τὸν κύριον), and has warned against falling prey to any philosophy. Through the first half of the chiasmus the contrast is heightened between the empty deceit of philosophy that rests on mere human tradition or worldly principles, and the way of Christ who is himself the embodiment of the whole fullness of deity. His death, burial and resurrection, and the believer's identification with the whole process in baptism, illustrate the ἐνέργεια of God.

F′ (2.13) marks a change in standpoint[57] indicated by the change of subject from 'you' to 'he',[58] but is much more closely linked with F than some analyses indicate.[59] F′ begins to describe what the resurrection life *means* for the believer. There is a formal parallelism in the way that the thoughts of being buried and raised with Christ in F are set alongside the ideas of being dead and made to live with him in F′. Baptism is the burial of one long since dead because of trespasses and uncircumcision of flesh. While literally true if addressed to Gentiles, it may be that 'uncircumcision' must be understood in a symbolic way, representing alienation from God. 'You' are made alive together with Christ, just as surely as he is raised from the dead, all 'our' trespasses having been forgiven.[60] It may be that χαρίζομαι is used here because

---

57. Dibelius-Greeven, *Kolosser*, p. 31; Lohse, *Colossians*, p. 106; O'Brien, *Colossians*, p. 121.

58. 'He' is taken to refer to 'God', as this seems demanded by the sense.

59. E.g., Bruce, *Colossians*, p. 106, who starts a new section here.

60. There is a var. lec. that would read ἡμᾶς (𝔓⁴⁶ B 33 88 etc.) for ὑμᾶς (ℵ* A C K etc.) following συνεζωοποίησεν—probably caused by the following

it is an appropriate verb to use in the context of the cancellation of a debt.[61] It is only in F′ and E′ that 'you' gives way to 'we', an example of a 'shift and reversion' at the centre of a chiasmus.[62] In respect of the need for forgiveness, Paul identifies himself with his readers.

The link between sin and death hardly needs elaboration, but the concept of having been made alive needs further amplification, particularly in regard to what has happened to sin. In a simple way Paul says that trespasses have been forgiven, but now, in E′ (2.14), he must look to the question of how it has been brought about. At the heart of this syntactically complex element is the phrase τὸ καθ' ἡμῶν χειρόγραφον. This could have its background in Judaism, where the relationship between humankind and God can be described as that between debtor and creditor.[63] The χειρόγραφον, the handwritten or signed certificate of indebtedness,[64] implies a situation brought by humans upon themselves. In this respect it stands in contrast to the circumcision described as ἀχειροποίητος in E. The divine initiative in E is contrasted with humanity's failings in E′. The position of humankind vis-à-vis the χειρόγραφον is clear: it is καθ' ἡμῶν, a position further reinforced by the description ὃ ἦν ὑπεναντίον ἡμῖν.

The occurrence of τοῖς δόγμασιν is problematical as it can be construed either with χειρόγραφον ('a certificate of indebtedness because of the regulations') or with the following relative clause ('which stands against us because of the regulations'). The overall meaning, however, is clear. There stands against Paul and his readers a cheirograph, which is linked to a failure to obey the δόγματα. It is possible that this refers to the Jewish commandments, or ordinances, since this term is sometimes used of them in Hellenistic Judaism,[65] although it could have wider reference to *any* laws. The link with B is further strengthened by the fact that, in Jewish eyes, the supreme symbol of the covenant enshrining the δόγματα was circumcision. In E the old circumcision is found wanting, and is replaced by one made

ἡμῖν—cf. Metzger, *Text*, p. 623. It is omitted altogether in א² D G P etc., possibly thought to be superfluous—cf. O'Brien, *Colossians*, p. 123.

61. Cf. Lk. 7.42-43; O'Brien, *Colossians*, pp. 123-24.

62. See 1.4.2 a above.

63. Lohse, Colossians, p. 108.

64. O'Brien, *Colossians*, p. 125.

65. Lohse, *Colossians*, p. 110; *et al.*—though not elsewhere by Paul—but cf. Eph. 2.15.

without hands. In E′ the certificate of indebtedness, the legacy of the old system, is cancelled too.[66]

The χειρόγραφον is dealt with decisively by the death of Jesus: it is blotted out (ἐξαλείψας), set aside (ἦρκεν ἐκ τοῦ μέσου) and nailed (προσηλώσας) to the cross—a piling up of incompatible metaphors! Although rather fanciful, it is suggested that this last feature could be a reference to the historical nailing of humankind's accusation against Jesus to his cross. Now *God* nails the χειρόγραφον against *humanity* there![67]

The formal symmetry of the chiasmus is at its weakest in this pair of elements. It has been argued that one such pair does not necessarily mean that an otherwise well-founded example of chiasmus must be rejected,[68] but care has to be taken not to make the concept of chiasmus so elastic that it becomes able to accommodate *any* contrary evidence, and, consequently, to make it degenerate into a theory inherently incapable of being falsifiable.[69] Equally, however, the problem must not be exaggerated, and if, as has been argued above, E contains a vivid metaphor for the death of Christ in the idea of the stripping off the body of flesh and an allusion to the believer's identification with that event, then E′ may well help to clarify how the believer benefits by it in the metaphor of the cancelling and nailing of the bond to the cross. It may be observed, too, that the metaphor of E would speak more to those of a Jewish background, while those of E′, and especially the concept of the cheirograph, would be more widely understood.[70]

5.3.3. *Outwards from the Centre*

D′ (2.15) is no less complex exegetically than E′. Among the many inter-related issues to be considered are the relationship of τὰς ἀρχὰς καὶ τὰς ἐξουσίας in D′ with ἀρχῆς καὶ ἐξουσίας in D, the subject and

---

66. There are other interpretations of χειρόγραφον, notably that of Bandstra, *Law*, pp. 158-63, who sees it in terms of a book containing people's evil deeds. Bandstra's position is critically discussed and rejected in O'Brien, *Colossians*, pp. 124-25.

67. Wright, *Colossians*, p. 113; O'Brien, *Colossians*, p. 126.

68. See 1.4.3 f above.

69. It was suggested in 1.4.3 f above that the presence of an asymmetrical pair in an otherwise clear example may serve to draw attention to that pair.

70. E. Lohse, 'χειρόγραφον', *TDNT*, IX, p. 435 shows that χειρόγραφον was known as a note of indebtedness in the Graeco-Roman world; cf. also Carr, *Angels*, pp. 53-58, 61.

meaning of ἀπεκδυσάμενος in D′ and its relationship with
ἀπεκδύσει in E, the implications of θριαμβεύσας and the question of
whether ἐν αὐτῷ in D′ refers to Christ or the cross.[71]

The best approach to this element is through the controlling metaphor
which may be either ἀπεκδυσάμενος (the majority choice) or
θριαμβεύσας.[72] It will be argued here that a more satisfactory account
of ἀπεκδυσάμενος can be given if θριαμβεύσας is taken as that
metaphor.

The background of θριαμβεύω is that of the Roman triumph.[73] It
must be stressed that it does *not* mean to 'win a victory', but is related
to the subsequent acclamation of the victor,[74] making very doubtful the
rendering 'to triumph over' something, because of the implicit concept
of a battle fought and won over the object of the verb.[75] Thus, 'to
triumph over powers' carries with it the almost inevitable thought that
the powers are the defeated enemy. In New Testament times two
aspects of the one scene are possible: the *triumphator* leading his
victorious army, or driving his captives before him.[76] In D′ Christ is the

71. These questions have been recently re-explored in R. Yates, 'Colossians
2.15: Christ Triumphant', *NTS* 37 (1991), pp. 573-91.

72. The choice of Carr, *Angels*, p. 61, and Yates, 'Colossians', p. 574.
However, Yates does not justify his choice, and Carr gives as his reason an alleged,
but unclear, parallelism between 2.15 and 2.14.

73. Although, in an interesting article, Duff argues (in the context of 2 Cor. 2.14)
that it also had a wider, metaphorical usage of a god's epiphany procession. The god
was often portrayed as victorious, and the participant should be seen as 'captured,
not as a prisoner of war, but as a devotee of the deity' (P.B. Duff, 'Metaphor, Motif,
and Meaning: The Rhetorical Strategy behind the Image "Led in Triumph" in
2 Corinthians 2:14', *CBQ* 53 [1991], pp. 79-92, 87). My principal reason for not
suggesting this interpretation in the context of Colossians is that it becomes more
difficult to give an adequate account of ἀπεκδυσάμενος (see below)—although this
might be worthy of further exploration elsewhere.

74. O'Brien, *Colossians*, p. 128; Carr, *Angels*, p. 62; Yates, 'Colossians', p. 574.

75. Still supported, however, by, e.g., Wright, *Colossians*, p. 114, although he
does not think that the 'powers' are necessarily powers of evil.

76. The question mark over Pauline authorship of Colossians makes the interpretation of θριαμβεύω in the light of its other use (and its disputed meaning) in 2 Cor.
2.14 of limited value. In that context Paul may see himself and the other apostles as
part of the victorious army, rather than as prisoners, since those walking alongside
the victor's chariot with censers are not the captives, but the most honoured partici-
pants—Carr, *Angels*, pp. 62-63; *pace* O'Brien, *Colossians*, pp. 128-29; Furnish,
2 Corinthians, pp. 173ff.; *et al.* who suggest that Paul is a captive.

triumphator,[77] and in this context θριαμβεύω means 'to lead in a triumphal procession'.[78] Here the object of the verb is τὰς ἀρχὰς καὶ τὰς ἐξουσίας, apparently the same beings mentioned in 1.16, and, of course, the same group over which Christ has already been said to be head in D. Thus the rather colourless and bland statement of D has now become a vivid picture. Once this concept is recognized as central, the rest of the element falls into place. Up to this point, therefore, nothing demands that the principalities and powers need be inimical to Christ, and, indeed, if this interpretation is correct, they are part of the heavenly host.[79]

Sense can now be made of ἀπεκδυσάμενος, the middle voice of which must be given due weight. It is not the middle used as an active,[80] of which there are few examples in Paul (e.g., the use of τίθημι in 1 Cor. 12.28 and 1 Thess. 5.9—an accepted usage by Paul's day[81]). This makes the fairly common translation 'having disarmed the powers...' an impossible one.[82] Even if the translation 'having stripped the principalities and powers'[83] were accepted, it begs the questions as to what precisely was removed (their weapons, their power, their dignity?) and what the possible background could be (a battlefield where an army is disarmed, or a royal court where public officials are degraded by being stripped of their dignity?)[84]

The other use of ἀπεκδύομαι in Colossians (3.9) refers to the removal of clothes, the same general background as ἀπέκδυσις in E.[85] Carr is sure that a consistent account of the term arises from the background to the pageantry of the not unfamiliar Roman triumph, a significant part of the preparation for which was the putting-off of the

77. Yates, 'Colossians', pp. 578-80 makes the point well.

78. G. Delling, 'θριαμβεύω', *TDNT*, III, p. 160; cf., too, BAGD; *pace* O'Brien, *Colossians*, p. 128, who suggests 'to lead *as a conquered enemy* in a victory parade', but without any evidence (italics mine), and against the principle that *enemies* are driven, but the *army* is led (cf. Yates, 'Colossians', pp. 579-80).

79. But see below on ἐδειγμάτισεν.

80. *Pace* Lohse, *Colossians*, p. 111; O'Brien, *Colossians*, p. 127.

81. Cf. BDF §316.1i.

82. Carr, *Angels*, p. 59, traces this to Jerome's substitution of *exspolians* for the *exuens se* of the Vet. Lat.

83. That of, e.g., O'Brien, *Colossians*, p. 127.

84. The alternatives are briefly discussed in O'Brien, *Colossians*, p. 127.

85. The intensified form is more likely to refer to a *total* undressing, rather than a *violent* removal (cf. Carr, *Angels*, p. 60).

battle-dress of the victor and the putting-on of the *triumphator's* prescribed and recognized ceremonial dress. In this context it might be speculated that the battle-dress of Christ was his flesh, although the participle can equally well stand in an absolute sense, and would mean 'having prepared himself'.[86]

Yates concludes that ἀπεκδυσάμενος picks up the same bold metaphor of death as is implied by ἀπέκδυσις in E: the stripping off refers to Christ's body of flesh in death.[87] It is not impossible either that the baptismal language of the central elements is impinging on D'.[88] In the one term, therefore, it may be legitimate to hold in constructive tension both the metaphor of Christ's stripping himself in death, and of the believer's identification with that death in baptism.

An implicit change of subject has been imported into the sentence, replacing 'God' (the implied subject of the last verb, ἦρκεν) with 'Christ'.[89] This may be nothing more than a subconscious slip on Paul's part.

The object of ἐδειγμάτισεν is now seen to be τὰς ἀρχὰς καὶ τὰς ἐξουσίας, creating a potential problem for the view upheld here that the principalities and powers are not necessarily hostile, in that a number of the more recent commentators find in δειγματίζω the idea of exposing something in a way that implies disgrace.[90] Carr insists that the word, rare within and beyond the New Testament, is neutral, meaning only 'to publicize', and would fit naturally in the present context.[91] Abbott lends his weight by suggesting that the overtones of shame are present only in the more common compound, παραδειγματίσαι.[92]

---

86. Carr, *Angels*, p. 61; a rendering described as 'weak' in Yates, 'Colossians', p. 578.

87. Discussed at length by Yates, 'Colossians', pp. 583-90.

88. So Martin, *Colossians*, p. 81. In 3.9, 10, 12 the baptismal practice of divesting oneself and re-robing is suggested.

89. Carr, *Angels*, p. 59, thinks that the change is with ἐξαλείψας. He justifies this by the parallel structure that he postulates for 2.14 and 15—unconvincing, since making 'Christ' the subject throughout 2.14 simply serves to introduce a new set of problems.

90. Lohse, *Colossians*, p. 112; Martin, *Colossians*, p. 88; *et al.* O'Brien, *Colossians*, p. 128, stops a little short of this, saying that it means 'to show them in their true character', but still carrying overtones of shame in his treatment.

91. Carr, *Angels*, p. 63; so, too, Yates, 'Colossians', p. 580.

92. Abbott, *Ephesians*, p. 261; O'Brien makes the same point, but a little ambivalently.

Because of its rarity, the question of whether or not shame is implied is surely open-ended, and must be decided by the context, where the individual's view of 'principalities and powers' will determine its overtones. The phrase ἐν παρρησίᾳ takes, according to Carr, its usual sense 'boldly', so intensifying ἐδειγμάτισεν. Finally, ἐν αὐτῷ will refer to the cross. The very place where the cheirograph was nailed becomes the place where Christ leads his triumph.

If the principalities and powers are not evilly-intentioned, who or what are they? For Carr[93] they are 'angel figures of the heaven of God, not demonic beings or fallen angels'; for Abbott[94] they are the angels responsible for the law. It might be best to suggest, in a broad paraphrase, that they are straightforwardly 'all beings with influence', and that a more precise identification of a specific group or functionality is not necessary. In 1.16 the clear emphasis is on the supremacy of Christ over *all*,[95] just as in 2.10 it is Christ's headship that is in view, not over a *specific* group of beings, but over *all* such with influence (ἡ κεφαλὴ πάσης ἀρχῆς καὶ ἐξουσίας). Thus in 2.15 all with influence belong to Christ's triumphal armies, but are there only to participate in the public celebration of his splendour.

In summary, therefore, there is a significant correspondence between D and D'. What is more natural than he who is ἡ κεφαλὴ πάσης ἀρχῆς καὶ ἐξουσίας leading them in his triumph after dealing with the cheirograph? The use of ἀπεκδυσάμενος, which appears to have been inspired by ἀπέκδυσις in E, is more in the nature of an incidental parallelism, resuming part of the thought of E and linking D' to E', rather than being the central thought of D', which lies in the concept of the triumph.[96]

Because of the complexity of the issues involved, it is not practical to examine competing views of 2.15. However, a very condensed review

---

93. Carr, *Angels*, p. 77.

94. Abbott, *Ephesians*, p. 261.

95. πᾶς occurs seven times in 1.15-20.

96. The above discussion is obviously based on Carr's approach. Clearly, Carr is not beyond criticism, and his whole thesis has been questioned on a number of counts, and especially by his highly contentious, and quite unlikely, proposal of interpolation in Eph. 6.12. Cf. C.E. Arnold, 'The 'Exorcism' of Ephesians 6:12 in Recent Research', *JSNT* 30 (1987), pp. 71-87. I would maintain, however, that his interpretation of principalities and powers *in Colossians* is both consistent and reasonable, particularly in regard to his dealing with the widely made assumption of hostility between the powers and Christ.

of how some others have construed the various parts of the verse is possible by noting (a) O'Brien's paraphrase: 'Having stripped the principalities and powers of their authority and dignity God exposed their utter helplessness for all to see, leading them in his triumphal procession in Christ';[97] (b) Bruce's translation: 'He stripped the principalities and powers and made a public example of them, triumphing over them by it' (the cross);[98] and (c) Lohse's translation: God 'who stripped the powers and principalities and put them on public display, who triumphed over them in him'.[99]

The transition to C' (2.16, 17) is easy for those who regard the now defeated 'hostile powers' as being connected with the pointless regulations that are detailed next. Another approach, however, may be possible. In terms of the progress of the thought of the passage, the questions of food, drink and so on are not to be associated with the powers and authorities of D', but with the δόγματα of E'. Christ has dealt with the χειρόγραφον and its related δόγματα on the cross and has held his triumph, affirming his status as victor. Who is to judge (cf. Rom. 8.1, 33-34)? The Colossians are 'fulfilled' in Christ (C) and need nothing else.

The five areas of prohibition in C' are grouped into three by the use of ἐν (twice, and ἐν μέρει in the third use): food, drink and the observation of special days. There are three different ways of understanding them:

a. They accurately reflect the teachings of a specific system.
b. The language is polemical and reflects *Paul's understanding* of a specific heretical system.[100]
c. These are themes that Paul uses as representative and characteristic, not of a specific system, but of *many* philosophies.

The huge variety of suggestions[101] and the absence of any consensus as to the identification of any group definitely known to have been active

97. O'Brien, *Colossians*, p. 102.
98. Bruce, *Colossians*, pp. 107-108.
99. Lohse, *Colossians*, p. 92.
100. See further 5.5 below.
101. More than 40 are identified in J.J. Gunther, *St Paul's Opponents and their Background: A Study of Apocalyptic and Jewish Sectarian Teachings* (NovTSup, 35; Leiden, 1973), pp. 3-4, although many of them could be grouped under broader headings.

in the first century appear to lead inexorably to one of two conclusions: viz., the Colossians are being confronted by a heretical group otherwise unknown, or the warnings are directed against *potential* problems rather than a single, coherent system,[102] with the use of τίς reinforcing its generalized nature.

In the rather enigmatic 2.17 the regulations are described as σκιὰ τῶν μελλόντων. O'Brien is correct that this should be seen from the standpoint of the period when the legalistic restrictions of 2.16 were in force, and that the best translation is 'a shadow of the things that were to come'.[103] The contrast of the σκιά and the εἰκών belongs to current philosophical categories, although, in this instance, as happens elsewhere in Hellenistic literature, σῶμα can be used instead of εἰκών to express the true reality.[104] Paul is playing here with the diversity of meaning of σῶμα.[105] It or its root has already occurred in C and E, and will occur again in A'. The suggestion[106] might be made that there is a specific linkage with C where σωματικῶς is used because Paul wants to insist that the fullness of divinity resides in Christ *in bodily form* or reality. Now, in C', he is again emphasizing that the *reality* (σῶμα) is τοῦ Χριστοῦ. Best is correct when he concludes that the 'body of Christ' metaphor is not in view here,[107] although it does act as the stimulus for its introduction in 2.19. It is just possible that Paul deliberately exploits a *double entendre*.[108] Whatever the overtones, however, at the surface level, Paul affirms that the substance or reality *belongs* to Christ.[109]

From the point of view of the hypothesis of a chiastic pattern, it might be said that there is a stronger balance between the beginning of 2.16 and 2.8, with the two imperatives. This need not be so, however, since Paul restarts his list in 2.18 with another unusual verb, καταβραβεύω,[110] which, along with συλαγωγέω in 2.8, has overtones of robbery. If those who see a link between σωματικῶς in 2.9 and σῶμα

---

102. Further considered in 5.5 below.

103. O'Brien, *Colossians*, p. 140; so, too, Bruce, *Colossians*, p. 116.

104. Lohse, *Colossians*, p. 116.

105. In a vaguely similar way that he has played with πλήρωμα within C.

106. With Lohse, *Colossians*, p. 100 n. 48.

107. Cf. E. Best, *One Body in Christ* (London, 1955), pp. 121-22.

108. So Wright, *Colossians*, p. 121.

109. O'Brien, *Colossians*, pp. 140-41; Bruce, *Colossians*, pp. 116-17.

110. Defined in BAGD as 'decide against (as umpire), *rob of a prize*, condemn τινά' (italics mine). See, too, Bruce, *Colossians*, p. 117 n. 111.

in 2.16 are correct, then the balance between the two elements lies here, and Paul is seen to break his exhortations of 2.16 and 18 in order to interject his observation about shadow and reality at just the appropriate point to create that balance. There is also some symmetry between their endings: human tradition is described as being οὐ κατὰ Χριστόν in B, and those who try to disqualify them, or rob them of the prize through such teaching in B′ are οὐ κρατῶν τὴν κεφαλήν, widely agreed to be a reference to Christ.

Yet again, B′ (2.18-19a) is an element of considerable exegetical complexity. Paul urges that the Colossians do not let anyone rob them of their prize,[111] and then continues a description of false practices and those 'delighting in' (θέλων ἐν) them.[112] The first of these is described by ταπεινοφροσύνη, which is the usual New Testament word for 'humility', and which apparently can be used in both a good or pejorative sense depending on the context. In a pejorative sense it might be rendered 'self-abasement'. This is followed by the phrase θρησκείᾳ τῶν ἀγγέλων. The fact that ἐν is not repeated is commonly taken to imply that it is closely linked in the apostle's mind with ταπεινοφροσύνη. The main problem, though, lies in the understanding of the worship of angels. The two main approaches to it take the genitive either as objective ('worship directed towards angels')[113] or as subjective ('worship which angels perform').[114] This controversy *is* of considerable importance for those who are searching for a single 'philosophy' or 'heresy' that is under attack, particularly if they are keen to stress its Jewish elements, because of the relative scarcity of information about heterodox Jewish attitudes to angels and their worship. In the line taken in this study, the matter is of relatively little consequence, because it is taken as one example of the kind of belief and practice that Paul deprecates, whether from a system that encourages the worship of angels by its devotees or from a system that claims knowledge of how angels worship.[115]

111. καταβραβευέτω—so Lohse, *Colossians*, p. 117.
112. So O'Brien, *Colossians*, p. 142; Wright, *Colossians*, p. 121.
113. Perhaps the majority view, represented by, e.g., Lohse, *Colossians*, p. 118; Martin, *Colossians*, p. 93, and the view that I would support.
114. Argued for notably by F.O. Francis, 'Humility and Angelic Worship in Col. 2.18', in Francis and Meeks (eds.), *Conflict*, pp. 163-95; also Carr, *Angels*, p. 71.
115. But see 5.5 below.

The next phrase ἃ ἑόρακεν ἐμβατεύων is very obscure.[116] Francis argues that the unexpressed object of ἐμβατεύων is the heavenly realm. It may be that Francis is right, and that a suitable translation might be 'which he has seen upon entering', the antecedent of 'which' being 'the worship of angels',[117] with the possibility of its even being used in an ironical way.[118] On the other hand, 'entering' could feasibly refer to some initiation rite.[119]

The third phrase is a little simpler as it speaks of the misguided devotee being puffed up ὑπὸ τοῦ νοὸς τῆς σαρκὸς αὐτοῦ. Whether this is translated in terms of 'his unspiritual mind'[120] or 'his carnal mind',[121] the use of σάρξ should not be overlooked. Whatever any followers of a philosophy may claim for their system, it is the product of a mind set on the flesh (cf. Rom. 8.7)—it is merely 'the tradition of men' (B). The alternatives 'according to the tradition of men', or 'according to the principles of the world' on the one hand, and 'according to Christ' on the other admit no compromise. Anyone espousing a 'philosophy' cannot at the same time claim to be adhering to Christ as the head.[122] This is further reinforced by 2.21-23 where the slightly ironical *gradatio* Μὴ ἅψῃ μηδὲ γεύσῃ μηδὲ θίγῃς[123] is specifically said to be κατὰ τὰ ἐντάλματα καὶ διδασκαλίας τῶν ἀνθρώπων.

The chiasmus has come full circle, and there is little surprise when there is a reintroduction of a metaphor of growth in A' (2.19b). The immediate trigger for it appears to be the use of κεφαλή in B'. Thus, in A' it is the whole body that now grows, nourished by the head. In A the

116. Discussed in F.O. Francis, 'The Background of EMBATEYEIN (Col. 2.18) in Legal Papyri and Oracle Inscriptions', in Francis and Meeks (eds.), *Conflict*, pp. 197-207.

117. So O'Brien, *Colossians*, p. 135.

118. Cf. Wright, *Colossians*, p. 123.

119. So Bruce, *Colossians*, pp. 117-22, and discussed in detail in Francis, 'Background', pp. 197ff.

120. So O'Brien, *Colossians*, p. 135.

121. Bruce, *Colossians*, p. 117.

122. Lohse, *Colossians*, p. 121.

123. The spirit of which is neatly captured by O'Brien, *Colossians*, p. 149: 'Do not handle! Do not taste! Do not even touch!'—he suggests that they are examples of the sorts of false regulations encountered. Wright, *Colossians*, p. 126, calls it 'an upward rise in absurd scrupulosity'!

believer as an individual appears to be more prominent,[124] although the idea of their togetherness is implied in ἐποικοδομούμενοι. In A´ growth is only possible when the various members remain attached to the body. It is interesting that the verb συμβιβάζω is used again here. It has occurred earlier in Col. 2.2 where O'Brien[125] discusses whether it should be taken as 'unite, knit together', or in its other sense of 'teach, instruct'. He chooses the latter sense for 2.2 because it better fits the immediate context of 'knowledge', 'understanding' and 'wisdom'. There is little doubt that in this present passage the former sense is intended. What may be of some significance is that this word with a *double entendre* has been chosen for A´, in view of the specific reference to teaching in A. The Greek speaker hears both meanings, and does not have to choose between them.

5.4. *Colossians 2.6-19 in its Wider Context in the Letter*

5.4.1. *The Chiasmus and Colossians 2.20*

It is worth noting Col. 2.20 in a little more detail, beginning with the conditional Εἰ ἀπεθάνετε σὺν Χριστῷ (cf. Rom. 6.8). This protasis may provide some confirmation of the interpretation of circumcision in E being understood in terms of the believers' death with Christ since there is no other reference to the believers' dying with Christ in this passage. In 2.20 they die ἀπὸ τῶν στοιχείων τοῦ κόσμου.[126] Bandstra puts the relevant question: 'Does Paul elsewhere say that Christians have died to the angelic, cosmic or demonic powers?'[127] However, Paul does say that Christians have died to the law (Rom. 7.4; Gal. 2.19), that is, to a system. Taking τὰ στοιχεῖα τοῦ κόσμου as 'the principles of the world' at least provides a parallel usage.

The translation of the participial phrase ὡς ζῶντες ἐν κόσμῳ, widely rendered 'as if you still lived in the world',[128] may not convey Paul's meaning at all accurately. His point is that the Colossians actually *do* live

124. *Pace* Lohse, *Colossians*, pp. 92ff., who interprets the whole passage in terms of the 'community'.

125. O'Brien, *Colossians*, p. 93.

126. Paul's habit in the phrase 'dying to sin' or 'law' is to use the dative, rather than ἀπό, the effect of which is to increase the sense of separation.

127. Bandstra, *Law*, p. 68. This question has little force for those who deny Pauline authorship.

128. This, or similar, is assumed by Bruce, *Colossians*, p. 123; O'Brien, *Colossians*, p. 149; Wright, *Colossians*, p. 125; *et al.*

in the world; a more satisfactory translation would be 'as those living in the world'. To render this phrase as if it conveyed the sense of need to escape from the 'world' may be congenial to those who identify the στοιχεῖα τοῦ κόσμου with cosmic forces, but what Paul is actually doing is underlining the fact that those in the world do not need to conform to the δόγματα. They have 'received Christ Jesus as Lord' (2.6), their new standing being confirmed in their baptism, with all that it means (F and F'). Having died to the 'teachings of the world', they need to recognize how irrelevant they are, even though they still live in the world (2.20).[129]

There is a problem as to whether τί...δογματίζεσθε is a hypothetical question or not. With δογματίζω it seems likely that Paul picks up the language of E' and issues a warning rather than an accusation[130] because there is no other evidence that the Colossian Christians have *actually* submitted to such regulations. Paul's appeals throughout this section suggest that he fears that they may succumb to pressure, rather than that they actually have already done so.

5.4.2. *The Chiasmus as Part of the Letter as a Whole*
It is important to see if this approach to Col. 2.6-19 is in keeping with the rest of the letter. The thanksgiving and prayer are very positive (1.3-14) with no hint of any problems in relation to deviations from the gospel. Indeed, Epaphras has told Paul of their love in the Spirit (1.8). His prayer is that they might 'walk worthy' (1.10), with no suggestion that they were not doing so, or were once, but no longer. From his prayer, which ends with his description of Christ's work on their behalf (1.12-14), he moves naturally into the much studied little section on the supremacy of Christ (1.15-20). While this *may* be pre-formed material, it provides the first use of some terms that occur again later in the letter, and notably in the chiasmus.[131] The 'once—now' comparison of 1.21-23. does not suggest any problems, until the first conditional of the letter

129. Cf. Rom. 8.12; 7.6.

130. Hooker, *Adam*, pp. 123, 133; Wright, *Colossians*, p. 125, although I disagree with his translation of the participial phrase ὡς ζῶντες...

131. The function of 1.15-20 in relation to the wider letter is discussed by Fowl, *Story*, pp. 123-54, who concludes that the relationship is complex. Fowl is right insofar as he suggests (*Story*, p. 145) that 1.15-20 provides the basis from which Paul can combat pressure to add to, or to subvert, the Colossians' experience of Christ (although I disagree with his conclusion that a specific heresy is being countered).

in 1.23: ἔι γε ἐπιμένετε τῇ πίστει... The implied exhortation is that they continue as they have been doing, rather than expressing a need for repentance from error.

Paul now moves into a section dealing with his own ministry and how he sees it (1.23b–2.5), both in general terms, and in relation to the Colossians. He wants them to have the full riches of complete understanding (2.2), so that they may not be deceived by persuasive speech (πιθανολογία: 2.4)—an ideal opportunity for a hint that there was heresy among them that needed to be dealt with. Instead, Paul immediately and positively praises their good order and firmness (2.5).

The connective οὖν introduces the chiastic section, prefaced by an appeal for right living, again with no hint that anything is amiss. Metaphors of growth and consolidation (A) are followed by a warning against the empty deceit of 'philosophy' based on human traditions and worldly principles rather than on Christ (B), whose sufficiency, with the fullness of Godhead dwelling in him *bodily* (C), and headship over all with influence (D) is stressed. In highly colourful language that might mean more to Jew than Gentile, an identification is suggested between believers and the death of Christ (E), with whom believers are figuratively united in both death and resurrection by baptism (F), a practice obliquely alluded to in the introductory verse. It is explained that the figurative death and resurrection of the believers is linked with sin and its forgiveness (F'), involving the nailing of the charge-sheet against the sinner, with its details of breaches of the law, to the cross (E'), using language that might mean more to a Gentile than that used in E. The efficacy of the death of Christ is celebrated in a triumph in which Christ as *triumphator* leads his armies (D'). Looking back to C, the Colossians are urged not to let anyone sit in judgment over them in matters such as food, drink and holy days that have only an appearance of the *substance* that in actuality belongs to Christ (C'). Using often obscure language, the Colossians are again urged to let no-one involve them in religious practices that serve only to demonstrate the failure of those endorsing them to hold fast to the head (B'), from whom growth comes for the whole body (A').

At a few points in the chiasmus Paul looks back to the language of 1.15-20, although, in fact, the paucity of references is somewhat surprising.[132] 'It is possible, therefore, that Paul's purpose in citing the

---

132. Sappington's conclusion, *Revelation*, pp. 174-75. He also summarizes the allusions.

hymn was more general than is usually assumed.'[133] What is equally possible is that the hymn was used as the starting-point for a more generalized discussion of the lordship of Christ, and the believer's relationship to him, rather than the rebuttal of specific heresy.

The importance of the baptismal metaphor[134] is frequently underestimated in the analysis of the epistle as it moves towards its paraenetic section, since it is this metaphor that provides the thread that ties the development of Paul's thought together. From the possible veiled allusion in 2.6, it assumes a central role in the chiasmus, to reappear at 2.20 with the idea of dying with Christ to worldly principles. Col. 2.20-23 is focused negatively (in the sense that it again urges the Colossians *not* to become entangled with the kind of human precepts and doctrines already warned against in the chiasmus), but then, in 3.1, the same baptismal metaphor is developed in a very positive way, picking up the idea of rising with Christ (once more from the centre of the chiasmus). Two 'catalogues' follow in 3.5-9 and 3.12-14, the first being of vices which have to be 'put to death' (looking back to 2.13), and the second consisting of virtues to be 'put on' as in the re-robing after baptism. Other baptismal allusions appear to be present in 3.9, 10 and 14. Such an analysis shows the whole of 2.6–3.17 to be a carefully developed section, the prime focus of which is the key concept of the believers' identification with the death and resurrection of Christ as expressed in baptism, and the outworking of that identification in the transformed life.[135]

The section on the Christian household (3.18–4.1) continues the theme of the transformed walk, and is followed by a number of briefer injunctions (4.2-6), including the plea to be watchful or on their guard (4.2). As the letter moves into its concluding section, Tychicus is to be sent specifically to encourage their hearts (4.8, καὶ παρακαλέσῃ τὰς καρδίας ὑμῶν) with the very positive note maintained to the end (cf., too, Epaphras's prayer in 4.12).

133. Sappington, *Revelation*, p. 176.

134. Its central place is well highlighted in Meeks, *Urban Christians*, p. 127, seeing the whole letter as a 'reminder of baptism' (quoting with approval N.A. Dahl, 'Anamnesis: Mémoire et commémoration dans le christianisme primitif', *ST* 1 [1947], pp. 69-95) and finding the theme of the letter in Col. 2.6-7.

135. This is not to deny the place of the warnings, although the chiastic pattern shows that they are significant but secondary.

5.5. *The Colossian 'Heresy'*

Although it is not directly linked to the identification of the chiasmus, some attention should be given to the discussion of the alleged Colossian 'heresy'. Thus, while it is true that many of the prohibitions appear to have their provenance in Hellenistic, or some form of heterodox, Judaism, no-one has adequately demonstrated the existence of a contemporaneous system that exactly accords with the categories cited by Paul. For Wright it is a polemic against Judaism.[136] For Lightfoot it was a gnosticizing Essene Judaism.[137] It is not surprising that Jewish ideas figure large in the list of prohibitions because of Paul's experience of those who would proclaim a 'different gospel' (Gal. 1.6). The date of origin of some of these systems is a problem.[138] Other solutions go beyond Judaism altogether, and see the Colossians contending with a pagan mystery-type cult.[139] The whole matter becomes even more difficult when some resort to postulating the existence of an otherwise unknown eclectic system.[140] The fact that so many backgrounds are suggested may actually reinforce the line taken throughout this chapter that Paul simply lists, in his own terminology, some of the many prohibitions and practices that he knows to have been a danger to newer Christians.

Interpreting the Colossian situation becomes no easier with the growing awareness of the problems of listening to 'one end of a telephone conversation'.[141] Difficulties faced by those suggesting that

136. Wright, *Colossians*, pp. 24-30.

137. J.B. Lightfoot, 'The Colossian Heresy', in Francis and Meeks (eds.), *Conflict*, pp. 13-59; Abbott, *Ephesians*, pp. xlviii-l; cf. Bruce, *Colossians*, pp. 17-26, obviously still influenced by Lightfoot.

138. Meeks's observations that the conventional categories used in describing urban Judaism in Paul's day suffer from 'vagueness, anachronism, and inappropriate definition' (*Urban Christians*, p. 33) can usefully be kept in mind throughout this discussion!

139. So M. Dibelius, 'The Isis Initiation in Apuleius and Related Initiatory Rites', in Francis and Meeks (eds.), *Conflict*, pp. 61-122.

140. E.g., G. Bornkamm, 'The Heresy of Colossians', in Francis and Meeks (eds.), *Conflict*, pp. 123-46, whose system includes elements from Iranian myth and Chaldean influences, combined with a gnosticized Judaism; Martin, *Colossians: Church*, pp. 4-20, suggests a syncretism of free-thinking Judaism and speculative ideas of Greek religion.

141. Hooker, *Adam*, p. 121; developed in Barclay, 'Mirror-reading', p. 74.

Paul is describing and countering a specific heretical system include the problems of how accurately Paul is reflecting or using *their* language, or if he is using *his own* (perhaps not totally unbiased) version[142] of it (e.g., τὰ στοιχεῖα τοῦ κόσμου, θρησκείᾳ τῶν ἀγγέλων, etc.) Decisions have to be taken about unusual vocabulary, viz., whether it is used because it is part of the opponents' stock-in-trade or whether it is simply a phrase that Paul does not habitually use.[143] An added twist is provided in Colossians because, if the author is other than Paul, it cannot be said with any certainty what the Colossian author's customary language is.

Barclay has highlighted some of the pitfalls of mirror-reading:

a. undue selectivity in identifying the most relevant statements;
b. over-interpretation of language as either belonging to the opponents or being used as rebuttal where none is intended;
c. mishandling polemics by failing to identify deliberate polarization, for example, on the author's part (or, perhaps, irony);
d. latching on to particular words and phrases and 'hanging a whole thesis on those flimsy pegs'.[144]

Arguably, Lightfoot's widely influential study[145] has fallen into some, if not all, of Barclay's pitfalls. To highlight only one or two of Lightfoot's points, he begins by distinguishing two groups of 'disturbing elements' at Colossae, that is, those from Judaism (Col. 2.11, 16, 17, 21-23), whose presence 'a mere glance...suffices to detect', and 'an element of theosophic speculation' with 'a tendency to interpose certain spiritual agencies, intermediate beings, between God and man, as the instruments of communication and the objects of worship'.[146] Starting from this premise, he is almost inevitably led to his conclusion of a gnosticizing Essene-type Judaism. Thus, he implies that there is evidence of Essene

---

142. Keck's suggestion (*Letters*, p. 19) that Paul did not misunderstand or misrepresent the situations he addressed is too facile. While I would not be happy with suggestions of *deliberate* misrepresentation, I would not suggest either that it was in Paul's best interest to present the 'opponents' in the best possible light. A degree of bias would surely not be unexpected. It appears, also, that Paul's knowledge of the Colossian situation was second-hand—cf. Col. 1.7, 8.

143. These issues are well described in Barclay, 'Mirror-reading', pp. 79-82.

144. Barclay, 'Mirror-reading', pp. 79-82.

145. Lightfoot, 'Heresy', pp. 13-59.

146. Lightfoot, 'Heresy', p. 13.

scrupulosity in Paul's allusions to food and drink in 2.16, 21.[147] But what evidence is there that the Colossian 'heretics' took their inspiration from Essenism or that Paul is reflecting *Essene* concerns at all, and not some otherwise unknown group's teaching? What evidence is there that Essenism had penetrated to the Lycus valley?[148] This may well be over-interpretation on Lightfoot's part, as well as being a mishandling of polemics in what Paul may intend as an ironical dismissal in 2.21 of petty rules and regulations.

In a similar fashion, what Lightfoot translates as 'the worship of angels' is linked very tenuously with the Essenes. He himself is only able to conclude rather weakly,

> At all events we seem to be justified in connecting it (i.e. Essene angelology) with the self imposed service and worshipping of angels at Colossae: and we may well suspect that we have here a germ which was developed into the Gnostic doctrine of aeons or emanations.[149]

This is surely a prime example of latching on to a particular phrase (the context and translation of which in Colossians is notoriously complex) and hanging a doctrine thereon, the 'peg' being quite unable to support it.[150]

A more careful methodology is therefore needed for mirror-reading Colossians. For a polemical context, Barclay offers a sevenfold method-ology.[151] It may be argued that Colossians is polemical only to a very limited extent because of the lack of evidence of a specific situation in his mind, and to that extent Barclay's methodology may not be completely applicable. Certainly, the theme to which Paul returns most often and most clearly is that of the believers' walk (1.10: περιπατῆσαι ἀξίως τοῦ κυρίου), but there is a marked lack of clarity about many of

---

147. Lightfoot, 'Heresy', pp. 20-21.

148. Martin, *Colossians: Church*, p. 16.

149. Lightfoot, 'Heresy', p. 22.

150. Another supposed key-word has been πλήρωμα—cf. Martin, *Colossians: Church*, p. 5; Bruce, *Colossians*, p. 24 and many more. To those who would argue that better models have been found than Lightfoot's in the last 100 years, I would reply that (a) Lightfoot's study has been widely influential, and (b) *all such approaches* seem to start from the assumption of the presence of a heretical group, when careful reading of Colossians makes it clear that such an assumption is a con-siderable one that I believe cannot be justified.

151. Barclay, 'Mirror-reading', pp. 84-85: these criteria are type of utterance, tone, frequency, clarity, unfamiliarity, consistency, historical plausibility.

the key phrases relating to the alleged heresy. Indeed, it may well be that
the contentious issues raised by the interpretation of these problematical
phrases have, almost subconciously, caused modern interpreters, trying
to make sense of what they see as a coherent heresy, to place much
more emphasis on this aspect of the letter than Paul ever intended. While
there are themes in Colossians unfamiliar from Paul's wider theology,
doubts about Pauline authorship clouds this criterion. On the criteria of
consistency and historical plausibility, no really consistent picture
emerges of any 'opponents', and a number of reconstructions are based
on questionable evidence on grounds of historical plausibility in the first
century.

5.6. *Conclusion*

The identification of the chiasmus in Col. 2.6-19 makes two
contributions to current debate. Because the chiasmus is centred on
2.12, 13, it shows how the emphasis in 2.6-19 is actually on *the positive
nature of the Colossians' life in Christ and what that means in terms of
identification with him* rather than on a 'heresy'. That the Colossians, as
all new Christians, will come under pressure from other competing
religious or philosophical systems is beyond doubt. But whether Jewish,
Hellenistic or syncretistic in tenor, Paul's appeal is that they remember
that their sole allegiance is not to any δόγματα but to Christ, shown by
their baptism with all its richness of meaning.

Secondly, the chiastic pattern has shown how Paul develops his
thought logically and consistently, with the second half of the pattern
balancing and complementing the first. When he warns, in a general and
unthreatened way, against 'philosophy and empty deceit', he is thinking
of *any* teaching other than the gospel, and uses illustrative examples
from different backgrounds including Judaism. Although not directly
related to the chiastic pattern as such, by interpreting τὰ στοιχεῖα τοῦ
κόσμου in terms of wordly principles or teaching, and the ἀρχαί and
ἐξουσίαι as neutral rather than hostile beings, along with the general
tone of the passage, there has been no need to speculate on systems and
practices about which there is sometimes scant evidence for dates and
spheres of influence.

Warning, nevertheless, is still a very real part of Paul's reason for
writing, but it is the warning of those who must be on their guard,
rather than the rebuking of those who have already succumbed, the

letter being motivated by Paul's concern for a group of Christians, about whom he consistently holds very positive feelings.

It must be clearly stated that it is possible to accept the presence of the chiasmus without the corollary that no specific heresy is in mind. The presence of the chiasmus does not preclude the possibility of στοιχεῖα being interpreted in a personalized-cosmological sense, or of principalities and powers being inimical to Christ, and so on, but the problem remains as to why the warning here is so different in tone from Galatians.[152]

If Colossians is a polemical text of the same type as Galatians, the mirror in which it is read produces a highly indistinct image. Those who begin from the assumption that the letter must be a response from Paul, provoked by the presence of a heretical group, find that group portrayed by the categories of Colossians 2. However, without that assumption it is a reasonable conclusion that this is a positive, warm letter, written out of a genuine pastoral concern for a group of Christians that Paul does not know personally, but who will inevitably come under pressures as a legacy of their former lives. His message to them is to stand firm, to continue to walk worthily (1.10, 23; 2.4-5, 6; 3.1, etc.; 4.12) and to be on their guard (2.8, 16, 18, 20; 4.2)!

---

152. A distinction that loses its force if Colossians is not by Paul.

Chapter 6

ROMANS 5.12-21: A PASSAGE OF CONTRASTS

6.1. *Introduction*

In common with so many of the Pauline letters, the new awareness of
rhetorical/literary analysis is making an impact on the study of Romans.[1]
Within the letter few would deny that Rom. 1.16–4.25 constitutes a
closely reasoned section. However, that consensus disappears when the
precise function of Romans 5 in Paul's train of thought is sought. Some
see it as the beginning of the next major section ending at 8.39;[2] some
see it as the end of the previous section;[3] others describe the whole of

1. See, e.g., N. Elliott, *The Rhetoric of Romans: Argumentative Constraint and
Strategy and Paul's Dialogue with Judaism* (JSNTSup, 45; Sheffield, 1990);
M.R. Cosby, 'Paul's Persuasive Language in Romans 5', in Watson (ed.)
Persuasive Artistry, pp. 209-26; M.C. de Boer, *The Defeat of Death: Apocalyptic
Eschatology in 1 Corinthians 15 and Romans 5* (JSNTSup, 22; Sheffield, 1988). It
is interesting that de Boer has been aware of a 'certain syntactical pattern' (*Defeat*,
p. 157) in Rom. 5.12-21 that leads him to a chiastic-like (although he does not use
the term) analysis with a number of points of contact with that which I propose,
although I reached my conclusions about the passage before I was aware of his work—
see further 6.4.2 below. Cf., too, N.A. Dahl (assisted by P. Donahue), *Missionary
Theology in Romans* (Minneapolis, 1977), p. 79; Dunn, *Romans*, pp. lix-lx; *et al.* In
a recent work, Thompson (*Clothed*, pp. 200-207) has proposed the presence of a
chiasmus (adapted from a suggestion in Parunak, 'Techniques', p. 543) in Rom.
14.13-21, and uses it to draw out some exegetical implications. Myers, 'Inversion',
pp. 30-47, has also suggested a number of chiasms in Rom. 3–8—see 1.4.1 above.
2. So Cranfield, *Romans*, p. 254—Cranfield discusses the main options at
pp. 252-55; E. Käsemann, *Romans* (trans. G.W. Bromiley; Grand Rapids, 1980),
p. 131; A.J.M. Wedderburn, *The Reasons for Romans* (Edinburgh, 1991), p. 130.
3. W. Sanday and A.C. Headlam, *The Epistle to the Romans* (Edinburgh, 5th
edn 1902), p. xlviii; D.T. Zahn, *Der Brief des Paulus an die Römer* (Leipzig, 1910),
p. 241; F.F. Bruce, *The Epistle of Paul to the Romans* (TNTC; London, 1963),
p. 67; Dunn, *Romans*, p. 242 (although recognizing that it prepares the way for
Rom. 6–8).

ch. 5 as transitional with elements that look both back and forward;[4] others again find only 5.1-11 to be the transitional section.[5] To some extent, these divisions reflect different understandings of the apostle's flow of thought.

In Elliott's thesis that the letter constitutes a tightly formed rhetorical unity arising 'from his (Paul's) apostolic commission to "secure the obedience of faith among the Gentiles" (Rom. 1.5)',[6] Romans 5 is seen as a transitional and 'pivotal'[7] section within the letter's argumentative macro-structure. Specifically within Rom. 5.1-11, and pointing to the thrice-repeated καυχώμεθα (5.2, 3, 11), he suggests that 5.1-11 brings the extended argument of the previous four chapters to its conclusion: the Christian's only proper boast is in the gracious saving initiative of God. At this point the 'reorientation of christology in 5.12-21 becomes the apocalyptic-theocentric anchor for the extended qualification of the Christian "boast" in Romans 6–11'.[8] Elliott's view of Romans obviously differs from many earlier approaches. Without arguing for its validity, it is interesting that, yet again, both parts of Romans 5 are given a key role.

If it is deemed necessary to attach labels to the various sections, it may be best to regard 5.1-11 as having a dual function. It appears to act both as a preliminary conclusion to what precedes it,[9] opening with the briefest possible summary of what Paul has been arguing for from 1.16 (Δικαιωθέντες οὖν ἐκ πίστεως...) and yet contains new ideas that stem from the list of some of the momentous consequences of that justification.

Thus, in 5.1-11 Paul is at pains to stress the positive consequences of justification by faith. He begins with peace (5.1) and access (5.2), but there is more, as the basic statement (or exhortation—καυχώμεθα) about rejoicing in hope is expanded by the use of οὐ μόνον δέ...ἀλλὰ καί (cf. 8.23; 9.10; 2 Cor. 8.19) to include rejoicing in sufferings, with an attendant and much longer list of consequences. In a similarly expansive vein, Paul goes on to underscore the generosity of the nature of the

---

4. M. Black, *Romans* (NCB; Grand Rapids, 1973), p. 81; Dahl, *Missionary Theology*, p. 91.
5. Ziesler, *Romans*, p. 135.
6. Elliott, *Rhetoric*, p. 290.
7. De Boer, *Defeat*, p. 147, too, uses the same terminology.
8. Elliott, *Rhetoric*, p. 227.
9. Dahl, *Missionary Theology*, p. 82.

divine love in 5.6-8. God's saving act is simply 'incommensurable'.[10]

Two statements follow, parallel in form and content insofar as both start from the fact of the believers' having been given a right standing with God; both go on to deduce salvific consequences of the divine action, and both have the form of the *argumentum a minori ad maius* (5.9, 10).[11] The syntactical form of 5.10 is that of a conditional clause followed by a principle clause beginning with πολλῷ μᾶλλον. In 5.9 πολλῷ μᾶλλον is also used, although the protasis is expressed elliptically by the participle δικαιωθέντες.[12] The section ends with another use of the construction first encountered in 5.3: οὐ μόνον δέ...ἀλλὰ καί.

The matter of the proportionality in God's dealing with the believer forms the thread that runs through Romans 5. It first occurs in 5.1-11, and then, as will be shown below, helps determine the shape of the chiastic pattern of 5.12-21.[13] In fact, more often than not in 5.12-21 the proportionality might be more accurately described as a *disproportionality*. Thus, 'Paul is at pains, not to balance sin and grace, but to tip the scales decisively in favour of the latter'.[14]

The syntactical construction of 5.1-11 is important because of the way in which 5.12-21 is now developed. Even with a superficial reading, it shows how Paul 'feels his way through a complex series of points and counterpoints as he searches for a complete and thoroughly satisfying formulation on Adam and Christ'.[15] These very points and counterpoints exhibit a marked degree of symmetry in what may be a highly

---

10. Käsemann, *Romans*, p. 137.

11. Cranfield, *Romans*, p. 265; Käsemann, *Romans*, p. 137, suggests that the conclusion of 5.7 is in the same category.

12. Cranfield, *Romans*, p. 266.

13. I use the term 'proportionality' in a broad sense to cover both comparisons and contrasts ('*As/as not* proposition X, *so* proposition Y') as well as pairs of statements in which one is juxtaposed with the other in such a way as to create a proportionate *imbalance*, or a 'disproportionality'. In this chapter these statements typically, though not uniquely, take the form '*If* proposition X is true, *much more* will proposition Y be true'.

14. J.T. Kirby, 'The Syntax of Romans 5.12: A Rhetorical Approach', *NTS* 33 (1987), pp. 283-86, 284-85.

15. Swee-Hwa Quek, 'Adam and Christ according to Paul', in D.A. Hagner and M.J. Harris (eds.), *Pauline Studies: Essays Presented to Professor F.F. Bruce on his 70th Birthday* (Exeter, 1980), pp. 67-79, 70.

developed chiasmus that helps clarify Paul's flow of thought.[16]

There is, of course, a dauntingly large literature on this passage, inspired not only by the notorious problems of 5.12, but also by the background to the Adam/Christ comparisons, and the whole area of Pauline anthropology.[17] While important in their own right, these areas cannot be explored in this context. It is the intention of this chapter to show in a new way *how* Paul constructs his argument.

6.2. *A Hypothetical Chiastic Pattern for Romans 5.12-21*

The chiasmus suggested here has affinities with that in Eph. 1.3-10[18] to the extent that it is syntactically based. In this instance it stems from the symmetrical disposition of a number of conditional and comparative statements balanced around a central point. Thus, *without examining the content at this stage*, it is noted that, after a comparison drawn using ὡς...οὕτως in 5.15, a conditional sentence in the form εἰ γὰρ...πολλῷ μᾶλλον follows. The situation is reversed in 5.17, 18, where a conditional sentence, again using εἰ γὰρ...πολλῷ μᾶλλον is followed by a comparison using ὡς...οὕτως. This pattern is reinforced by the observation that there is verbal identity between the opening phrases of the two conditional clauses (εἰ γὰρ τῷ τοῦ ἑνὸς παραπτώματι). It thus seems at least possible, *on syntactical grounds alone*, to suggest a five-member chiasmus encompassing 5.15 to 5.18:

D 5.15a Ἀλλ' οὐχ ὡς τὸ παράπτωμα, οὕτως καὶ τὸ χάρισμα·

E 5.15b εἰ γὰρ τῷ τοῦ ἑνὸς παραπτώματι οἱ πολλοὶ ἀπέθανον,
πολλῷ μᾶλλον ἡ χάρις τοῦ θεοῦ καὶ ἡ δωρεὰ ἐν χάριτι τῇ
τοῦ ἑνὸς ἀνθρώπου Ἰησοῦ Χριστοῦ εἰς τοὺς πολλοὺς
ἐπερίσσευσεν.

F 5.16 καὶ οὐχ ὡς δι' ἑνὸς ἁμαρτήσαντος τὸ δώρημα·
τὸ μὲν γὰρ κρίμα ἐξ ἑνὸς εἰς κατάκριμα,
τὸ δὲ χάρισμα ἐκ πολλῶν παραπτωμάτων εἰς δικαίωμα.

---

16. *Pace* C.K. Barrett, *A Commentary on the Epistle to the Romans* (BNTC; London, 1962), p. 110, who feels that the thought of the paragraph is not clearly set out.

17. Representative bibliographies may be found in Cranfield, *Romans*, pp. 270-71 n. 1; Käsemann, *Romans*, p. 140; Dunn, *Romans*, pp. 269-70.

18. See 2.3 above.

Ε΄ 5.17 εἰ γὰρ τῷ τοῦ ἑνὸς παραπτώματι ὁ θάνατος
ἐβασίλευσεν διὰ τοῦ ἑνός, πολλῷ μᾶλλον οἱ τὴν περισσείαν
τῆς χάριτος καὶ τῆς δωρεᾶς τῆς δικαιοσύνης λαμβάνοντες ἐν
ζωῇ βασιλεύσουσιν διὰ τοῦ ἑνὸς Ἰησοῦ Χριστοῦ.

Δ΄ 5.18 Ἄρα οὖν ὡς δι' ἑνὸς παραπτώματος εἰς πάντας
ἀνθρώπους εἰς κατάκριμα, οὕτως καὶ δι' ἑνὸς δικαιώματος
εἰς πάντας ἀνθρώπους εἰς δικαίωσιν ζωῆς·

The next step, however, is to ask if this is the full extent of the chiasmus.
The unit 5.12-21 begins and ends with ὥσπερ...οὕτως constructions—
although it must not be assumed that καὶ οὕτως in 5.12 means the
same as οὕτως καί in 5.21, and it must be noted that there is a third
ὥσπερ...οὕτως construction in 5.19, raising the problem of why 5.12
has been chosen to balance 5.21, and not some other combination. This
again must be left to the detailed discussion below. Finally, the term
νόμος occurs only in 5.12 and 5.20.[19]
   This leads to the following complete pattern:

A 5.12 Διὰ τοῦτο ὥσπερ δι' ἑνὸς ἀνθρώπου ἡ ἁμαρτία εἰς τὸν
κόσμον εἰσῆλθεν καὶ διὰ τῆς ἁμαρτίας ὁ θάνατος, καὶ
οὕτως εἰς πάντας ἀνθρώπους ὁ θάνατος διῆλθεν, ἐφ' ᾧ
πάντες ἥμαρτον·

B 5.13 ἄχρι γὰρ νόμου ἁμαρτία ἦν ἐν κόσμῳ, ἁμαρτία δὲ οὐκ
ἐλλογεῖται μὴ ὄντος νόμου,

C 5.14 ἀλλὰ ἐβασίλευσεν ὁ θάνατος ἀπὸ Ἀδὰμ μέχρι
Μωϋσέως καὶ ἐπὶ τοὺς μὴ ἁμαρτήσαντας ἐπὶ τῷ ὁμοιώματι
τῆς παραβάσεως Ἀδὰμ, ὅς ἐστιν τύπος τοῦ μέλλοντος.

D 5.15a Ἀλλ' οὐχ ὡς τὸ παράπτωμα, οὕτως καὶ τὸ χάρισμα·

E 5.15b εἰ γὰρ τῷ τοῦ ἑνὸς παραπτώματι οἱ πολλοὶ ἀπέθανον,
πολλῷ μᾶλλον ἡ χάρις τοῦ θεοῦ καὶ ἡ δωρεὰ ἐν χάριτι τῇ
τοῦ ἑνὸς ἀνθρώπου Ἰησοῦ Χριστοῦ εἰς τοὺς πολλοὺς
ἐπερίσσευσεν.

F 5.16 καὶ οὐχ ὡς δι' ἑνὸς ἁμαρτήσαντος τὸ δώρημα·
τὸ μὲν γὰρ κρίμα ἐξ ἑνὸς εἰς κατάκριμα,
τὸ δὲ χάρισμα ἐκ πολλῶν παραπτωμάτων εἰς δικαίωμα.

19. Although, of course, the sceptic is right to point out that κατάκριμα occurs
only in 5.16 and 18, and to ask why these are not balanced.

E′ 5.17 εἰ γὰρ τῷ τοῦ ἑνὸς παραπτώματι ὁ θάνατος
ἐβασίλευσεν διὰ τοῦ ἑνός,
πολλῷ μᾶλλον οἱ τὴν περισσείαν τῆς χάριτος καὶ τῆς
δωρεᾶς τῆς δικαιοσύνης λαμβάνοντες ἐν ζωῇ
βασιλεύσουσιν διὰ τοῦ ἑνὸς Ἰησοῦ Χριστοῦ.

D′ 5.18 Ἄρα οὖν ὡς δι' ἑνὸς παραπτώματος εἰς πάντας
ἀνθρώπους εἰς κατάκριμα,
οὕτως καὶ δι' ἑνὸς δικαιώματος εἰς πάντας ἀνθρώπους εἰς
δικαίωσιν ζωῆς·

C′ 5.19 ὥσπερ γὰρ διὰ τῆς παρακοῆς τοῦ ἑνὸς ἀνθρώπου
ἁμαρτωλοὶ κατεστάθησαν οἱ πολλοί, οὕτως καὶ διὰ τῆς
ὑπακοῆς τοῦ ἑνὸς δίκαιοι κατασταθήσονται οἱ πολλοί.

B′ 5.20 νόμος δὲ παρεισῆλθεν ἵνα πλεονάσῃ τὸ παράπτωμα· οὗ
δὲ ἐπλεόνασεν ἡ ἁμαρτία, ὑπερεπερίσσευσεν ἡ χάρις,

A′ 5.21 ἵνα ὥσπερ ἐβασίλευσεν ἡ ἁμαρτία ἐν τῷ θανάτῳ, οὕτως
καὶ ἡ χάρις βασιλεύσῃ διὰ δικαιοσύνης εἰς ζωὴν αἰώνιον διὰ
Ἰησοῦ Χριστοῦ τοῦ κυρίου ἡμῶν.[20]

While this pattern shows some grammatical balance around its centre, and may indicate that the whole passage begins and ends in a similar way with the use of some kind of ὥσπερ constructions, this is still far short of a convincing demonstration of a chiasmus extending from 5.12-21 (including the balancing of 5.14 and 19 with apparently no significant objective parallels).

Some general observations may help to begin the process of confirming the presence of the chiasmus. In 1.6.1 above it was suggested that it strengthens a potential chiasmus when it can be shown that balancing is occurring at more than one level. Here, the disposition of the related terms ἁμαρτία and παράπτωμα in the chiasmus should not be overlooked. Of the ten occurrences of ἁμαρτία and its cognates, nine are in A, B, C, C′, B′ and A′. Of the six occurrences of παράπτωμα and its cognates, five are in D, E, F, E′ and D′. It seems clear that, for whatever reason (the use of ἁμαρτία for sin in the sense of 'missing a mark', and παράπτωμα for a fall or 'first deflection from uprightness'?),[21] there is a strong preference shown for the use of the one term at the beginning and end of the pattern, and of the other at its centre.

20. A copy of this chiastic pattern is included in the Appendix.
21. Sanday and Headlam, *Romans*, p. 140; *et al.*

Likewise, an indication that rhetorical considerations have been influential in the framing of the sequence of comparisons is the predominance of terms ending in -μα[22] towards the centre. Of the nine occurrences of nouns ending in -μα (either nominative or accusative singular), eight are in C, A and C': two in C (παράπτωμα, χάρισμα), and no less than five in A (δώρημα, κρίμα, κατάκριμα, χάρισμα and δικαίωμα), and one in C' (κατάκριμα).

Three elements, D, F and D', consist of antitheses so compressed that they contain no verbs at all.[23]

The presence of a minor chiasmus in the crosswise disposition of the terms sin-death-death-sin in 5.12 has also been quite widely noted.[24] It probably has no real significance for the exegesis of the passage, but is another, albeit small, indication of the fact that this passage was carefully crafted.

In methodological terms, the viability of the hypothetical structure is inextricably tied up with conclusions about the relationship between form and content in the section. If it is deemed to have been necessary to manipulate the content of the passage in order to mould it into the chiastic form, then the pattern will be rightly rejected as an imposed artifice. Form should enhance the impact of the content.[25]

6.3. *The Exegesis of the Hypothetical Chiasmus: From Centre to Periphery*

Since the exegesis of this section has been the subject of a great many studies, there may be little to be gained by approaching it yet again in the conventional manner. However, the special nature and functions of the centre of a chiasmus have already been highlighted.[26] It will be argued that 5.16 is a good example of the centre acting as the focal point, illustrating the way in which some chiasms can be read from the

---

22. Noted by Dunn, *Romans*, p. 271; de Boer, *Defeat*, p. 157. See, too, BDF §488.3.

23. Noted, too, by de Boer, *Defeat*, p. 157.

24. M. Dibelius, 'Vier Worte des Römerbriefs, 5,5; 5,12; 8,10; 11,30s', *SymBU* 3 (1944), pp. 3-17, 8; see, too, U. Wilckens, *Der Brief an die Römer* (EKKNT; 2 vols.; Neukirchen–Vluyn, 1978), p. 315; Cosby, 'Persuasive Language', p. 220; *et al.*

25. An alternative surface structure for the passage is discussed in 6.4.2 below.

26. See 1.6.2 a above.

centre outwards. Thus, the method followed in this selective exegesis will
be to proceed by examining the balanced pairs of elements outwards to
the edge of the chiasmus, this having the advantage of postponing discussion of A and A′ (which undoubtedly contain the unit's most difficult
exegetical judgments) until as much insight as possible has been gained
into Paul's manner of arguing in 5.12-21. Later, an account of the
sequential development of his thinking is given.[27]

6.3.1. *The Central Element, F (5.16)*

The absence of verbs throughout F highlights the compressed antithetical style[28] that is a feature of this passage, but it does not obscure Paul's
point of the contrast that exists between the effect of one man's sinning
and the free gift (δώρημα). This, it is suggested, is the dominant (but
not, of course, the sole) thought of the chiasmus that will be worked out
in the series of parallels and contrasts.[29]

If 5.12-21 were being discussed in sequential order, it would have
been noted that the opening statement of F, καὶ οὐχ ὡς δι' ἑνὸς
ἁμαρτήσαντος τὸ δώρημα, stands out because it is formulated in an
unusual way in the context of the many comparisons and contrasts of
this passage, since ὡς stands alone without the parallel form seen elsewhere.[30] It is recognized, however, that at some level there is a link
between this verse and 5.15a, insofar as the καὶ οὐχ ὡς of 5.16 looks
back to ἀλλ' οὐχ ὡς in 5.15a.

The remainder of F is an expansion of 5.16a using μὲν...δέ in a way
unique in 5.12-21, thus creating a well-formed antithesis[31] and a clear
internal parallelism. Paul does introduce a slight ambiguity by not
making clear whether the judgment ἐξ ἑνός follows one *trespass*[32]
or one *man*.[33] Not much appears to rest on the choice since the
deed belongs to the doer. It may even be possible that Paul uses the

27. See 6.4 below.
28. Sanday and Headlam, *Romans*, p. 140.
29. See further 6.4.1 below.
30. A point well made by Swee-Hwa Quek, 'Adam', p. 70, who makes a
detailed study of the structure of the comparisons in this passage. De Boer, *Defeat*,
pp. 157, 159, supplies 'so also' to 5.16a, a necessary (but unjustifiable) addition in
order to harmonize the structure of 5.15 with 5.16, 17 in his scheme. See further
6.4.2 below.
31. Cosby, *Persuasive Language*, p. 222.
32. So, e.g., Barrett, *Romans*, p. 114.
33. E.g., Cranfield, *Romans*, p. 286.

ambiguity to allow the phrase to be understood as 'the judgment following one-man-and-his-tresspass brought condemnation'.[34]

When he considers the free gift (substituting χάρισμα for δώρημα), the contrast is immediately made, as ἐξ ἑνός and its result (κατάκριμα) is set against ἐκ πολλῶν παραπτωμάτων, and its result (δικαίωμα). As κατάκριμα stands at the end of the old age, so δικαίωμα forms the goal of the new.[35] It is widely suggested that δικαίωμα is used for rhetorical purposes to provide a formal counterpart to κατάκριμα,[36] but it can still be given its full weight of meaning if we see δικαίωμα bearing to δικαίωσις the relation of an act completed to an act in process.[37] There is, however, no inherent logic in Paul's statements,[38] no *a priori* reason why κατάκριμα should stem ἐξ ἑνός, but δικαίωμα should flow ἐκ πολλῶν παραπτωμάτων. Instead, Paul highlights the disproportionality between the effects of Adam's action and the χάρισμα in what is the most startling expression of the paradox of grace in the whole passage. Thus, if from one sin came condemnation, the result of many sins might be reasonably expected to be universal condemnation. Instead, such is the shocking and surprising character of God's grace, δικαίωμα ensues! Perhaps nowhere else in the chiasmus is the overturning of expectations so graphically portrayed, as Paul returns again to the nature and role of the grace of God, a controversial doctrine that he has already shown to be at the heart of his gospel (e.g., Rom. 3.8; 4.4-5; 5.6-11) and which will continue to occupy him after this chiastic section (6.1-4; 15; etc.).

6.3.2. *E (5.15b) and E´ (5.17)*

These paired elements are strikingly close in thought, both using εἰ γάρ...πολλῷ μᾶλλον constructions, and sharing identical opening phrases. A number of commentators[39] suggest a Semitic use of οἱ πολλοί (the many), in which it is not so much 'many contrasted with all', but 'many contrasted with one' that is in view. There may be a

---

34. Cf. Dunn, *Romans*, p. 280.

35. O. Michel, *Der Brief an die Römer* (KEK; Göttingen, 14th edn, 1978), p. 190.

36. Cranfield, *Romans*, p. 287 n. 2; *et al.*

37. So Sanday and Headlam, *Romans*, p. 141.

38. Barth, *Romans*, p. 176.

39. Barrett, *Romans*, p. 114; Michel, *Römer*, p. 188; D. Zeller, *Der Brief an die Römer* (RNT; Regensburg, 1985), p. 118; *et al.*

further indication that this is indeed how Paul is thinking when it is noticed that in the protasis of E', he adds the apparently redundant phrase διὰ τοῦ ἑνός (looking back to οἱ πολλοί in E?) Thus, each protasis is saying substantially the same: through one man's sin, death reigned, or 'the many' died.

Clearly, too, there are similarities in the πολλῷ μᾶλλον clauses: the occurrence of χάρις, δωρεά, the use of περισσεύω and its cognate noun, and the phrase 'the one man Jesus Christ'. However, E' complements E by adding two ideas, significant to Paul, to it. In E no attempt is made to define what is meant by ἡ δωρεὰ ἐν χάριτι. In E' it is revealed as being ἡ δωρεὰ τῆς δικαιοσύνης. Likewise, in E there is no hint of the *effect* of ἡ χάρις τοῦ θεοῦ καὶ ἡ δωρεὰ ἐν χάριτι. In E' it is discovered that the recipients ἐν ζωῇ βασιλεύσουσιν. Thus, E' appears to recapitulate E and expand its thinking.

De Boer interestingly notes the forensic nature of the language of 5.15, and, in line with his theory of the cosmological-apocalyptic nature of Paul's discussion of death, observes that the forensic statements of 5.15 ('by the tresspass the many died'; 'the grace of God...abounded for the many') are transformed in 5.17 into cosmologically oriented statements ('by the tresspass *death reigned*'; 'those who receive the abundance of grace...shall *reign in life*.').[40] In this sense, too, E' expands the thought of E.

When evidence of the presence of a chiasmus is being sought, it might be reasonable to expect that, at least occasionally, an indication is given that the person writing is aware of the pattern being produced. There may be such an instance in E and E'. If the structure of the apodosis of E is examined, it contains an unexpected inversion: instead of οἱ πολλοί, ἡ χάρις becomes the subject of the apodosis. It is at least plausible to suggest that this was done to stress the divine initiative in grace. What is intriguing, however, is that there is a similar inversion in E' that needlessly produces a 'clumsiness' in the Greek.[41] The more natural expression in E' would have led to a contrast between death reigning (in the protasis) and life reigning (in the apodosis), whereas Paul appears deliberately to have used the circumlocutary phrase οἱ τὴν περισσείαν...λαμβάνοντες.[42] This appears to be a conscious mirroring

40. De Boer, *Defeat*, p. 163 (italics his).
41. Barrett's description, *Romans*, p. 115.
42. Cf. Cranfield, *Romans*, pp. 287-88.

of the structure of E in E′, demonstrating a distinct rhetorical sophistication in terms of chiastic awareness.[43]

6.3.3. D (5.15a) and D′ (5.18)

Again, Paul's compressed style is immediately apparent. Both D and D′ are constructed around ὡς οὕτως καί phrases with no verbs expressed. It is almost universally accepted that in D a 'negative comparison' or contrast is being made.[44] Thus, the 'act of sin' (παράπτωμα) and the gift or 'act of grace' (χάρισμα)[45] stand in sharp contrast: the one is not like the other. There is no balance between the two: the χάρισμα is disproportionate to the act of sin. Element D′ puts flesh, as it were, on the bare bones of D. The ὡς clause of D′ describes in an elliptical summary the effect of the transgression, and the οὕτως clause amplifies the χάρισμα, here characterized by δικαίωμα.

Caragounis has a novel approach to 5.15a (and 5.16a), treating them both as rhetorical questions, introduced by the negative οὐ and expecting an affirmative answer.[46] The main significance of his paper does not lie so much in this debatable conclusion[47] as in the points he makes on the way to it.[48] Here it is sufficient to note that he argues that the dissimilarity between Adam and Christ is adequately highlighted by the use of terms like παράπτωμα and χάρισμα *per se*, and that the theme of the entire paragraph is the parallel or similarity between them, with the use of πολλῷ μᾶλλον serving not to underline a difference but to emphasize that similarity. While Caragounis may have a point, since the main contrasts in the traditional approach are in 5.15a and 5.16a, the μέν...δέ construction in 5.16bc relies for its effectiveness in the contrast between one and many. It remains the suggestion of this study that the *theme* is much more adequately described in terms of the

---

43. *Contra* Cosby, 'Persuasive Language', p. 223, who misses the presence of the chiasmus and thus concludes that 'Paul's language...does not exhibit rhetorical sophistication at this stage'.

44. See 6.3.4 below for the significance of this in relation to τύπος.

45. Barrett's translations, *Romans*, p. 113.

46. C.C. Caragounis, 'Romans 5.15-16 in the Context of 5.12-21: Contrast or Comparison?', *NTS* 31 (1985), pp. 142-48, 144-45. His translation of the syntactically unique (in the New Testament) 5.15a is, 'But does not the free gift operate like the trespass?' ('Contrast', p. 144; see 'Contrast', p. 147 n. 12 for a survey of the use of ὡς in the New Testament.)

47. Not accepted by Dunn, *Romans*, p. 271, although he gives no reasons.

48. See 6.4.2 below.

disproportionality of sin and grace in their inter-relationship. The use of πολλῷ μᾶλλον is not to emphasize similarity, but rather to underscore that very disproportionality. The typology between Adam and Christ (focused on the former's disobedience and the latter's obedience),[49] while much more than incidental, is not central, but is brought in as an illustrative analogy.[50]

Thus, in D, by beginning with 'Αλλ' οὐχ, Paul draws back from immediately developing the idea of Adam as a type of Christ.[51] Significantly, the contrast that he does make in D is not between *Adam and Christ directly* so much as between the consequences and the effects of their actions.[52] More than that, however, the contrast may actually be between Adam's action and *God's action*. In this passage the χάρισμα appears to be from *God*, in so far as in E it is ἡ χάρις τοῦ θεοῦ (although it is certainly effected through Christ).[53]

Just as there is a simple internal syntactical balance within D, with each phrase consisting of one noun with its definite article, the much longer D′ is equally carefully balanced internally. This may be represented schematically thus:

"Αρα οὖν ὡς
    δι' ἑνὸς παραπτώματος   εἰς πάντας ἀνθρώπους   εἰς κατάκριμα,
οὕτως καὶ
    δι' ἑνὸς δικαιώματος   εἰς πάντας ἀνθρώπους   εἰς δικαίωσιν ζωῆς·

The addition of ζωῆς is significant in that it is in an emphatic position in its phrase, appearing to draw further attention to itself by deliberately upsetting the structural balance. ζωῆς, best taken as a genitive of

---

49. See 6.3.4 below.
50. See further 6.4.2 below.
51. See 6.3.4 below.
52. Cf. Keck, *Letters*, p. 116; Zahn, *Römer*, p. 274; likewise Cranfield, *Romans*, p. 283: of Adam, 'it is to be noted that it is precisely his παράβασις... and its results which constitute him the τύπος τοῦ μέλλοντος'; Swee-Hwa Quek, 'Adam', p. 70.
53. I recognize that this may be somewhat modified in the following clause which, however, is widely regarded as obscure. I would take 'the gift' as being the 'gift of righteousness' (as made plain in E′)—so Cranfield, *Romans*, pp. 285-86. ἡ δωρεά is closely linked with ἐν χάριτι, the whole being a gift-in-grace, inextricably linked with 'the one man Jesus Christ'. Perhaps he is thinking of the grace of God *embodied* in Christ. It is difficult to be sure of Paul's meaning.

result,[54] is the result of the whole process that stems from the χάρισμα, and may stand as a one-word summary of the theological imbalance implicit in the 'negative comparison' of D. The transgression is not like the free gift, because the free gift leads to *life*,[55] with all its implications in terms of justification.

Thus, the function of E′ *in the argument* (as distinct from its function in the chiasmus) is to act as a summary and first development ("Αρα οὖν...) of the two negative contrasts of D and F, each with its corresponding conditional, E and E′.[56] Picking up παράπτωμα from D and κατάκριμα from F, it summarizes the positive contrast between the sinful act and its effect, and the act of righteousness and its effect, encapsulating the disproportionality implied by the two εἰ γὰρ...πολλῷ μᾶλλον clauses, and in a syntactical formulation that is the precise positive counterpart of D (D: οὐχ ὡς...οὕτως καί; D′: ὡς...οὕτως καί)

6.3.4. C (5.14) and C′ (5.19)

This may at first sight appear to be the weakest link in the chiasmus, with the occurrence of the participle ἁμαρτήσαντας in C and ἁμαρτωλοί in C′ not being of any striking significance. If a balance exists, it must be one of content.[57]

C appears to make a simple statement. The result of sin is death's universal reign from Adam to Moses, even over those who sinned in a different way from Adam. It is only, in fact, in this period that everyone died as a consequence of Adam's fall.[58] At this stage law had no part to play.[59] It is important to notice that the last relative clause of C gives the first clear hint since the beginning of the passage that there is some kind of comparison to be made between Adam and Christ.

C′ consists of another ὥσπερ...οὕτως καί sentence, the two halves of which are very finely balanced in a manner, and using a syntactical

54. Cranfield, *Romans*, p. 289; Ziesler, *Romans*, p. 151; *et al.*

55. Cf. ἐν ζωῇ in E′.

56. So, e.g., Caragounis, 'Contrast', p. 143, although I disagree with his logic in then suggesting that 5.18 is the conclusion of the comparison of 5.12, especially since he himself acknowledges that 5.18 is assertion and not argument. It is *assertion* precisely because its function is summary. The significant relationship between the chiastic form and the content will be discussed in 6.4.2 below.

57. But see 6.2 above for the disposition of ἁμαρτία and παράπτωμα in the chiasmus.

58. Dahl, *Missionary Theology*, p. 91.

59. See further 6.3.5 below.

form, reminiscent of D' (but, unlike D', using verbs). It is *not*, however, simply a restatement of D'.[60] Rather, it is a necessary and new component of Paul's argument, required to elucidate, in a very significant way, the whole basis of the 'relationship' between Adam and Christ that allows Paul to use τύπος of Adam.[61] The term τύπος has a technical usage in biblical literature, and 'usually refers to a correspondence in characteristics or historical pattern between two realities, with one as the enhancement or fulfilment of the other'.[62] However, it is important to recognize the discontinuity in Paul's thought at this point. With the last clause of C, Paul seems ready to go on to expand the comparison begun in A (5.12), but cannot do so without first making two *contrasts* between the effects of the respective actions associated with the two,[63] this suggesting that the substance of the contrasts is more pressing in his thinking than the formulation of the comparison.[64]

Thus, the introductory γάρ in C' may be consciously used. Up to this point the whole discussion has been in abstract, generalized terms and the Romans have not been told of the nature of Adam's sin that has had such far-reaching consequences for the many. This is defined in C' as 'disobedience', and shows 'obedience' to be the contrasting aspect of the life of Christ that made possible the justification of the many. This

60. *Pace* Barrett, *Romans*, p. 117; *et al.* Cf. Käsemann's description (*Romans*, p. 157) that 5.19 'repeats, supports and elucidates' what is said in 5.18, although there is more than this in view. Cosby, 'Persuasive Language', p. 224, calls 5.18, 19 'two beautifully balanced antitheses'.

61. With the great majority, I understand τοῦ μέλλοντος as being a messianic designation; *pace* J.A.T. Robinson, *The Body* (London, 1952), p. 35 n. 1, and R. Scroggs, *The Last Adam: A Study in Pauline Anthropology* (Oxford, 1966), pp. 80-81, whose identification of τοῦ μέλλοντος with Moses or 'man under the law' has not been widely accepted.

62. Ziesler, *Romans*, p. 148, reflecting the thinking of many others.

63. Cf. Dunn, *Romans*, p. 293. Cranfield is aware of this delay in the out-working of the comparison, and draws attention to it more than once: 'The relative clause ὅς ἐστιν τύπος τοῦ μέλλοντος is a very clear hint of the comparison, for the completion of the formal statement of which we have still to wait until v. 18f' (Cranfield, *Romans*, p. 283). De Boer, *Defeat*, p. 160, too, makes a similar link. However, the phrases in 5.18 δι' ἑνὸς παραπτώματος and δι' ἑνὸς δικαιώματος are, as it were, the consequence of the typology that is *rooted* in the disobedience of the former and the obedience of the latter: see below.

64. Otherwise, why should he postpone the comparison by interposing qualifications to the as yet unmade comparison? Caragounis, 'Contrast', p. 144, highlights this point.

insight is of much more than passing interest for Paul, as can be seen by the way that he later develops the specific concept of the 'obedience of faith' in 6.12-19.[65]

Therefore, the facile assumption should not necessarily be made that Paul intended to create a type–antitype comparison based on Adam and Christ beginning in D, with its opening juxtaposition of adversative and negative ('Αλλ' οὐχ...) In the section that extends from D to D' it is Adam's sin with its effects and God's χάρισμα, χάρις, δώρημα and δωρεά that are primarily in view. In the same way, Paul appears to have consciously to link the direct contrast of the actions of Adam and Christ in C' to the less immediate contrast of D' by means of the construction ὥσπερ γὰρ...οὕτως καὶ, making specific for the first time the way in which Adam may properly be said to be a type of Christ.

6.3.5. B (5.13) and B' (5.20)

A more striking balance exists between B and B': sin, before and after the law. Although these verses have great theological importance, in terms of the chiastic pattern, they can be dealt with in very brief compass.

It is only in these two elements that the term νόμος occurs in the chiasmus. In B Paul affirms that sin was in the world ἄχρι νόμου, but was not counted as such. The law is the factor that disturbs the analogy in contrast between Adam and Christ.[66] The question of the function of the law in relation to sin has only been partially answered earlier in the letter (cf. 3.20, 31; 4.13-15). Now Paul addresses it directly, but his answer lies in the reading of B and B' together. In B' the corollary to B is stated first—law came in to increase the trespass—and then the new thought is added to it to the effect that, where sin increased, grace abounded all the more.

6.3.6. A (5.12) and A' (5.21)

The difficulties of A in its construction, translation and attendant theological implications are legion, and cannot all be addressed in this

---

65. Thompson, *Clothed*, p. 83; *et al.* See 6.4.1 below.

66. Dahl, *Missionary Theology*, p. 91. It is interesting that no one gives an adequate explanation of the sudden re-introduction of the concept of law in 5.20. In particular, Cosby's careful rhetorical analysis is quite silent on the rhetorical status of 5.20 in a passage in which he finds so much other evidence of rhetorical skill ('Persuasive Language', p. 224). On the basis of the chiastic patterning, its reoccurrence is neither unexpected nor surprising.

context. Thus, without any detail of the history of its interpretation, the translation of ἐφ' ᾧ is taken as 'because' with the majority of modern commentators.[67]

In terms of the chiasmus, however, a major problem that has to be considered is whether or not Paul intended his readers to see a balance between ὥσπερ...καὶ οὕτως in 5.12 and ὥσπερ...οὕτως καί in 5.21. In favour of agreeing that he did is the fact that there have already been two other pairs of elements (D and D', E and E') that have shared a common grammatical structure. On the other hand, the only other occurrence of ὥσπερ...οὕτως καί is in C' where there is no grammatical balancing with C.

More fundamental, however, is the long-standing objection that καὶ οὕτως is quite different in meaning from οὕτως καί, and that the latter order is consistently found when it is used to introduce the apodosis after ὡς, ὥσπερ and so on. In contrast, καὶ οὕτως means 'and so' or 'and thus', with the implication of result or manner. In addition, if the clause is taken as an apodosis, it seems to yield an unsatisfactory comparison: the entry of sin and death through one man, and the coming of death to all because all sinned.[68]

The best recent attempt at arguing that the καὶ οὕτως clause was intended as the apodosis is that of Kirby.[69] His objections to the 'traditional' approach that translates καὶ οὕτως as 'and thus', making the verse an unfinished construction later to be resumed (or otherwise, depending on the commentator), can be summarized thus:

a. The traditional approach assumes a 'violent anacolouthon' and needs 'to posit a lengthy and cumbersome ellipsis' in a passage that otherwise shows a 'careful, even elegant, finish', pointing to 5.15 as an example.

b. On the traditional view, 5.13-14 'must be taken as a long aside that Paul could not resist interjecting even at such a closely argued juncture of his thought'.

67. Many commentators provide surveys of that history. Particularly helpful are those in Käsemann, *Romans*, pp. 147-49, and Cranfield, *Romans*, pp. 274-79.

68. So Cranfield, *Romans*, p. 272 n. 5; *contra* Barrett, *Romans*, p. 110, whose translation runs, 'As through one man sin entered the world (and through sin came that man's death), so also death came to all men, because they all sinned'. He does not seek to justify this translation, or the addition of 'that man's' before the first 'death'.

69. Kirby, 'Syntax', pp. 283-86.

c.   The ὥσπερ/οὕτως correlation is so frequent in this passage
     that Paul is obviously using it as a structural device. In all other
     places (5.15, 18, 19, 21; 6.4, 19) ὥσπερ is explicitly answered
     by οὕτως.

In response to Kirby's first point, the anacolouthon is certainly 'sudden',
but it need not merit the description 'violent'. It is reasonable to suggest
that, for Paul, the issues raised in the protasis concerning Adam, sin and
death, and, in particular, the need to make the link between Adam's sin
and the readers' condition, have taken precedence in his mind over the
need to provide an immediate apodosis. Likewise, the ellipsis may be
lengthy (indeed, it may be considerably longer than Kirby suggests), but
it is *cumbersome*, only if its elegant chiastic ordering is not perceived.

His second point is curious: it is precisely *because* the passage is
closely argued that the aside appears, as Paul sees the opportunity to
deal with the problems associated with Adam's sin and humankind's situation, apparently not wanting to delay consideration until later. Nor is
his third point as strong as it may first appear, because the *first occurrence* of ὥσπερ in Romans 5 is in 5.12. If 5.12 had stood in the middle
or at the end of the series of such correlations, it could have been argued
that Paul might have been expected to have maintained consistency in
usage. On the other hand, the combination of ὥσπερ with the less usually found καὶ οὕτως could well have acted as a trigger for Paul to
make much more use of ὥσπερ in a passage full of antitheses in its
more normal ὥσπερ...οὕτως καὶ formulation.

Kirby's arguments do not counterbalance the weight of the more
traditional approach to the problem, either in his criticisms of it, or,
indeed, in his defence of his own translation: 'just as through one man
(*sc.* Adam) sin came into the world, and through sin death, *so too* (*sc.*
through one man, Adam) death came to all men'.[70] This is unconvincing
because it leads to a very weak comparison inasmuch as the counterbalance to the emphatically placed and (in terms of Paul's argument)
highly significant phrase δι᾽ ἑνὸς ἀνθρώπου is absent from the apodosis, and must be supplied by Kirby.

The emphatic position of δι᾽ ἑνὸς ἀνθρώπου in the protasis and the
suggestion that there should be something of equivalent emphasis in the
apodosis[71] is significant, especially since so many rhetorically inspired

---

70. Kirby, 'Syntax', p. 284.
71. Cranfield, *Romans*, p. 272 n. 5.

details have been observed in the remainder of the passage. Maillot, too, taking it as a comparative sentence,[72] argues that it is answered by εἰς πάντας ἀνθρώπους, creating a disproportionality (Maillot's term) between cause and consequence. While there is such a disproportionality created, he may have confused a *comparative* sentence (just as...so also) with one of result or consequence, in which καὶ οὕτως means 'and so'. In this instance what is present is not a disproportionate *comparison* in 5.12 so much as disproportionate *consequence*.

Among the suggested solutions of the broken construction of 5.12, perhaps the most common regards 5.18a as repeating the substance of the original protasis, with 5.18b supplying the 'missing' apodosis;[73] others find the comparison completed in 5.19;[74] others, again, think that he leaves it uncompleted.[75]

It can be understood why many are attracted to 5.18 and 5.19 as the likely conclusions of the broken construction, if for no other reason than the fact that they are sequentially the closest candidates. There are two objections, however, to these:

a. Neither the protasis in 5.18 or 19 adequately sums up 5.12. The better of the two is 5.19, with its emphasis on the spread of sin through the disobedience of one man, but 5.12 speaks of sin *and death* entering through one man, and spreading to all men.

b. There is no phrase in the apodoses of 5.18,19 that corresponds to the prominence of δι' ἑνὸς ἀνθρώπου in 5.12. In 5.18 δι' ἑνὸς δικαιώματος in the apodosis clearly responds to δι' ἑνὸς παραπτώματος in the protasis.

Likewise, there is nothing that serves this function in 5.19, with its careful internal parallelism.

This leads to the suggestion that, in fact, the protasis of A′ best resumes the thought of A.[76] The apodosis of A′ may now be seen as a

---

72. A. Maillot, *L'épitre aux Romains* (Paris, 1984), pp. 143-44.

73. Cf. Cranfield, *Romans*, p. 273; Barth, *Romans*, p. 181; Bruce, *Romans*, p. 130; Caragounis, 'Contrast', p. 144; Dunn, *Romans*, pp. 282-83; Käsemann, *Romans*, p. 155; Myers, 'Inversion', p. 39.

74. E.g., Zahn, *Römer*, p. 285; Black, *Romans*, p. 86.

75. Sanday and Headlam, *Romans*, p. 132.

76. De Boer, *Defeat*, p. 162, comes to the same conclusion, highlighting the difference in terminology between the protasis of 5.18 and 5.12. I note that the same

very appropriate and effective correlative to A—and especially so as there is now a balancing phrase in A′ that carries equal emphasis to δι’ ἑνὸς ἀνθρώπου in A, viz. its final words, διὰ ’Ιησοῦ Χριστοῦ τοῦ κυρίου ἡμῶν. The whole tragedy of sin and death unfolds through the action of one man; the whole victory is accomplished equally through 'our Lord Jesus Christ'.[77]

This, in fact, accords well with Sanday and Headlam's interesting proposal in regard to Paul's original intention in A. They suggest that he was going to write:

> ὥσπερ δι’ ἑνὸς ἀνθρώπου ἡ ἁμαρτία εἰς τὸν κόσμον εἰσῆλθεν, καὶ διὰ τῆς ἁμαρτίας ὁ θάνατος...οὕτως καὶ δι’ ἑνὸς ἀνθρώπου ἡ δικαιοσύνη εἰσῆλθεν, καὶ διὰ τῆς δικαιοσύνης ἡ ζωή.[78]

While they themselves conclude that the structure is unfinished, it is intriguing that each one of their suggested ideas occurs in the apodosis of A′, with the sole exception of the idea of 'reigning' replacing that of 'entering'.

The possibility of the apodosis of 5.12 being supplied in 5.21 is not widely discussed.[79] Perhaps it has been thought to be unlikely because of their 'sequential' distance apart. But when the passage is seen as a chiasmus, two of the great strengths of this suggestion are the chiastic proximity of 5.12 and 5.21 (in terms of the fact that they are in parallel elements), and the rounding off of the passage in a rather striking manner, tying beginning and end firmly together. Furthermore, in substance A′ stands as an excellent comment on Michel's observation in relation to F, that as κατάκριμα stands at the end of the old age, so δικαίωμα is the goal of the new.[80]

combination of ideas (with the substitution of παράπτωμα for ἁμαρτία) is present in E′, but this, of course, is not a candidate because it is part of one of the arguments *a fortiori* rather than part of a comparative sentence.

77. De Boer, *Defeat*, p. 163, makes the same point: 'while the protasis of v. 12a-b *begins* with the phrase "through one human being"...the apodosis in v. 21b *ends* with the phrase "through Jesus Christ our Lord"...'

78. Sanday and Headlam, *Romans*, p. 132. De Boer, *Defeat*, p. 162, supplies a virtually identical apodosis.

79. But see de Boer, *Defeat*, pp. 162-63. Maillot, *Romains*, p. 152, specifically links the two in the suggestion that they have the same form (a comment with which I disagree—see above), but makes nothing of it in exegesis.

80. Michel, *Römer*, p. 190.

6.4. *The Sequential Progress of Paul's Thought in Romans 5.12-21*

6.4.1. *The Chiasmus and Paul's Flow of Thought*

Up to this point, 5.12-21 has been examined from the artificial perspective of looking backwards and forwards from the central affirmation F, but the unfolding of Paul's thought must now be considered sequentially. First, if an overview of the passage is sought, it may be suggested that Paul moves from the reign of sin and death initiated by Adam to the reign of grace and righteousness brought about through Christ. Thus, as a brief sketch, A, B and C deal with the world and history of the first Adam; D brings the first hint of the profound discontinuity and utter dissimilarity between the two worlds; E summarizes the old order and gives the first statement of the new, leading into F, with its balanced, almost cryptic style, but making the central statement of the difference between the two orders. Moving out from the centre, E′ spells out some of the unstated inferences of E, defining for the first time the free gift as 'righteousness', and the effect of God's grace in terms of reigning in life. D′ picks up the discontinuity between the two orders hinted at in D, and quantifies that discontinuity in the light of the discussion of E, F and E′. C′ defines the nature of Adam's παράβασις, and, by so doing, illustrates how Adam is a type of Christ. B′ and A′ in turn pick up the themes of B and A, and in each case show how the new order stands over against the old, overcoming it. The passage is a masterpiece of construction and of chiastically progressive argument!

Such then is the skeleton of Paul's thought. To add flesh, it is recalled that in Romans 4 Paul has used Abraham's situation to demonstrate his thesis that justification is by faith. This, in turn, provides the starting point for Romans 5, with its briefest of summaries (Δικαιωθέντες οὖν ἐκ πίστεως...) and the beginning of his exploration of some of the consequences of that justification. But the wonder of God's action captures Paul's imagination: at the right time, Christ died for the ungodly (5.6), the willing sacrifice of one on behalf of the many.[81]

Perhaps the seeds that later germinate into the discussion of 5.12-21

---

81. Dunn, *Romans*, p. 266; Cosby is very aware of the rhetorical crafting of the beginning of Rom. 5. He finds the technique of *transitio* in 5.1, 2, briefly recalling what has gone before and hinting at what is to follow next ('Persuasive Language', p. 213), followed by a *gradatio* that builds to a rhetorical climax in 5.5 ('Persuasive Language', p. 214).

can be found in 5.6, as Paul feels the need to redefine the nature of the relationship between Christ and the 'ungodly', but this time more closely than before. The disproportionality in God's love becomes strikingly clear for him in the climactic chain of 5.7-8: laying down one's life for a just man is extraordinary. How much more so is Christ's death for the sinner? God's love is out of all proportion to 'our' deserving. By this point, the idea of the death of Christ has moved into the forefront of his thinking (four times in 5.6-8), and he follows this with two arguments *a fortiori* in 5.9, 10, using the εἰ...πολλῷ μᾶλλον construction in two succeeding sentences.[82] In 5.9 the idea of God's wrath (which has earlier been discussed at length in association with judgment in, for example, 2.1-10; 3.5-8) reappears, and in 5.10 the new concept of reconciliation is introduced, both in the context of the death of Christ.

It is quite understandable that Paul should want to go on to explore further the nature of the relationship between those needing to be reconciled (here, of course, God and sinful man), in terms of where each stands, and what each has done or is expected to do. On this basis Rom. 5.12a *is* clearly and logically connected with 5.1-11 as Paul embarks on his new point. He may well have intended to write a 'regular' ὥσπερ...οὕτως καί comparative sentence, but as soon as he reaches δι' ἑνὸς ἀνθρώπου, he realizes that he has opened up a new and more urgent problem that follows on from 5.8-10: how the fact of one man's sinning affected all other individuals, leading to the universal reign of death, making all people enemies.

Thus, Paul goes off at a tangent, describing the chain reaction that shows how all die because all sin. But now a new difficulty lies in the role of *law* in all this, especially since the relationship between law and sin has been prominent in his thinking from as far back as 2.12. However, 5.13 is his first statement of the *temporal* relationship between the two, although more in the nature of an allusion. In C he returns to the theme of the reign of death over all sinners, setting it in the 'historical' context of the pre-law days 'from Adam to Moses',[83] and

82. It should be noted, of course, that εἰ is actually missing from the first, the protasis being implicit in the participle δικαιωθέντες.

83. Sanders, *Paul*, pp. 24 and 35-36, finds 'a certain awkwardness' in Paul's attempt to connect the law to universal sinfulness, suggesting an inconsistency between Rom. 2 and 5.12-14. Law 'is required for sin to be counted', but then 'it was counted anyway'. The inconsistency may not be as apparent as he suggests, but I agree that the introduction of the concept of law in the chiasmus is a little awkward.

signalling the fact that there is an as yet unspecified comparison between the two in the concept of the τύπος.

In fact, he then immediately backs away from direct comparison and instead asserts that the relationship is essentially one of dissimilarity,[84] beginning with a firmly negative comparison (D) that does not directly relate to Adam and Christ anyway, so much as to the outworked effect of their actions. Thus, D sets up the contrast, which E expands into a statement *a minori ad maius*, asserting the disproportionality[85] that exists between the effects of sin and grace.

This leads immediately to the central affirmation of the total dissimilarity (again in the form of the negative comparison in F) between the effects of one man's sinning and the δώρημα. This is the crucial statement that describes the focus of Paul's thought: the one man's sinning leads to condemnation and judgment; the free gift after many transgressions leads to righteousness. Disproportionate indeed! But the impact of this element is not sufficiently described by such a concept. The feature that must have so astonished the Romans is the completely unexpected outworking of the opening assertion of F (καὶ οὐχ ὡς δι' ἑνὸς ἁμαρτήσαντος τὸ δώρημα·) as the free gift after many transgressions is both dramatically and climactically revealed as δικαίωμα, the final word at the end of a carefully crafted element.

E′ is another *argumentum a minori ad maius* that emphasizes further the disproportionality in terms of the abundance of grace, and clarifies what Paul means by the 'gift', identifying it with righteousness ('the gift of righteousness'). In D′ he can now make a fuller statement of the dissimilarity hinted at in D, but doing so positively, summarizing 5.15-17.

So far, however, the discussion of the spread and effect of sin has been in general terms. His readers have not yet been told wherein Adam's sin lay, nor in what concrete respect he was a type of Christ. Paul now specifies in C′ that it was the disobedience of the former that resulted in the many being made sinners, and the obedience of the latter that resulted in the many being made righteous.

As the chiastic pattern moves to completion, Paul comes back in B′ to the role of law, and uses the opportunity once more to highlight the disproportionality between sin and grace.

Having now dealt to his own satisfaction with the way that Adam's

84. Not really 'antithetische Typologie' (Michel, *Römer*, p. 185), a term which 'is liable to be misleading in this connexion' (so Cranfield, *Romans*, p. 273).

85. 'If statement X is true, much more is statement Y true.'

actions affected the many in the reign of death, he can return to his original intention. Without this time mentioning Adam's role specifically, he recapitulates A in the protasis of A', and proclaims the reign of grace through righteousness resulting in eternal life—all accomplished 'through our Lord Jesus Christ'. But now the very disproportionality that he has been at pains to stress produces a new problem: should believers continue in sin so as to encourage a disproportionate increase in grace? And so ch. 6. begins.

In Rom. 6.1-14 Paul answers his questions essentially by an appeal to their (i.e., Paul's and the Romans') common experience of baptism[86] and what it means. Continuing in sin is ruled out because of the believers' baptism into the death of Christ. Further identification with Christ is encouraged as Paul begins to develop the link between the obedience of Christ (from 5.19) and the believers' obedience to the 'standard of teaching' (6.17).

6.4.2. *The Chiasmus and the Surface Structure of Paul's Thought*

In this passage the possibility must be considered that there is a more obvious structure than that suggested by the chiastic pattern. In such a scheme the comparison of 5.12 is broken by the parenthetical aside of 5.13, 14. Such a view suggests that the introduction of the notion of Adam as τύπος is followed by two connected negative comparisons in 5.15a ('Αλλ' οὐχ ὡς...) and 5.16a (καὶ οὐχ ὡς...), each with its explanatory εἰ γὰρ...πολλῷ μᾶλλον construction. An inference is drawn from these in 5.18 ("Αρα οὖν...) and, at the same time, the broken comparison of 5.12 is concluded in 5.18, 19. The role of law is further emphasized in 5.20, and Paul reaches his conclusion in 5.21.

Just how superficial this may be, however, is clearly indicated by Caragounis:

> Furthermore, to start a comparison (v. 12), then break it off and insert a parenthesis (vv. 13-14), then treat of a difference in order to preclude any misunderstanding (vv. 15-17) of a comparison that has not yet been made(!)[87] and finally, repeat the comparison's first part and then add the other (v. 18), is, indeed, a very muddled procedure![88]

---

86. Dahl, *Missionary Theology*, p. 84.
87. The exclamation mark is Caragounis's.
88. Caragounis, 'Contrast', p. 144.

It is the suggestion of this study that the modern preoccupation of the 'history of religions' school with the background and development of the Adam–Christ typology[89] has, perhaps subconsciously, shifted the emphasis of much contemporary exegesis towards the Adam–Christ antithesis, whereas the focus of Paul's thought is to be found elsewhere. The chiasmus clearly suggests that the purpose of the typology lies in the disobedience/obedience antithesis of C'. The function in the argument of the adversative ἀλλά in 5.15a is to move the reader away, at least at this point, from overhasty comparison between Adam and Christ.

Thus, in D (5.15a) the antithesis between παράπτωμα and χάρισμα is set up, to be developed into the statement of the disproportionality between them in E (5.15b), where the use of παράπτωμα in the protasis and χάρις in the apodosis should be observed.

A close examination of the relationship between 5.15 and 5.16, 17, however, shows how differently 5.17 relates to 5.16 when compared with how 5.15b relates to 5.15a despite the repetition of οὐχ ὡς and εἰ γάρ...πολλῷ μᾶλλον. Thus:

a. In 5.16 there is no οὕτως καί as in 5.15.

b. Other rhetorical considerations are clearly at work in 5.16, as seen by the use of the series of -μα terms,[90] and the carefully balanced μὲν/δέ phrases, uniquely present in 5.12-21 at this point.

c. 5.17 manifestly picks up the vocabulary of 5.15b rather than 5.16. Thus, 5.17 uses both χάρις and δωρεά (as in 5.15b) rather than δώρημα and χάρισμα as in 5.16.

d. The identical opening phrases of 5.17 and 5.15b, the presence of the apparently redundant διὰ τοῦ ἑνός in 5.17, and the unexpected and slightly clumsy subject of the apodosis of 5.17 have all been noted in 6.3.2 above.

The cumulative impact of these observations is to give the impression that there is more happening in the structure of the passage than simply two negative comparisons joined by καί (5.16) and then expanded by subsequent conditional clauses. The compressed style of both 5.15a and 5.16a makes translation difficult, but there may not be, in fact, much difference at all in the two contrasts. In the first, 'transgression' and 'free gift' are contrasted; in the second, the 'gift' and what came '*through*

89. See Käsemann, *Romans*, pp. 142-47, for example.
90. See 6.2 above.

one man's sinning' are highlighted.[91] But the man and his sin are inseparable.[92]

There seems little question that the highly elliptical 5.16, with its concentration of nouns in -μα, would make an immediate impact on Paul's audience that would give 5.16 a higher profile in their minds (and in the rhetorical patterning of the passage) than if it were simply the second of two negative comparisons.

De Boer's analysis of the structure of 5.12-21 deserves closer consideration.[93] Laying out the passage in an indented fashion, he suggests 'a certain kind of correspondence' between 5.12a, b and 5.21, between 5.12c ('and so death spread...')-14 and 5.20, between 5.15-17 and 5.18-19. He finds the clearest correpondence between 5.12c-14 and 5.20, giving three reasons: the 'just as...so also' pattern is absent from them, both specifically mention the Law, and the passage is 'rather more easily comprehensible without them'.

With regard to the two units 5.15-17 and 5.18, 19, he suggests that they are 'discernible and complementary'. In the first unit two negative comparisons are formulated with explanatory expansions,[94] although the phrases of 5.16b, c 'disrupt the flow'.[95] Two positive comparisons follow, paralleled to each other in construction (5.18, 19).

In line with his general thesis that 5.12-21 represents a transition from the forensic terminology that characterizes the earlier part of Romans to the cosmological language typical of chs. 6–8,[96] he notes that in 5.12a, b and 5.21 sin, death and grace are personified as cosmological rulers in conflict, using none of the forensic terminology and motifs present in the intervening verses.[97] He concludes that 5.21a 'amounts to a reprise of the apodosis[98] of v. 12a-b' which is then completed by the apodosis of 5.21b.[99]

It is clear that de Boer has come close to the chiastic pattern proposed

---

91. Dunn, *Romans*, p. 280.
92. See 6.3.1 above on the ambiguous ἐξ ἑνός in 5.16b.
93. De Boer, *Defeat*, pp. 158-59.
94. De Boer, *Defeat*, p. 160.
95. De Boer, *Defeat*, p. 157.
96. De Boer, *Defeat*, p. 152.
97. De Boer, *Defeat*, p. 160. He cites transgression, tresspass, judgment, condemnation, free gift of righteousness and justification.
98. This should surely be the 'protasis'.
99. See further 6.3.6 above.

in this chapter, and, indeed, some of the points he makes serve to under-line that hypothesis, particularly, perhaps, in relation to E and E', and A and A'.[100] His analysis, however, has some weaknesses, including the following:

a. He does not give a convincing reason for 'dividing' 5.12 at καὶ οὕτως. His argument that 5.12 is 'rather long for a pro-tasis'[101] would be difficult to substantiate. Indeed, in de Boer's terminology the 'correspondence' between his second (5.12c-14) and second last (5.20) units is enhanced if 5.12c, d is assigned to the first unit.

b. Only a weak case can be built on the observation of the *absence* of forensic terminology in his first and last unit. This would be much more persuasive if the first and last units had used the only cosmological terminology in the passage, but, of course, it occurs throughout.[102]

c. By including 5.14 in his second unit, but 5.19 in his third last, he misses the opportunity to make the 'correspondence', of which he is nonetheless aware,[103] between the Adam–Christ typology and their respective disobedience and obedience.

d. He cannot give any adequate account of the function of 5.16b, c, although he notes their rhetorical crafting,[104] and consistently supposes an understood οὕτως in 5.16a in order to maintain the syntactical balance of his two central correspondences, without ever justifying such an assumption.

It is therefore suggested that, while de Boer's approach to the section is an interesting and helpful one that begins, as does the hypothesis of this chapter, with the observation of its syntactical patterns, the chiasmus proposed here accounts for these more satisfactorily. No elements are found to be intrusive,[105] and in particular the function of 5.16 as the centre of the chiasmus adequately explains its unique formulation in the section.

100. See respectively 6.3.2 and 6.3.5 above.

101. De Boer, *Defeat*, p. 160.

102. The odd verse division after 5.12b is also necessary to exclude the forensic terminology of 5.12c, d from the first unit.

103. De Boer, *Defeat*, p. 160.

104. De Boer, *Defeat*, p. 157.

105. With the exception, perhaps, to a very limited degree, of B (5.13).

6.5. *Conclusion*

As illustrated by the central element of the chiasmus, the focus of Paul's thought in this skilfully crafted passage that uses a blend of forensic and cosmological language is on the dissimilarity existing between the δώρημα and what came through one man's sinning. The judgment following one-man-and-his-sin is condemnation; the astonishing gift following many trespasses results in δικαίωμα. This is the disproportionality that Paul set out to highlight in the broken construction of 5.12, and that he finally formulates in 5.21: the reign of sin is superseded by the reign of grace through δικαιοσύνη resulting in eternal life. In this the Adam–Christ typology, in fact, plays a rather less major role than has sometimes been assumed, the typology lying in the relationship between Adam's disobedience and Christ's obedience. Another secondary, though significant theme, is the function of law in relation to sin. Paul's argument inevitably progresses to the questions of 6.1 as a consequence of his statement in 5.20 regarding the relationship between the law, sin and grace.

Chapter 7

CONCLUSIONS

Throughout this chapter caution should be exercised in making any generalized statements about *all* chiasms at the intermediate level on the basis of only five developed examples. The analysis of these five illustrates the flexibility of the chiastic technique, and may be enough to begin the process of identifying some of the most useful features of chiasmus for future study.

7.1. *Conclusions in Relation to Methodology*

7.1.1. *In Relation to the Requirements and Constraints in the Identification of a Chiasmus*

We are now in a position to review the methodological parameters set for this inquiry in the first chapter. Three requirements were suggested, without the fulfilment of which a proposed pattern would not be accepted as chiastic. These were, in brief: (a) the chiasmus will be present in the text, without resorting to textual emendation; (b) the symmetrical elements will be present in precisely inverted order; (c) the chiasmus will begin and end at a reasonable point.[1] The first and the second need no further comment, since only examples conforming to these have been considered. The third, however, raises some interesting issues.

The difficulty of defining a 'reasonable point' has already been alluded to.[2] Few would dismiss the patterns in Eph. 2.11-22 or Rom. 5.12-21 on the basis that they begin or end at *unreasonable points* in the text,[3] although the other three need further examination. Perhaps the

---

1. See 1.4.3 above.
2. See 1.4.3 above.
3. Although, of course, commentators can be found who might wish to further divide these units into more atomistic sub-units.

most helpful criterion in this respect is that of the *flow of syntax*.[4] The requirement might then be refined and restated in terms that a chiasmus will not break the flow of syntax. On this basis, Gal. 5.13–6.2 ends at an appropriate point *syntactically*. The question of whether it ends at an appropriate point otherwise will be considered later.[5]

Eph. 1.3-14 is a unique case in this study in that the chiamsus ends at 1.10 in the middle of a 'sentence'. However, even here evidence has been produced that 1.11 includes a semantically significant change of perspective that has been noticed by a number of commentators.[6] It is as though the great sentence draws breath at this point before continuing on its way. A break in the flow of syntax might further be described, therefore, as a break occurring between clauses. This proposal, too, accommodates the way in which Eph. 1.3-10 and Col. 2.6-19 begin with an introductory clause that is associated with, but is not part of, the chiasmus.[7]

It appears reasonable to suggest, therefore, that these three requirements remain in place for the study of chiasmus. A compelling argument would need to be presented before a chiastic pattern that clearly breaks the flow of syntax would be acceptable. As confidence is gained in the field, it might be possible at some point to relax the second prerequisite a little. It is not easy, however, to envisage circumstances in which the first might be set aside, without opening the door to the wholesale textual rearrangements and emendations of which I have been so critical in, for example, the recovery of 'hymnic' patterns.[8]

In relation to the other constraints,[9] particular attention throughout has been paid to examining the exegetical basis for the patterns, and, in the few cases where a term could be said to be 'commonly occurring', an attempt has been made to justify its chosen position in the chiasmus.

Not many non-balancing elements have been found. In some instances

4. This concept was suggested to me by Lincoln's discussion of the analysis of Eph. 1.3-14 (*Ephesians*, pp. 15-16, etc.), although he does not use it in relation to chiasmus.

5. See 7.2.2 below.

6. Notably, Caragaounis, *Mysterion*, pp. 34-35. Cf., too, Barth, *Ephesians*, p. 98, and Schille, *Hymnen*, pp. 66ff.: see further 2.5 above.

7. See further 7.2.1 below.

8. See, e.g., 2.2.1 above.

9. Four were suggested in 1.4.3 above: the avoidance of 'chiasmus by headings', the selective use of a commonly occurring term, the presence of non-balancing elements, and the presentation of a chiamus in an exegetical vacuum.

the balance has been weak,[10] but, once more, it has been possible to give a reasonable account of how such weakness came about, or why it might be present. It is worth while reiterating the point that this is a valid constraint: the presence of non-symmetrical elements must not be allowed to become a 'catch-all' to lend an appearance of validity to an otherwise weak pattern. In the examples presented above, the *strength* of the great majority of parallels have led to the conclusion that, on the balance of probability, a chiasmus was intended in the passage, despite the weakly balanced pair of elements.

Throughout the study, too, the principle of avoiding 'chiasmus by heading' has been advocated.[11] While maintaining that the underlying reasons for this are sound, in practice it might be argued that, when the basis of comparison of two elements relies on *content* rather than on *form*, the ensuing description of the relevant content of the element results in an implicit assignation of a 'heading' to that element. This having been said, however, the need for careful exegesis of the individual elements is not reduced.

7.1.2. *In Relation to the Process of Identifying a Chiasmus*

The 'experimenting'[12] required to identify a potential chiasmus is difficult to demonstrate since it is more naturally accommodated by a stage prior to writing. In the present context it is only the results of those 'experiments' deemed to have been successful that have been presented. However, in some examples (most notably in Gal. 5.13–6.2 and Rom. 5.12-21)[13] an element of experiment was present in so far as a strong central panel was first identified, and then developed outwards until the situation was reached when the chiastic patterning broke down.

The two-step procedure of identifying a potential chiasmus as far as possible, in the first instance, on the principle of observable, objective criteria (usually syntactical and verbal symmetries) has, in each case, produced the basis of a reasonable hypothesis that was then subjected to the second step of a careful (if, necessarily, selective) exegesis.[14] It is at

---

10. As in the elements on the extremities of Eph. 2.11-22, and E and É in Col. 2.6-19—see 3.3.2 and 5.3.2 respectively.

11. For the reasons, see 1.4.3 d above.

12. Alluded to in 1.4.4 above.

13. See 4.1 and 6.2 above, respectively.

14. 'Selective' in the sense that the constraints of space precluded the exploration of the study of sometimes great issues that sprang from a given text, but which

this juncture that an element of subjective judgment is required in order
to determine the point at which the hypothetical pattern can be considered to have been sufficiently well established to allow exegesis to move
beyond its first function of helping to determine the pattern into its
second function of producing new insight on the basis of a well-founded
pattern.[15]

Some further comment is necessary on the characteristics of chiasmus,[16] that stem from interaction with Lund's inappropriately described
'laws governing chiastic structure'.[17] This led to some tentative suggestions of frequently, though not necessarily universally, observed
characteristics of chiasmus. In brief, these are: (a) the shift at the
centre;[18] (b) the presence of introductory or concluding frame passages;
(c) the presence of directly paralleled elements within a chiasmus; (d) the
distribution of identical ideas at the extremes and the middle of a pattern;
(e) the approximately equal length of given pairs of balancing elements;
(f) the centre providing the focus of the author's thought.

The occurrence of a *shift and reversion at the centre* has been shown
to be a pervasive feature, strikingly present in Eph. 1.3-10,[19] marked in
Gal. 5.13–6.2,[20] present but not sharply defined in Col. 2.6-19,[21] and
clear in Rom. 5.12-21.[22] Only Eph. 2.11-22 appears not to have a

were not relevant for the study of the chiasmus.

15. Many instances could be produced: e.g., in Col. 2.6-19 (see 5.3.1 above), it
may be asked if the presence of the *hapax legomena* verbs συλαγωγέω and
καταβραβεύω in 2.8 and 2.18 (with their common background involving the concept of robbery) is to be seen as confirmatory of the chiastic pattern, or whether, the
presence of the chiasmus having been adequately demonstrated already, their
common background can then be stressed on the basis of their chiastic pairing. (But
see further 7.3 below on the relationship between corresponding elements in a chiasmus.) A different kind of example is provided in 2.4.2 and 2.4.4 above in relation
to the assigning of ἐν ἀγάπῃ and ἐν πάσῃ σοφίᾳ καὶ φρονήσει to a preceding or
subsequent clause. There should, in theory, be a point at which the assignation of
these phrases could be made on the basis of an established chiasmus, rather than their
remaining subject to more 'traditional' exegesis that often cannot come to a clear
decision one way or the other.

16. As described in 1.4.2 above.

17. Lund, *Chiasmus*, pp. 40-42.

18. Already modified by the description 'shift and reversion': see 1.4.2 above.

19. See 2.4.5 above.

20. See 4.2.7 above.

21. See 5.3.2 above.

22. See 6.3.1 above.

significant instance of this feature, although it is recalled that Westcott[23] draws attention to 'the abrupt, unprepared transition from τὰ ἀμφότερα' in I' (Eph. 2.15).[24] The latter immediately gives way to the former again for the remainder of the pattern.

This having been said, however, when the five presented examples (three of which are odd, and two are even chiasms)[25] are re-examined, the nature of the shift at the centre is interesting. Thus, an unexpected change of person is introduced and immediately left behind in Eph. 1.3-10 (odd), in Gal. 5.13–6.2 (odd),[26] and less clearly so in Col. 2.6-19 (an even chiasmus where the change from second person plural to first person plural is introduced in F', and continues in E', but is then left behind). The shift may be a sudden change in language or terminology (that may include the introduction of a new concept) as in Eph. 1.3-10 (with the introduction of the reference to the historic actions of Jesus in 1.7), in Gal. 5.13–6.2 (with its eschatological overtones in 5.21b), in Col. 2.6-19 (with the baptismal metaphor in 2.12, 13) and in Rom. 5.12-21 (with ὡς standing by itself in 5.16, and the carefully crafted μὲν...δέ antithesis).

It is clear that the range of changes that can be anticipated at the centre cannot be defined. The question arises, therefore, whether the presence of such a shift and reversion in a passage has any potential for the identification of a chiasmus, to the extent that an abrupt or unexpected change in a passage (particularly if the 'new' usage immediately gives way to the 'old' again) may alert the reader to the possibility of such a pattern. The problem is that any passage (chiastic or otherwise) will show 'shifts' as points are made and arguments are progressively developed. The combination of the facts that not every chiasmus shows the same kind of shift and reversion, and some chiasms may not exhibit the feature strongly at all makes the concept of the shift and reversion at the centre of the chiasmus of no use as a diagnostic tool for establishing the presence of a chiasmus. At some level, too, the presence of a 'shift' may be expected, or even required, as a corollary of the *definition* of a

---

23. Westcott, *Ephesians*, p. 38.

24. See 3.3.4 above.

25. Chiasms may be described as 'odd' if they have an odd number of elements (i.e., a unique central element) or 'even' if they have an even number of elements overall (i.e., a pair of balanced elements at the centre).

26. Although this aspect of the shift and reversion is weakened by the fact that the first person has already been used momentarily in Gal. 5.16.

chiasmus. This is particulary the case in an odd chiasmus, where the central element might be expected to stand out by dint of its unique nature. The conclusion, therefore, has to be drawn that, while it may be legitimate to look for a shift and reversion at the centre of a chiasmus, the presence of which has already been established by other criteria, the presence (or absence) of such a shift cannot be used as a diagnostic tool in the process of identifying a chiasmus. One, perhaps, can go no further than to conclude that a strong shift and reversion may serve to draw attention to the centre of an already established chiastic pattern.

Equally problematical is the concept of the *frame passage*. In fact, of the five developed examples, only two are associated with what Lund might have called 'frame passages'—those in Eph. 1.3-10 (or 1.3-14 if 1.11-14 could be seen as a concluding frame passage) and Col. 2.6-19.[27]

Of these two, it would appear that the former is a special case if the theory of Eph. 1.3-10 being preformed material can be upheld.[28] In this instance it has been suggested that the author's own ends have been served by the conscious incorporation and development of preformed material within the larger rhetorical unit of 1.3-14, the beginning of the next rhetorical unit being adequately signalled by the presence of Διὰ τοῦτο in 1.15. In fact, whether or not 1.3-10 is deemed to be preformed, the chiasmus is embedded in a longer rhetorical unit.

In the case of Col. 2.6-19, in Lund's terminology, 2.6 forms the introductory frame passage. In this example it could be argued that the *end* of the rhetorical unit is identical with the end of the chiasmus, although the *beginning* of the rhetorical unit occurs in the verse previous to the beginning of the chiasmus. One possible function of chiasmus in relation to the text was as a structuring device.[29] It seems possible at first sight to suggest that it has such a function in this instance, since it must appear obvious that 2.6 should be read with 2.7 rather than with 2.5.

In Lund's original treatment[30] the frame passage can apparently occur either before or after a chiasmus. In principle this need raise no

---

27. Bailey, *Poet*, p. 63, actually shows the first two words of Eph. 2.11-22 Διὸ μνημονεύετε outside of his chiastic pattern also.

28. See 2.5.4 above. It is worth repeating the point that the preformation of Eph. 1.3-10 is a somewhat speculative theory that was suggested by the subsequent way in which the chiasmus was developed in Ephesians. The possible rejection of theories of preformation in no way affects the identification of the chiasmus.

29. See 1.5.1 above.

30. Lund, *Chiasmus*, p. 40.

difficulty, but it does produce a tension if the primary (or, even, one of the paramount) functions of chiasmus in the text is as a structuring device. How can the identification of a chiasmus help determine the 'structure' of a passage if it may (or may not) be preceded and/or followed by a frame passage of an indeterminate length?[31]

The use of *directly paralleled sub-elements* within the chiastic framework was illustrated in Eph. 1.3-10, Eph. 2.11-22 and possibly in Gal. 5.13–6.2.[32] In connection with *the distribution of identical ideas at the extremes and centre* of a chiasmus, none of the examples have shown this particularly clearly, although in Col. 2.6-19 the allusion to baptism in 2.6 is picked up in 2.12 at the centre of the pattern and then recurs in 2.20 as the controlling metaphor of the next rhetorical unit.[33] Thus, while these features have been identified in some of the examples, they cannot be said to be characteristic of all chiasms.

The suggestion that *corresponding elements are of approximately the same length* has been found throughout all the examples, and is, therefore, one of the more widely present features. In Rom. 5.12-21 where element D corresponds to a relatively longer D′,[34] it was suggested that D′ clearly amplifies D.[35]

The problem of extrapolating from five examples to general statements about chiasmus of intermediate length reduces the usefulness of these suggested characteristics. They would appear to have little role in the initial determination of a chiasmus, although the presence of one or more of them may, to a degree, enhance the argument for the validity of a given pattern. In the longer term, however, it can be seen that, as more examples are identified, there is an ever-increasing possibility of building up a profile of what constitutes a 'typical' chiasmus. Even then, however, room will always need to be left for the example that, for some special effect, purpose or situation, has been deliberately created to be atypical.

31. This is further discussed in 7.2.1 below.
32. See the discussion in 4.2.1 above.
33. See 5.4.2 above.
34. See 6.3.3 above.
35. The discussion of the centre as the focus of the author's thought is found in 7.3 below.

7.2. *Review of the Functions of Chiasmus*

7.2.1. *In Relation to the Text*

It has been suggested that chiasmus may function as an art form, a mnemonic device and as a structuring device.[36] The first two of these suggested functions appear to need little comment. Thus, there is a marked aesthetic effectiveness in, for example, the chiasmus in Eph. 1.3-10, which has the (non-intentional) effect of heightening the pedestrian construction of 1.11-14. All the five developed examples occur in key passages in their respective letters, and it could be reasonably conjectured that the authors felt that these were worthy of committal to memory. However, both of these functions are, to a large extent, dependent on the *author's* viewpoint. Thus, for example in Eph. 1.3-10, what the author might see as the product of careful construction, another can dismiss as a 'monstrous conglomeration'.[37]

In this context the most intriguing suggestion remains that of Parunak,[38] who sees chiasmus as a structuring device. It cannot be denied that it *does* lend structure to a passage, setting it off from what surrounds it in the instances when there is no frame passage associated with the pattern. The point, however, is whether this is to be seen as a *function* of chiasmus, or as a more or less inevitable *consequence* of its presence in a passage. It is, of course, the recipients' inability to know in advance if a frame passage is present that makes the distinction relevant.

If such a structuring function is allowed, it may operate, theoretically, in one of two ways; it may either act as a means of identifying the chiasmus as a discreet unit of material that the author wishes to introduce into the main flow of the argument, thus assuming a function akin to that of the modern use of brackets, or, alternatively, highlighting a particularly important section in his argument by lending a higher degree of structure to the material encompassed by the chiasmus than to that which surrounds it. In the five presented examples, the second would appear to be the consistently observed feature.

There may, however, be another approach to this matter, although the small number of developed examples again prevents a generalized conclusion. Of the two with associated frame passages, Eph. 1.3-14 may be

---

36. These are discussed in 1.5.1 above.
37. Norden, *Agnostos Theos*, p. 253: see 3.1 above.
38. Parunak, 'Typesetting', pp. 153-68: see further 1.5.1 c above.

left aside as the special case of the incorporation of a (preformed) chiasmus into a larger and clearly defined rhetorical unit. However, in Col. 2.6-19 the question arises as to the extent to which 2.6 can be adequately described either as an 'introduction', or as a 'frame' to what follows. It may, in fact, be more accurately characterized as a *thema* or *topos* which is then developed in a section that is chiastically patterned.[39] The appeal to the Christians' walk in Christ, based upon their reception of the apostolic tradition and associated with the oblique reference to baptism,[40] could be very well described as the theme that was to be developed. That development is then lent shape and delineated by the chiastic pattern, and, indeed, links Col. 2.6 well to the focus of Paul's thought as revealed in the central elements F and F' (2.12, 13).[41]

It seems, therefore, that the use of chiasmus as a structuring device is not as straightforward as first appeared. It may be best to conclude that, as a consequence of its identification, a chiasmus may lend a degree of structure to a passage, but, because of the possibility of the presence of an introductory or appended section, it is not possible to assume that a chiasmus will precisely correspond to a rhetorical unit.

7.2.2. *In Relation to the Argument*
The basic premise that has been adopted in this connection is that form enhances content,[42] with the corollary that a valid chiasmus will not fragment an argument.[43] There is, of course, the ever-present danger of circularity in this, since, once the premise is stated, the exegesis would be expected to be pursued in such a way as would reinforce that premise so that it becomes a self-fulfilling statement.

39. This suggestion is based on W. Schenk's approach to 1 Cor. 15.1-11 ('Textlinguistische Aspekte der Strukturanalyse, dargestellt am Beispiel von 1 Kor XV. 1-11', *NTS* 23 [1976], pp. 469-77, esp. 470-71). He finds in this passage a 'Thema' which is then developed in a chiastically ordered 'Rhema' (his terms). This should be distinguished from Jeremias's approach in which he frequently found theme A juxtaposed with theme B, and then developed in the order B, A (Jeremias, 'Chiasmus', esp. pp. 152-56). Schenk's 'Thema' is the simple statement Γνωρίζω δὲ ὑμῖν, ἀδελφοί, τὸ εὐαγγέλιον (1 Cor. 15.1a) which is then amplified by means of a (supposed) chiasmus extending from 15.1b to 15.3a.

40. See further 6.3.1 above.

41. See, too, 5.3.2.

42. See 1.5.2 above.

43. This corollary was used in the criticism of Turner's chiastic analysis of Eph. 2.11-22—see 3.2 above.

In two of the five developed examples, however, the chiasmus has ended at a point where few, if any, commentators have previously identified a division in the text. In Eph. 1.3-14 some have identified the change of standpoint after 1.10 where it is suggested that the chiasmus ends,[44] but the case for a division between Gal. 6.2 and 6.3 has not been strongly championed at all. In this instance, however, there has been very little consensus as to any structure for the *sententiae*. The position adopted in this study has been that the use of γάρ in 6.3 heralds the first comment on the whole chiasmus with its warnings related to the fiasco of community dissension, with its loveless back-biting providing opportunity for the flesh.[45] Some commentators overlook the presence of γάρ completely,[46] while others suggest that it may be explanatory of something said previously.[47] It has been argued above that, far from fragmenting Paul's argument, the suggestion of the division occasioned by the end of the chiasmus at 6.2 has given 6.3 a new force and relevance.

In defence of the premise that, in the study of chiasmus, form enhances content, two observations must be made:

a. On most occasions, corresponding elements are found to deal with the same, or clearly related, subject matter. This is particularly striking when the second occurrence is not strictly necessitated by the flow of the argument (e.g., the second introduction of νόμος in Rom. 5.12-21; the recurrence of the growth metaphor at Col. 2.17b in Col. 2.6-19; the use of the concept of the 'law of Christ' in Gal. 6.2, looking back, it is argued, to 5.14 in the chiasmus in Gal. 5.13–6.2; etc.)[48]

b. In a significant number of instances commentators, unaware of a chiastic hypothesis, are found to have linked chiastically-balanced verses in such a way that the one reinforces the other.

The significance of the second observation must not be overplayed, however. It obviously could be countered that there are as many instances when commentators *fail* to make such a linkage, and many

---

44. See 2.3 above.

45. See further 4.5.2 above.

46. E.g., Bruce, *Galatians*, in both his translation (p. 259) and his comment (pp. 261-62).

47. As Longenecker, *Galatians*, p. 276.

48. See respectively 6.3.5, 5.3.3 and 4.2.1 above.

occasions when they make links that are not accommodated within the chiastic pattern.

In conclusion, therefore, it appears that the question of the function of chiasmus must remain open. While the examples developed have highlighted a number of possibilities, it may be that chiasmus did not have a single or a simple function, but was, in general terms, a *tool of rhetorical composition*, capable of functioning as an art form, an *aide-memoire*, acting as a structuring device as a consequence of its presence, while enhancing in a clear, yet flexible way (see further the next section) the impact of the argument. Of these possibilities, the most interesting and potentially rewarding observation is the interaction of form and content, the chiastic pattern relating sequentially distant elements in a way that has clear implications for exegesis.

7.3. *Chiasmus and Exegesis*

The study of New Testament and, therefore, Pauline rhetoric has become an important field in its own right in recent years. In this area the investigation of chiasmus has its place. However, if the presence of chiasmus in the Pauline letters is going to contribute to wider Pauline studies, then the relationship between chiasmus and exegesis assumes a central importance. This relationship can be described at two levels: (a) the use of exegesis as a tool for establishing the presence of chiasmus,[49] and (b) the use of the chiastic pattern as a basis for suggesting new exegetical insight.

The range of possible relationships between corresponding chiastic elements was described[50] in terms of syntactical balancing, balancing of significant key- or catch-words, and the balancing of concepts or ideas. The experience of developing the five examples in this study has shown that syntactical balancing and the balancing of key-words are useful diagnostic tools in the *identification* of chiasmus, whereas the balancing of concepts is the most fruitful area for new exegetical insight, although it also has a part to play, on occasion, in the establishing of the presence of a chiasmus (principally in the absence of the other two methods of balance that rely on more objective, formal criteria). However, in practically every instance examined, it has been suggested that there was a conceptual balancing in some way in corresponding elements, that

49. Already described in 7.1.2 above.
50. See 1.6.1 above.

consisted of either repetition (or recapitulation), contrast or expansion, or, indeed, a combination of these.

Despite the impossibility of *predicting* the nature of the exegetical balancing in a given pair of elements, the fact that new, and hitherto unsuspected, exegetical insights may be gained makes chiasmus, properly identified, a potentially powerful exegetical implement. In a given instance, therefore, what is usually weighed is a balance of probability concerning the relationship between two elements, into which comes other factors (like the use of a given term or concept elsewhere in the letter, and other wider exegetical implications). This makes the study of chiasmus fertile ground for exegetical inquiry, and has already brought to light a number of interesting possibilities.[51] Certainly the study of chiasmus is not a panacea for all the exegete's ills, but it does lead to new questions being asked of a passage, with the ensuing possibility of new answers.

Of considerable importance, too, is the way that the chiasmus reveals the author's movement of thought as a case is built. The chiastic pattern portrays that movement in an objective fashion. Thus, what may be dismissed as tautological in an argument assumed to be constructed in a typical Western sequential fashion is revealed as a repetition or recapitulation that lends body to a chiasmus. Allusions once thought to be weak because of their sequential separation become much stronger and more vivid because of their chiastic proximity.

In all of this, however, what has come through most clearly is the function of the centre of the chiasmus, whether that consists of a unique element or a pair of elements. In every example it has been argued that the centre has described the author's primary (though not, of course, sole) focus of interest.[52] Thus, in Eph. 2.11-22 it was suggested that the author's focus of thought was in the abrogation of the rigid system of

---

51. A good example of this was furnished in Eph. 1.3-10 in the possibility of understanding the content of μυστήριον in B´ (1.9a) by reference to its chiastic partner B (1.5) with its concept of the predestining of believers to adoption through Christ—see 2.4.3 above.

52. As usual, Eph. 1.3-14 is a special case inasmuch as the focus of interest of the author of the pre-formed chiasmus was the key role of the work of Christ in effecting the redemption of some, though not all, Jews (see further 2.7 above)—a point then used by the Ephesian author to distinguish 'we' (Jewish believers) from 'you' (Gentile believers) in 1.13 (see 2.5.3 above) in the first development of the chiasmus for the ends of the Ephesian author.

commandments and ordinances, with the stress on the present unity between Jewish and Gentile believers, a point that is consistently highlighted throughout the letter.[53]

In Gal. 5.13–6.2 this understanding of the role of the centre of the chiasmus (5.21b) has highlighted in a new way the prominence of the warning-note in the passage.[54] Paul's *principal* object is to counsel against the results of doing the works of the flesh, although he also provides a series of positive injunctions alongside the warning elements. This means that other themes, like that of the fruit of the Spirit, become subsidiary to the primary focus of thought.

The central elements in Col. 2.6-19, F and F′ (Col. 2.12 and 13 respectively), on the same basis, suggest that the focus here is on the positive nature of the believer's walk with Christ and what that means in terms of identification with him rather than on a 'heresy'. While it has been widely assumed that the centre of attention in this passage was the combatting of some heretical system, the chiastic pattern suggests otherwise.[55] This approach thus helps to add weight to the arguments of those like Hooker[56] who question whether there actually were false teachers at Colossae. The warnings about the empty deceit of philosophy are not insignificant, but are illustrative of the kind of practices against which the Colossians must be on their guard in their new walk as Christians. It is the outworking of that walk that is central to Paul's purpose.

Paul's focus in Rom. 5.12-21 was suggested by the central element F (Rom. 5.16) to have been the utter dissimilarity between the δώρημα and one man's sinning, and the astonishing outcome of the grace of God, viz., righteousness after many sins.[57] Again, this implies that the Adam–Christ typology may not have been as significant to him as has sometimes been assumed, since it has been shown that the typology lay in the relationship between Adam's disobedience and Christ's obedience.

Each of these conclusions has some importance, not just for the exegesis of the passage in which the chiasmus is found, but in a wider context. Thus, in each case it was found to be possible to integrate the focus of thought suggested by the chiastic pattern into the overall exegesis of

53. See 3.4 above.
54. See 4.3 above.
55. See particularly 5.5 above.
56. Hooker, *Paul*, pp. 121-36.
57. See 6.4.3 above.

Chiasmus in the Pauline Letters

the letter, an exercise that was undertaken at the appropriate point in each of the preceding chapters.

On occasion, therefore, while the nature of the balances between individual elements may be exegetically significant, the value of chiasmus in exegesis may be restricted to a degree by the unpredictability associated with the different ways of balancing two elements.[58] However, of all these exegetical possibilities the role of the centre as the focus of the author's thought is the one that appears to be the most consistently useful, both in our understanding of the thought of the individual chiasmus, and also in terms of its integration into the wider letter.

7.4. *Chiasmus and Hymns*

In light of the fact that two of the passages explored in the previous chapters (Eph. 1.3-14 and Eph. 2.11-22)[59] have been long considered by some to contain fragments of early Christian hymns, and that there has even been the suggestion that there is hymnic material embedded within Col. 2.6-19,[60] it may be worth exploring the relationship, if any, between chiasmus and the quest for early Christian hymns in a little more detail.

It should be noted in passing that this inquiry is not concerned with the observation of the presence of chiastic traits within passages claimed as 'hymns'. These are most frequently simple chiasms of the ABBA type.[61] Barth, at least, is so sure of the presence of 'chiasmsc features'[62] that he lists it as one of seven 'more or less fool-proof' indicators of the presence of hymns or confessions. Rather, the purpose of this section is

---

58. Account must also be taken of the fact that, occasionally, a pair of elements has been found in which it has been difficult to see any balance—as in E (Col. 2.11) and E' (Col. 2.14) in Col. 2.6-19 (see 5.3.2 above). This may be a failure on my part to understand how Paul is thinking, or a conscious or accidental introduction of an asymmetry on his part.

59. See 2.2.1 and 3.1 above respectively.

60. Schille, *Hymnen*, pp. 31-37; K. Wengst, *Christologische Formeln und Lieder des Urchristentums* (Gütersloh, 1972), pp. 186ff., suggests that Col. 2.13-15 was taken from a baptismal liturgy. These suggestions have not been widely supported.

61. Sanders, 'Hymnic Elements', p. 218 n. 22 points out that, in hymns, verbs in two (often parallel) lines may be found chiastically disposed, e.g. in Ps. 109.2b-3a.

62. Barth, 'Traditions', pp. 9-10.

to ask the more fundamental question as to the possibility that the general symmetry and balancing of cola associated with chiasmus at the intermediate level has, at least on some occasions, misled scholars into an attempted 'reconstruction' of an early Christian hymn.

It is now becoming accepted that the term 'Christian hymn' as used by Schille and Deichgräber in their influential studies in the field[63] may be a misnomer to the extent that it may include material of a broader confessional or liturgical nature.[64] This has been recently and well high-lighted by Fowl[65] who makes the perceptive comment that, while there are objective formal criteria that link many of these alleged 'hymns' to each other and differentiate them from the surrounding material, there is no valid reason to call these passages 'hymns' 'in any of the senses of "hymn" used by Schille, Deichgräber and others (i.e. a formalized expression of praise from the worship of the earliest church)'. He is pre-pared to go no further than to allow that they can be called 'hymns' only to the extent that they represent 'reflection on an exalted religious figure in language that could justifiably be called poetic'.

Schille himself is also aware of the problem of identifying hymns, especially because of our lack of knowledge of when or how they might have been used, and the fact that, according to him, they have to be reconstructed from larger texts into which they have been incorpo-rated.[66] Despite this, he identifies thirty or so examples!

Just as the effort to identify hymns by counting words and/or syllables and seeking thereby to identify 'balanced' strophes[67] has not been gen-erally accepted, so also attempts to make alleged hymns follow the rules of Greek scansion[68] have not been widely adopted. The expectation of what a hymn might be is often now couched in rather vague terms,

---

63. Schille, *Hymnen*; R. Deichgräber, *Gotteshymnus und Christushymnus der frühen Christenheit* (Göttingen, 1967); Wengst, *Formeln*, prefers to call them 'Lieder'; Deichgräber, *Gotteshymnus*, pp. 11-21, has a useful account of earlier scholarship on NT hymns.

64. Cf. Barth, 'Traditions', p. 9.

65. Fowl, *Story*, p. 16.

66. Schille, *Hymnen*, p. 11.

67. As in J. Schattenmann, *Studien zum neutestamentlichen Prosahymnus* (Munich, 1965).

68. Cf. B. Eckman, 'A Quantitative Metrical Analysis of the Philippians Hymn', *NTS* 26 (1979), pp. 258-66.

perhaps a passage with 'formal and stylistic characteristics, which could reasonably be called poetic'.[69]

It is, however, the problems associated with the 'reconstruction' of an alleged hymn that lead to so much uncertainty in the field. A fundamentally important, but frequently overlooked, problem that affects the 'recovery' of every hymn in which 'interpolations' have been made is that, if the trouble has been taken to insert extra text to adapt material for the author's own ends, there is no reason to imagine that the author would not omit other portions. Once this is recognized, there is no longer any reasonable hope of reconstruction of an original form.[70] In this connection, Fowl[71] makes some other telling points:

a.   Those seeking to reconstruct hymns make a fundamental, but ultimately often unjustifiable, assumption that the passages in question are quotations from pre-existing material.

b.   Such an assumption is particularly suspect in those letters where authorship is an issue, and especially so when the argument for pre-formulation rests on uniqueness of vocabulary.

c.   In many other places in the Pauline corpus there is no hesitancy to be explicit when the author presents pre-formulated material, or recounts what another has said as in 1 Cor. 11.23, Gal. 3.10 or 1 Tim. 5.18.

d.   The criterion of redactional activity to account for stylistic abnormality presupposes knowledge of a standard for what was stylistically conventional.[72]

e.   There are no pagan Hellenistic analogies to the stylistic features, like the repetition of relative pronouns and connecting words, commonly taken to indicate the presence of an embedded hymn.[73]

---

69. Fowl, *Story*, p. 24. Fowl later identifies hymns with 'poetic accounts of the nature and/or activity of a divine figure' (*Story*, p. 45).

70. Cf. Wright, 'Poetry', p. 445.

71. Fowl, *Story*, pp. 37-40.

72. Fowl, *Story*, pp. 14 and 39 points out the long-standing influence of E. Norden's *Der antike Kunstprosa* (Leipzig, 1898) and *Agnostos Theos* (Stuttgart, 1912) in describing both Hellenistic and Jewish stylistic conventions. While these were works which were pioneering in their day, the new interest in first-century rhetoric is adding greatly to our present understanding.

73. This point is made by K. Berger, 'Hellenistische Gattungen im Neuen Testament', *ANRW*, II.25.2, pp. 1031-432, 1168.

In addition to these points, the question of the *motive* for the Pauline authors to incorporate preformed material in what often appears to be a fragmented form must be raised. Leaving aside the fact that there is usually no explicit appeal to this material as a point of contact between writer and recipient or as a mutually recognized basis for the authors' exhortation, instruction and so forth, it is often difficult to see what they hope to achieve by appealing to it at all.[74]

Pursuing these points to their conclusion falls outside the scope of this study, but perhaps enough has been done to make plausible the suggestion that, in some instances at least, the character of a passage, formerly referred to as 'hymnic' may actually be better described by reference to the *rhetorical* compositional technique of chiasmus as in the case of Eph. 1.3-14, 2.11-22 and Col. 2.6-19.[75]

Some of the stylistic features,[76] therefore, that help set apart a passage from its context on occasion may not be 'hymnic', but features of chiasmus. Thus, repetitions may point, not to a hymnic refrain, but to corresponding elements of a chiasmus; the rhythmical quality of a piece of writing may arise from the frequently found characteristic that corresponding elements of a chiasmus approximate in length to one another; the fact that a 'hymn' may show an *inclusio* could be indicative of the greater degree of symmetry found in a chiasmus. Likewise, theories of rearrangement or interpolation in a hymn may be needed to account for the shift and reversion often found at the centre of a chiasmus, or to make elements that are actually chiastically balanced 'fit' into preconceived notions of early Christian poetry.

In addition, the fact should not be overlooked that the identification of the chiasmus in the three instances referred to above has been done without recourse to any theories of textual emendation or interpolation, and gives an account of the text as it stands.

74. On the other hand, it may be the reflection of the fact of the Pauline authors' returning to, and modifying for their own ends, a pattern of words well-known to them, perhaps even without conscious motive.

75. I do not intend to imply that all so-called hymns are actually chiasms, nor that a passage cannot be both a hymn and a chiasmus. It is obvious, too, that *chiasms themselves* may be material preformed for some purpose, whether confessional, liturgical or paraenetic, etc. Chiastic structures have also been suggested for other 'hymns'—notably for Col. 1.15-20 (cf. E. Bammel, 'Versuch zu Kol 1,15-20', *ZNW* 52 [1961], pp. 88-95; Wright, 'Poetry') and, much less convincingly, for Phil. 2.6-11 (Di Marco, 'Chiasmus 4. Teil', p. 27).

76. As, e.g., those noted by Barth, 'Traditions', p. 10.

The relationship between the fields of early Christian hymnology and chiasmus as a rhetorical compositional technique may well be one worthy of future exploration. Such an investigation might perhaps best begin by re-examining those passages most commonly assumed to show 'hymnic traits'.

7.5. Further Avenues for Exploration of Chiasmus in the Pauline Letters

In addition to exploring the links, if any, between chiasmus as a compositional technique and early Christian hymnology, a number of other matters may merit further investigation. Perhaps the most pressing need is the greater confidence that would ensue from the examination of other well-founded examples of chiasmus of intermediate length from the Pauline letters with the further refinements of methodological procedures and awareness of the types of exegetical insights that such study would produce.[77] Thus, some matters have already been, of necessity, left undecided because of the relatively small sample base used, for example, the function of chiasmus in relation to the text. Additional matters not yet touched on, and beyond the scope of this present study, such as the questions of the relationship between chiasmus and style, or chiasmus and subject matter, may yet prove to be significant.

In the study of Pauline letters one of the most long-running questions remains the relationship of Ephesians and Colossians, both to each other, and to the undisputed Paulines.[78] Of particular interest in this matter is the identification of the chiasmus in Eph. 1.3-10. If this hypothesis is accepted, and if the subsequent suggestion that it may well be preformed material developed for the Ephesian author's own ends can be sustained, then it would appear to be unlikely that Eph. 1.3-10 could be dependent on Colossians. However, it is recognized that such a conclusion stems from one hypothesis (the presence of the chiasmus) built upon another (the preformation of the material), and is therefore dependent upon the validity of both. By itself, the matter of the preformed Ephesian

---

77. Preliminary indications suggest that there may be similar chiasms present in, e.g., Col. 1.15-20, Eph. 2.1-10, 4.1-16 and Philemon. Detailed exegesis would be necessary to support these, and they are suggested here without implying that they are well-founded.

78. A convenient recent survey of this question and that of authorship is found in Lincoln, *Ephesians*, pp. xlvii-lxxiii.

chiasmus does not undermine the whole of the theory of Colossian priority, but, in this connection, Eph. 1.3-14 has long been considered a significant passage. Thus, Lincoln notes that Eph. 1.3-14 has 'a large number of parallels with Colossians'.[79] It has been the position adopted in this study that Eph. 1.3-14 is a passage of key significance within Ephesians itself. It therefore seems reasonable to examine in greater detail than has been possible here the use of this chiasmus within the remainder of Ephesians, and the nature of 'overlaps' in thought and/or terminology, not just with Colossians, but with the wider Pauline corpus in an attempt to assess the extent, if any, to which the theories of inter-dependency and priority are affected.

Another obvious avenue for exploration is to ask how the present study relates to the use of chiasmus elsewhere in the New Testament, as more and more examples are suggested, particularly from the Gospels and Acts. Of particular interest would be its functions in relation to text and argument in narrative or in parables (or even, perhaps, in apocalyptic).

In connection with the scale of chiasms, it was one of the stated aims of this study to advance investigation and debate about chiasmus from its presence at the micro-level to the intermediate level presently under consideration. It has been shown that, while the same basic definition covers both, the function of chiasmus may be quite different at the two levels. Thus, in simple ABBA chiasmus, the role of the centre has no great significance, in contrast to the intermediate level. Similarly, any structuring function of chiasmus is very limited at the micro-level.

Some of the most trenchant criticism of earlier work on chiasmus was reserved for those purporting to identify chiasmus on a massive scale.[80] Thus, the question now needs to be posed as to the relationship, if any, between chiasmus at the intermediate level, and at the macro-level (if convincing examples of the latter can be found). It must be asked whether it is possible to develop a methodology that can describe such macro-chiasmus, or if the concept of chiasmus ends with chiasmus of the scale identified in this study.

A proper appreciation of chiasmus in the Pauline letters, based on an adequate methodology and discussed within defined parameters, has

---

79. Lincoln, *Ephesians*, p. lii. See, too, p. lvi for words and ideas in the eulogy purporting to come from other letters. A much more detailed analysis can be found in E.J. Goodspeed, *The Meaning of Ephesians* (Chicago, 1933), pp. 82-89.

80. See especially 1.4.1 above.

been shown to be a potentially powerful tool both for rhetorical analysis and for exegesis that can reinforce existing exegetical judgments and give new insight into passages in which it is present. At a time when more and more chiasms are being identified, it is important that the methodology continues to be further refined so that the cutting edge of the tool remains sharp, in order to prevent the excesses that led to the justifiable scepticism of earlier years in relation to chiasmus.

APPENDIX

The Chiasmus in Ephesians 1.3-10

1.3 Εὐλογητὸς ὁ θεὸς καὶ πατὴρ τοῦ κυρίου ἡμῶν Ἰησοῦ Χριστοῦ, ὁ εὐλογήσας ἡμᾶς ἐν πάσῃ εὐλογίᾳ πνευματικῇ ἐν τοῖς ἐπουρανίοις ἐν Χριστῷ,

A {
{A₁ 1.4 καθὼς ἐξελέξατο ἡμᾶς ἐν αὐτῷ πρὸ καταβολῆς κόσμου,

{A₂ εἶναι ἡμᾶς ἁγίους καὶ ἀμώμους κατενώπιον αὐτοῦ (ἐν ἀγάπῃ),

B {
{B₁ ( ) 1.5 προορίσας ἡμᾶς εἰς υἱοθεσίαν διὰ Ἰησοῦ Χριστοῦ εἰς αὐτόν,

{B₂ κατὰ τὴν εὐδοκίαν τοῦ θελήματος αὐτοῦ,

C {
{C₁ 1.6 εἰς ἔπαινον δόξης τῆς χάριτος αὐτοῦ

{C₂ ἧς ἐχαρίτωσεν ἡμᾶς ἐν τῷ ἠγαπημένῳ.

D 1.7 Ἐν ᾧ ἔχομεν τὴν ἀπολύτρωσιν διὰ τοῦ αἵματος αὐτοῦ, τὴν ἄφεσιν τῶν παραπτωμάτων,

C′ {
{C₁′ 1.7c κατὰ τὸ πλοῦτος τῆς χάριτος αὐτοῦ

{C₂′ 1.8 ἧς ἐπερίσσευσεν εἰς ἡμᾶς (ἐν πάσῃ σοφίᾳ καὶ φρονήσει)

B′ {
{B₁′ ( ) 1.9 γνωρίσας ἡμῖν τὸ μυστήριον τοῦ θελήματος αὐτοῦ,

{B₂′ κατὰ τὴν εὐδοκίαν αὐτοῦ

A′ {
{A₁′ ἣν προέθετο ἐν αὐτῷ 1.10 εἰς οἰκονομίαν τοῦ πληρώματος τῶν καιρῶν,

{A₂′ ἀνακεφαλαιώσασθαι τὰ πάντα ἐν τῷ Χριστῷ, τὰ ἐπὶ τοῖς οὐρανοῖς καὶ τὰ ἐπὶ τῆς γῆς·

The Chiasmus in Ephesians 2.11-22

A   2.11 Διὸ μνημονεύετε ὅτι ποτὲ ὑμεῖς τὰ ἔθνη ἐν σαρκί,

B   οἱ λεγόμενοι ἀκροβυστία ὑπὸ τῆς λεγομένης περιτομῆς ἐν σαρκὶ χειροποιήτου,

C   12 ὅτι ἦτε τῷ καιρῷ ἐκείνῳ χωρὶς Χριστοῦ,

D   ἀπηλλοτριωμένοι τῆς πολιτείας τοῦ Ἰσραὴλ

E   καὶ ξένοι τῶν διαθηκῶν τῆς ἐπαγγελίας,

F   ἐλπίδα μὴ ἔχοντες καὶ ἄθεοι ἐν τῷ κόσμῳ.

$\{G_1$ 13 νυνὶ δὲ ἐν Χριστῷ Ἰησοῦ ὑμεῖς οἵ ποτε ὄντες μακρὰν

G {

$\{G_2$ ἐγενήθητε ἐγγὺς ἐν τῷ αἵματι τοῦ Χριστοῦ.

$\{H_1$ 14 Αὐτὸς γάρ ἐστιν ἡ εἰρήνη ἡμῶν, ὁ ποιήσας τὰ ἀμφότερα ἓν

H {

$\{H_2$ καὶ τὸ μεσότοιχον τοῦ φραγμοῦ λύσας, τὴν ἔχθραν ἐν τῇ σαρκὶ αὐτοῦ,

I   15 τὸν νόμον τῶν ἐντολῶν ἐν δόγμασιν καταργήσας,

Ι´   ἵνα τοὺς δύο κτίσῃ ἐν αὐτῷ εἰς ἕνα καινὸν ἄνθρωπον

$\{H_1´$ ποιῶν εἰρήνην, 16 καὶ ἀποκαταλλάξῃ τοὺς ἀμφοτέρους ἐν ἑνὶ

H´ {   σώματι τῷ θεῷ διὰ τοῦ σταυροῦ,

$\{H_2´$ ἀποκτείνας τὴν ἔχθραν ἐν αὐτῷ.

$\{G_1´$ 17 καὶ ἐλθὼν εὐηγγελίσατο εἰρήνην ὑμῖν τοῖς μακρὰν

G´ {

$\{G_2´$ καὶ εἰρήνην τοῖς ἐγγύς·

F´   18 ὅτι δι᾽ αὐτοῦ ἔχομεν τὴν προσαγωγὴν οἱ ἀμφότεροι ἐν ἑνὶ πνεύματι πρὸς τὸν πατέρα.

E´   19 Ἄρα οὖν οὐκέτι ἐστὲ ξένοι καὶ πάροικοι,

D´   ἀλλὰ ἐστὲ συμπολῖται τῶν ἁγίων καὶ οἰκεῖοι τοῦ θεοῦ,

C´   20 ἐποικοδομηθέντες ἐπὶ τῷ θεμελίῳ τῶν ἀποστόλων καὶ προφητῶν, ὄντος ἀκρογωνιαίου αὐτοῦ Χριστοῦ Ἰησοῦ,

B´   21 ἐν ᾧ πᾶσα οἰκοδομὴ συναρμολογουμένη αὔξει εἰς ναὸν ἅγιον ἐν κυρίῳ,

A´   22 ἐν ᾧ καὶ ὑμεῖς συνοικοδομεῖσθε εἰς κατοικητήριον τοῦ θεοῦ ἐν πνεύματι.

The Chiasmus in Galatians 5.13–6.2

{a₁   5.13 Ὑμεῖς γὰρ ἐπ᾽ ἐλευθερίᾳ ἐκλήθητε, ἀδελφοί· μόνον μὴ τὴν
{   ἐλευθερίαν εἰς ἀφορμὴν τῇ σαρκί,
A {a₂   ἀλλὰ διὰ τῆς ἀγάπης δουλεύετε ἀλλήλοις.
{a₃   14 ὁ γὰρ πᾶς νόμος ἐν ἑνὶ λόγῳ πεπλήρωται, ἐν τῷ· ἀγαπήσεις τὸν
       πλησίον σου ὡς σεαυτόν.

B   15 εἰ δὲ ἀλλήλους δάκνετε καὶ κατεσθίετε, βλέπετε μή ὑπ᾽ ἀλλήλων
       ἀναλωθῆτε.

C   16 Λέγω δέ, πνεύματι περιπατεῖτε καὶ ἐπιθυμίαν σαρκὸς οὐ μὴ
       τελέσητε.

D   17 ἡ γὰρ σὰρξ ἐπιθυμεῖ κατὰ τοῦ πνεύματος, τὸ δὲ πνεῦμα κατὰ
       τῆς σαρκός, ταῦτα γὰρ ἀλλήλοις ἀντίκειται, ἵνα μὴ ἃ ἐαν θέλητε
       ταῦτα ποιῆτε.

E   18 εἰ δὲ πνεύματι ἄγεσθε, οὐκ ἐστὲ ὑπὸ νόμον.

F   19 φανερὰ δέ ἐστιν τὰ ἔργα τῆς σαρκός, ἅτινά ἐστιν πορνεία,
       ἀκαθαρσία, ἀσέλγεια, 20 εἰδωλολατρία, φαρμακεία, ἔχθραι, ἔρις,
       ζῆλος, θυμοί, ἐριθεῖαι, διχοστασίαι, αἱρέσεις, 21 φθόνοι, μέθαι,
       κῶμοι, καὶ τὰ ὅμοια τούτοις,

G   21b ἃ προλέγω ὑμῖν, καθὼς προεῖπον ὅτι οἱ τὰ τοιαῦτα πράσσοντες
       βασιλείαν θεοῦ οὐ κληρονομήσουσιν.

F´   22 ὁ δὲ καρπὸς τοῦ πνεύματός ἐστιν ἀγάπη χαρά εἰρήνη,
       μακροθυμία χρηστότης ἀγαθωσύνη, πίστις 23 πραΰτης ἐγκράτεια·

E´   23b κατὰ τῶν τοιούτων οὐκ ἔστιν νόμος.

D´   24 οἱ δὲ τοῦ Χριστοῦ Ἰησοῦ τὴν σάρκα ἐσταύρωσαν σὺν τοῖς
       παθήμασιν καὶ ταῖς ἐπιθυμίαις.

C´   25 Εἰ ζῶμεν πνεύματι, πνεύματι καὶ στοιχῶμεν.

B´   26 μὴ γινώμεθα κενόδοξοι, ἀλλήλους προκαλούμενοι, ἀλλήλοις
       φθονοῦντες.

{a₁´   6.1 Ἀδελφοί, ἐὰν καὶ προλημφθῇ ἄνθρωπος ἔν τινι παραπτώματι,
       ὑμεῖς οἱ πνευματικοὶ καταρτίζετε τὸν τοιοῦτον ἐν πνεύματι
A´ {   πραΰτητος, σκοπῶν σεαυτὸν μὴ καὶ σὺ πειρασθῇς.
{a₂´   2 Ἀλλήλων τὰ βάρη βαστάζετε,
{a₃´   καὶ οὕτως ἀναπληρώσετε τὸν νόμον τοῦ Χριστοῦ.

The Chiasmus in Colossians 2.6-19

2.6 Ὡσ οὖν παρελάβετε τὸν Χριστὸν Ἰησοῦν τὸν κύριον, ἐν αὐτῷ περιπατεῖτε

A 2.7 ἐρριζωμένοι καὶ ἐποικοδομούμενοι ἐν αὐτῷ καὶ βεβαιούμενοι τῇ πίστει καθὼς ἐδιδάχθητε, περισσεύοντες ἐν εὐχαριστίᾳ.

B 2.8 Βλέπετε μή τις ὑμᾶς ἔσται ὁ συλαγωγῶν διὰ τῆς φιλοσοφίας καὶ κενῆς ἀπάτης κατὰ τὴν παράδοσιν τῶν ἀνθρώπων, κατὰ τὰ στοιχεῖα τοῦ κόσμου καὶ οὐ κατὰ Χριστόν·

C 2.9 ὅτι ἐν αὐτῷ κατοικεῖ πᾶν τὸ πλήρωμα τῆς θεότητος σωματικῶς, 2.10a καὶ ἐστὲ ἐν αὐτῷ πεπληρωμένοι,

D 2.10b ὅς ἐστιν ἡ κεφαλὴ πάσης ἀρχῆς καὶ ἐξουσίας.

E 2.11 Ἐν ᾧ καὶ περιετμήθητε περιτομῇ ἀχειροποιήτῳ ἐν τῇ ἀπεκδύσει τοῦ σώματος τῆς σαρκός, ἐν τῇ περιτομῇ τοῦ Χριστοῦ,

F 2.12 συνταφέντες αὐτῷ ἐν τῷ βαπτισμῷ, ἐν ᾧ καὶ συνηγέρθητε διὰ τῆς πίστεως τῆς ἐνεργείας τοῦ θεοῦ τοῦ ἐγείραντος αὐτὸν ἐκ νεκρῶν·

F′ 2.13 καὶ ὑμᾶς νεκροὺς ὄντας [ἐν] τοῖς παραπτώμασιν καὶ τῇ ἀκροβυστίᾳ τῆς σαρκὸς ὑμῶν, συνεζωοποίησεν ὑμᾶς σὺν αὐτῷ, χαρισάμενος ἡμῖν πάντα τὰ παραπτώματα.

E′ 2.14 ἐξαλείψας τὸ καθ᾽ ἡμῶν χειρόγραφον τοῖς δόγμασιν ὃ ἦν ὑπεναντίον ἡμῖν, καὶ αὐτὸ ἦρκεν ἐκ τοῦ μέσου προσηλώσας αὐτὸ τῷ σταυρῷ·

D′ 2.15 ἀπεκδυσάμενος τὰς ἀρχὰς καὶ τὰς ἐξουσίας ἐδειγμάτισεν ἐν παρρησίᾳ, θριαμβεύσας αὐτοὺς ἐν αὐτῷ.

C′ 2.16 Μὴ οὖν τις ὑμᾶς κρινέτω ἐν βρώσει καὶ ἐν πόσει ἢ ἐν μέρει ἑορτῆς ἢ νεομηνίας ἢ σαββάτων· 2.17 ἅ ἐστιν σκιὰ τῶν μελλόντων, τὸ δὲ σῶμα τοῦ Χριστοῦ.

B′ 2.18 μηδεὶς ὑμᾶς καταβραβευέτω θέλων ἐν ταπεινοφροσύνῃ καὶ θρησκείᾳ τῶν ἀγγέλων, ἃ ἑόρακεν ἐμβατεύων, εἰκῇ φυσιούμενος ὑπὸ τοῦ νοὸς τῆς σαρκὸς αὐτοῦ, 2.19a καὶ οὐ κρατῶν τὴν κεφαλήν,

A′ 2.19b ἐξ οὗ πᾶν τὸ σῶμα διὰ τῶν ἁφῶν καὶ συνδέσμων ἐπιχορηγούμενον καὶ συμβιβαζόμενον αὔξει τὴν αὔξησιν τοῦ θεοῦ.

The Chiasmus in Romans 5.12-21

A   5.12 Διὰ τοῦτο ὥσπερ δι᾽ ἑνὸς ἀνθρώπου ἡ ἁμαρτία εἰς τὸν κόσμον εἰσῆλθεν καὶ διὰ τῆς ἁμαρτίας ὁ θάνατος, καὶ οὕτως εἰς πάντας ἀνθρώπους ὁ θάνατος διῆλθεν, ἐφ᾽ ᾧ πάντες ἥμαρτον·

B   5.13 ἄχρι γὰρ νόμου ἁμαρτία ἦν ἐν κόσμῳ, ἁμαρτία δὲ οὐκ ἐλλογεῖται μὴ ὄντος νόμου,

C   5.14 ἀλλὰ ἐβασίλευσεν ὁ θάνατος ἀπὸ Ἀδὰμ μέχρι Μωϋσέως καὶ ἐπὶ τοὺς μὴ ἁμαρτήσαντας ἐπὶ τῷ ὁμοιώματι τῆς παραβάσεως Ἀδὰμ, ὅς ἐστιν τύπος τοῦ μέλλοντος.

D   5.15a Ἀλλ᾽ οὐχ ὡς τὸ παράπτωμα, οὕτως καὶ τὸ χάρισμα·

E   5.15b εἰ γὰρ τῷ τοῦ ἑνὸς παραπτώματι οἱ πολλοὶ ἀπέθανον, πολλῷ μᾶλλον ἡ χάρις τοῦ θεοῦ καὶ ἡ δωρεὰ ἐν χάριτι τῇ τοῦ ἑνὸς ἀνθρώπου Ἰησοῦ Χριστοῦ εἰς τοὺς πολλοὺς ἐπερίσσευσεν.

F   5.16 καὶ οὐχ ὡς δι᾽ ἑνὸς ἁμαρτήσαντος τὸ δώρημα· τὸ μὲν γὰρ κρίμα ἐξ ἑνὸς εἰς κατάκριμα, τὸ δὲ χάρισμα ἐκ πολλῶν παραπτωμάτων εἰς δικαίωμα.

É   5.17 εἰ γὰρ τῷ τοῦ ἑνὸς παραπτώματι ὁ θάνατος ἐβασίλευσεν διὰ τοῦ ἑνός, πολλῷ μᾶλλον οἱ τὴν περισσείαν τῆς χάριτος καὶ τῆς δωρεᾶς τῆς δικαιοσύνης λαμβάνοντες ἐν ζωῇ βασιλεύσουσιν διὰ τοῦ ἑνὸς Ἰησοῦ Χριστοῦ.

D́   5.18 Ἄρα οὖν ὡς δι᾽ ἑνὸς παραπτώματος εἰς πάντας ἀνθρώπους εἰς κατάκριμα, οὕτως καὶ δι᾽ ἑνὸς δικαιώματος εἰς πάντας ἀνθρώπους εἰς δικαίωσιν ζωῆς·

Ć   5.19 ὥσπερ γὰρ διὰ τῆς παρακοῆς τοῦ ἑνὸς ἀνθρώπου ἁμαρτωλοὶ κατεστάθησαν οἱ πολλοί, οὕτως καὶ διὰ τῆς ὑπακοῆς τοῦ ἑνὸς δίκαιοι κατασταθήσονται οἱ πολλοί.

B́   5.20 νόμος δὲ παρεισῆλθεν ἵνα πλεονάσῃ τὸ παράπτωμα· οὗ δὲ ἐπλεόνασεν ἡ ἁμαρτία, ὑπερεπερίσσευσεν ἡ χάρις,

Á   5.21 ἵνα ὥσπερ ἐβασίλευσεν ἡ ἁμαρτία ἐν τῷ θανάτῳ, οὕτως καὶ ἡ χάρις βασιλεύσῃ διὰ δικαιοσύνης εἰς ζωὴν αἰώνιον διὰ Ἰησοῦ Χριστοῦ τοῦ κυρίου ἡμῶν.

BIBLIOGRAPHY

Abbott, T.K., *A Critical and Exegetical Commentary on the Epistles to the Ephesians and to the Colossians* (ICC; Edinburgh, 1897).

Abbott-Smith, G., *A Manual Greek Lexicon of the New Testament* (Edinburgh, 3rd edn, 1937).

Arnold, C.E., *Ephesians: Power and Magic. The Concept of Power in Ephesians in Light of its Historical Setting* (SNTSMS, 63; Cambridge, 1989).

—'The "Exorcism" of Ephesians 6.12 in Recent Research', *JSNT* 30 (1987), pp. 71-87.

Aune, D., Review of Betz, *Galatians, RSR* 7 (1981), pp. 323-28.

Bailey, K.E., *Poet and Peasant, and Through Peasant Eyes: A Literary-Cultural Approach to the Parables of Luke* (Grand Rapids, 1983).

Bammel, E., 'Versuch zu Kol 1,15-20', *ZNW* 52 (1961), pp. 88-95.

Bandstra, A.J., *The Law and the Elements of the World: An Exegetical Study in Aspects of Paul's Teaching* (Kampen, 1964).

Barclay, J.M.G., 'Mirror-reading a Polemical Letter: Galatians as a Test Case', *JSNT* 31 (1987), pp. 73-93.

—*Obeying the Truth: A Study of Paul's Ethics in Galatians* (SNTW; Edinburgh, 1988).

Barrett, C.K., 'The Allegory of Abraham, Sarah and Hagar in the Argument of Galatians', in Friedrich *et al.* (eds.), *Rechtfertigung*, pp. 1-16.

—*A Commentary on the Epistle to the Romans* (BNTC; London, 1962).

—*The First Epistle to the Corinthians* (BNTC; London, 2nd edn, 1971).

—*Freedom and Obligation: A Study of the Epistle to the Galatians* (London, 1985).

Barth, M., *The Broken Wall* (London, 1960).

—*Ephesians* (AB; 2 vols.; New York, 1974).

—Review of Bligh, *Galatians in Greek, CBQ* 30 (1968), pp. 76-79.

—'Traditions in Ephesians', *NTS* 30 (1984), pp. 3-25.

Basset, S.E., *The Poetry of Homer* (SCL, 15; Berkeley, 1938).

—Ὕστερον πρότερον Ὁμηρικῶς (HSCP, 31; Cambridge, MA, 1920).

Beasley-Murray, G.R., *Baptism in the New Testament* (London, 1962).

Bengel, J.A., *Gnomon Novi Testamenti* (Tübingen, 1742).

Berger, K., 'Hellenistische Gattungen im Neuen Testament', *ANRW*, II.25.2, pp. 1031-1432.

Best, E., *One Body in Christ* (London, 1955).

Betz, H.D., *Galatians: A Commentary on Paul's Letter to the Churches in Galatia* (Hermeneia; Philadelphia, 1979).

—'The Problem of Rhetoric and Theology according to the Apostle Paul', in Vanhoye (ed.), *Paul*, pp. 16-48.

—Review of Bligh, *Galatians in Greek, JBL* 89 (1970) pp. 126-27.

Black, C.C., 'Keeping up with Recent Studies, XVI: Rhetorical Criticism and Biblical Interpretation', *ExpTim* 100 (1989), pp. 252-58.

Black, M., *Romans* (NCB; Grand Rapids, 1973).

Bligh, J., *Galatians: A Discussion of St Paul's Epistle* (Householder Commentaries; London, 1969).

—*Galatians in Greek: A Structural Analysis of St Paul's Epistle to the Galatians* (Detroit, 1966).

Boer, M.C. de, *The Defeat of Death: Apocalyptic Eschatology in 1 Corinthians 15 and Romans 5* (JSNTSup, 22; Sheffield, 1988).

Boers, H., 'The Form Critical Study of Paul's Letters. 1 Thessalonians as a Case Study', *NTS* 22 (1976), pp. 140-58.

Boismard, M.E., *Le prologue de S. Jean* (Paris, 1953).

Bonner, S.F., *Education in Ancient Rome: From the Elder Cato to the Younger Pliny* (London, 1977).

Bornkam, G., 'The Heresy of Colossians', in Francis and Meeks (eds.), *Conflict*, pp. 123-46.

Borse, U., *Der Brief an die Galater* (RNT; Regensburg, 1984).

Boys, T., *Key to the Book of Psalms* (London, 1825).

—*Tactica Sacra* (London, 1824).

Breck, J., 'Biblical Chiasmus: Exploring Structure for Meaning', *BTB* 17 (1986), pp. 70-74.

Brinsmead, B.H., *Galatians: Dialogical Response to Opponents* (SBLDS, 65; Chico, CA, 1982).

Bruce, F.F., *The Epistles to the Colossians to Philemon and to the Ephesians* (NICNT; Grand Rapids, 1984).

—*The Epistle to the Galatians: A Commentary on the Greek Text* (NIGTC; Grand Rapids, 1982).

—*The Epistle of Paul to the Romans* (TNTC; London, 1963).

Bultmann, R., *Der Stil der paulinischen Predigt und die kynisch-stoische Diatribe* (Göttingen, 1910).

Burton, E. De W., *A Critical and Exegetical Commentary on the Epistle to the Galatians* (ICC; Edinburgh, 1920).

Caird, G.B., *Paul's Letters from Prison* (Oxford, 1976).

Cambier, J., 'La bénédiction d'Eph 1.3-14', *ZNW* 54 (1963), pp. 58-104.

Caragounis, C.C., *The Ephesian Mysterion* (Lund, 1977).

—'Romans 5.15-16 in the Context of 5.12-21: Contrast or Comparison?', *NTS* 31 (1985), pp. 142-48.

Carr, W., *Angels and Principalities* (Cambridge, 1981).

Clark, D.J., 'Criteria for Identifying Chiasm', *LB* 35 (1974), pp. 63-72

Collins, J.J., 'Chiasmus, the "ABA" Pattern and the Text of Paul', in *Studiorum Paulinorum Congressus Internationalis Catholicus 1961* (Rome, 1963), II, pp. 575-83.

Cosby, M.R., 'Paul's Persuasive Language in Romans 5', in Watson (ed.), *Persuasive Artistry*, pp. 209-26

Cranfield, C.E.B., *A Critical and Exegetical Commentary on the Epistle to the Romans* (ICC; 2 vols.; Edinburgh, 1975).

Dahl, N.A., 'Anamnesis: Mémoire et commémoration dans le christianisme primitif', *ST* 1 (1947), pp. 69-95.

Dahl, N.A. (assisted by P. Donahue), *Missionary Theology in Romans* (Minneapolis, 1977).

Deichgräber, R., *Gotteshymnus und Christushymnus der frühen Christenheit* (Göttingen, 1967).

Dewey, J., 'The Literary Structure of the Controversy Stories in Mark 2.1–3.6', *JBL* 92 (1973), pp. 394-401.

Dibelius, M., *An die Kolosser, Epheser an Philemon* (HNT, 12; Tübingen, 3rd rev. edn, 1953).

—'The Isis Initiation in Apuleius and Related Initiatory Rites', in Francis and Meeks (eds.), *Conflict*, pp. 61-122.

—'Vier Worte des Römerbriefs, 5,5; 5,12; 8,10; 11,30s', *SymBU* 3 (1944), pp. 3-17.

Di Marco, A., 'Der Chiasmus in der Bibel 1. Teil', *LB* 36 (1975), pp. 21-97.

—'Der Chiasmus in der Bibel 4.Teil', *LB* 44 (1979), pp. 3-70.

Duff, P.B., 'Metaphor, Motif and Meaning: The Rhetorical Strategy behind the Image "Led in Triumph" in 2 Corinthians 2:14', *CBQ* 53 (1991), pp. 79-92.

Duncan, G.S., *The Epistle of Paul to the Galatians* (London, 1934).

Dunn, J.D.G., *Romans* (WBC, 38A, 38B; Dallas, 1988).

Ebeling, G., *The Truth of the Gospel: An Exposition of Galatians* (trans. D. Green; Philadelphia, 1985).

Eckman, B., 'A Quantitative Metrical Analysis of the Philippians Hymn', *NTS* 26 (1980), pp. 258-66.

Ellicott, C.J., *Ephesians* (London, 1855).

Elliott, N., *The Rhetoric of Romans: Argumentative Constraint and Strategy and Paul's Dialogue with Judaism* (JSNTSup, 45; Sheffield, 1990).

Exum, C., and C.H. Talbert, 'The Structure of Paul's Speech to the Ephesian Elders (Acts 20,18-35)', *CBQ* 29 (1967), pp. 233-36.

Fischer, K.M., *Tendenz und Absicht des Epheserbriefes* (Gottingen, 1973).

Forbes, J., *Analytical Commentary on the Epistle to the Romans* (Edinburgh, 1868).

Fowl, S.E., *The Story of Christ in the Ethics of Paul: An Analysis of the Function of the Hymnic Material in the Pauline Corpus* (JSNTSup, 36; Sheffield, 1990).

Francis, F.O., 'The Background of EMBATEYEIN (Col.2.18) in Legal Papyri and Oracle Inscriptions', in Francis and Meeks (eds.), *Conflict*, pp. 197-207.

—'Humility and Angelic Worship in Col. 2.18', in Francis and Meeks (eds.), *Conflict*, pp. 163-95.

Francis, F.O., and W.A. Meeks (eds.), *Conflict at Colossae* (Missoula, MT, 1975).

Friedrich, J., *et al.* (eds.), *Rechtfertigung: Festschrift für E. Käsemann zum 70. Geburtstag* (Tübingen, 1976).

Furnish, V.P., *II Corinthians* (AB, 32A; New York, 1984).

—*Theology and Ethics in Paul* (Nashville, 1968).

Galbiati, E., *La struttura letteraria dell' Esodo* (Rome, 1956).

Giavini, G., 'La struttura letteraria dell'inno cristologico di Col.1', *RivB* 15 (1967), pp. 317-20.

—'La structure littéraire d'Eph. 2.11-22', *NTS* 16 (1970), pp. 209-11.

Gnilka, J., *Der Epheserbrief* (HTKNT; Freiburg, 1971).

Goodspeed, E.J., *The Meaning of Ephesians* (Chicago, 1933).

Grelot, P., 'La structure d'Ephésiens 1,3-14', *RB* 96 (1989), pp. 193-209.

Gunther, J.J., *St Paul's Opponents and their Background: A Study of Apocalyptic and Jewish Sectarian Teachings* (NovTSup, 35; Leiden, 1973).

Guthrie, D., *Galatians* (The Century Bible NS; London, rev. edn, 1974).

Hagner, D.A., and M.J. Harris (eds.), *Pauline Studies: Essays Presented to Professor F.F. Bruce on his 70th Birthday* (Exeter, 1980).

Hansen, G.W., *Abraham in Galatians: Epistolary and Rhetorical Contexts* (JSNTSup, 29; Sheffield, 1989).

Haupt, E., *Der Brief an die Epheser* (Göttingen, 1902).

Hays, R.B., 'Christology and Ethics in Galatians: The Law of Christ', *CBQ* 49 (1987), pp. 268-90.

—*The Faith of Jesus Christ: An Investigation of the Narrative Substructure of Galatians 3:1–4:11* (SBLDS, 56; Chico, CA, 1983).

Hengel, M., *Judaism and Hellenism* (trans. J. Bowden; 2 vols.; Philadelphia, 1974).

—*The Pre-Christian Paul* (London, 1991).

Hooker, M.D., *From Adam to Christ: Essays on Paul* (Cambridge, 1990).

Houlden, J.L., *Paul's Letters from Prison* (Harmondsworth, 1970).

Innitzer, T., 'Der "Hymnus" im Epheserbrief 1.3-14', *ZKT* 28 (1904), pp. 612-21.

Jebb, J., *Sacred Literature* (London, 1820).

Jeremias, J., 'Chiasmus in den Paulusbriefen', *ZNW* 49 (1958), pp. 145-56.

Käsemann, E., *Commentary on Romans* (trans. G.W. Bromiley; Grand Rapids, 1980).

Keck, L.E., *Paul and his Letters* (Proclamation Commentaries; Philadelphia, 2nd edn, 1988).

Kennedy, G.A., *New Testament Interpretation through Rhetorical Criticism* (Chapel Hill, NC, 1984).

Kirby, J.C., *Ephesians, Baptism and Pentecost* (London, 1968).

Kïrby, J.T., 'The Syntax of Romans 5.12: A Rhetorical Approach', *NTS* 33 (1987), pp. 283-86.

Kuck, D.W., 'Each Will Bear his Own Burden: Paul's Creative Use of an Apocalyptic Motif', *NTS* 40 (1994), pp. 289-97.

Kuhn, K.G., 'Der Epheserbrief im Lichte der Qumrantexte', *NTS* 7 (1960), pp. 334-46.

Lagrange, M.J., *Saint Paul, épitre aux Galates* (EBib; Paris, 1950).

Lausberg, H., *Elemente der literarischen Rhetorik* (Munich, 1963).

—*Handbuch der literarischen Rhetorik* (2 vols.; Munich, 1960).

Lightfoot, J.B., 'The Colossian Heresy', in Francis and Meeks (eds.), *Conflict*, pp. 13-59.

—*St Paul's Epistle to the Galatians* (London, 2nd edn, 1866).

Lincoln, A.T., *Ephesians* (WBC, 42; Dallas, 1990).

Lohmeyer, E., 'Das Proömium des Epheserbriefs', *TBl* (1926), pp. 120-25.

Lohse, E., *Colossians and Philemon* (trans. W.R. Poehlmann and R.J. Karris; Philadelphia, 1971).

Longenecker, R.N., *Galatians* (WBC, 41; Waco, TX, 1990).

Lowth, R., *De sacra poesi Hebraeorum praelectiones academicae* (Oxford, 1821).

Lund, N.W., *Chiasmus in the New Testament: A Study in Formgeschichte* (Chapel Hill, NC, 1942).

—'Chiasmus in the Psalms', *AJSL 49* (1933), pp. 281-312.

—'The Presence of Chiasmus in the New Testament', *JR* 10 (1930), pp. 74-93.

—'The Presence of Chiasmus in the Old Testament', *AJSL* 46 (1930), pp. 104-26.

Maillot, A., *L'épitre aux Romains* (Paris, 1984).

Man, R.E., 'The Value of Chiasm for New Testament Interpretation', *BSac* 141 (1984), pp. 146-57.

Manson, T.W., Review of Lund, *Chiasmus, JTS* 45 (1944), pp. 81-84.

Marcus, J., *The Mystery of the Kingdom* (SBLDS, 90; Atlanta, 1986).

Marrou, H.I., *A History of Education in Antiquity* (London, 1956).

Martin, R.P., *Carmen Christi: Philippians 2:5-11 in Recent Interpretation and in the Setting of Early Christian Worship* (SNTSMS, 4; Cambridge, 1967).

—*Colossians: The Church's Lord and the Christian's Liberty* (Exeter, 1972).

—*Colossians and Philemon* (NCB; London, 1974).

—*2 Corinthians* (WBC, 40; Waco, TX, 1986).

Masson, C., *L'épître de Paul aux Ephésiens* (Neuchâtel, 1953).

Maurer, C., 'Der Hymnus von Epheser 1 als Schlüssel zum ganzen Briefe', *EvT* 11 (1951–52), pp. 151-72.

Meeks, W.A., Review of Betz, *Galatians, JBL* 100 (1981), pp. 304-306.

—*The First Urban Christians: The Social World of the Apostle Paul* (New Haven, 1983).

—'The Image of the Androgyne: Some Uses of a Symbol in Earliest Christianity', *HR* 13 (1974), pp. 165-208.

Metzger, B.M., *A Textual Commentary on the Greek New Testament* (London, 1975).

Michel, O., *Der Brief an die Römer* (KEK; Göttingen, 14th edn, 1978).

Miesner, D.R., 'Chiasm and the Composition and Message of Paul's Missionary Sermons' (unpublished ThD Thesis, Concordia Seminary in Exile [Seminex] in Cooperation with Lutheran School of Theology at Chicago, 1974).

Mitton, C.L., *Ephesians* (NCB; London, 1981).

Morgan, R., with J. Barton, *Biblical Interpretation* (Oxford, 1988).

Moule, C.F.D., *The Epistles of Paul the Apostle to the Colossians and to Philemon* (Cambridge, 1968).

—'"Fulness" and "Fill" in the New Testament', *SJT* 4 (1951), pp. 79-86.

Moulton, J.H., *A Grammar of New Testament Greek*. I. *Prolegomena* (Edinburgh, 3rd edn, 1908).

Mussner, F., *Der Brief an die Epheser* (ÖTKNT, 10; Gütersloh, 1982).

—*Der Galaterbrief* (HTKNT, 9; Freiburg, 1974).

Myers, C.D., 'Chiastic Inversion in the Argument of Romans 3–8', *NovT*, 35 (1993), pp. 30-47.

Myres, J.L., *Herodotus, Father of History* (Oxford, 1953).

Neill, S., and N.T. Wright, *The Interpretation of the New Testament: 1861–1986* (Oxford, 2nd edn, 1988).

Norden, E., *Agnostos Theos: Untersuchung zur Formengeschichte religiöser Rede* (Stuttgart, 4th edn, 1956).

—*Der antike Kunstprosa* (Leipzig, 1898).

Norrman, R., *Samuel Butler and the Meaning of Chiasmus* (London, 1986).

Norwood, G., *Pindar* (SCL, 19; Berkeley, 1945).

O'Brien, P.T., *Colossians, Philemon* (WBC, 44; Waco, TX, 1982).

—'Ephesians 1; An Unusual Introduction to a New Testament Letter', *NTS* 25 (1979), pp. 504-16.

O'Neill, J.C., *The Recovery of Paul's Letter to the Galatians* (London, 1972).

Odeberg, H., *The View of the Universe in the Epistle to the Ephesians* (Lund, 1934).

Oepke, A., *Der Brief des Paulus an die Galater* (THKNT, 9; Berlin, 5th edn, 1984).

Overfield, P.D., 'Pleroma: A Study in Content and Context', *NTS* 25 (1978–79), pp. 384-96.

Parunak, H. van D., 'Oral Typesetting: Some Uses of Biblical Structure', *Bib* 62 (1981), pp. 153-68.

—'Transitional Techniques in the Bible', *JBL* 102 (1983), pp. 525-48.

Percy, E., *Die Probleme der Kolosser- und Epheserbriefe* (Lund, 1946).

Perelman, C., and L. Olbrechts-Tyteca, *The New Rhetoric: A Treatise on Argumentation* (trans. J. Wilkinson and P. Weaver; Notre Dame, 1969).

Pogoloff, S.M., 'Isocrates and Hermeneutics', in Watson (ed.), *Persuasive Artistry*, pp. 338-362.

Radday, Y.T., 'Chiasmus in the Old Testament', in Welch (ed), *Chiasmus*, pp. 50-117.

Robbins, V.K., *Jesus the Teacher* (Philadelphia, 1984).

—'Writing as a Rhetorical Act in Plutarch and the Gospels', in Watson (ed.), *Persuasive Artistry*, pp. 142-68.

Robinson, J.A., *St Paul's Epistle to the Ephesians* (London, 2nd edn, 1909).

Robinson, J.A.T., *The Body* (London, 1952).

Robinson, T.H., *The Gospel of Matthew* (MNTC; London, 1928).

Roetzel, C.J., 'Jewish Christian–Gentile Christian Relations: A Discussion of Eph. 2.15a', *ZNW* 74 (1983), pp. 81-89.

Roon, A. van, *The Authenticity of Ephesians* (Leiden, 1974).

Sanday, W., and A.C. Headlam, *A Critical and Exegetical Commentary on the Epistle to the Romans* (ICC; Edinburgh, 5th edn, 1902).

Sanders, E.P., *Paul, the Law and the Jewish People* (Philadelphia, 1983).

Sanders, J., 'Hymnic Elements in Ephesians 1–3', *ZNW* 56 (1965), pp. 214-32.

Sappington, T.J., *Revelation and Redemption at Colossae* (JSNTSup, 53; Sheffield, 1991).

Schattenmann, J., *Studien zum neutestamentlichen Prosahymnus* (Munich, 1965).

Schenk, W., 'Textlinguistische Aspekte der Strukturanalyse, dargestellt am Beispiel von 1Kor XV.1-11', *NTS* 23 (1976), pp. 469-77.

Schille, G., *Frühchristliche Hymnen* (Berlin, 1962).

Schlier, H., *Der Brief an die Epheser: Ein Kommentar* (Düsseldorf, 7th edn, 1971).

—*Der Brief an die Galater* (KEK, 7; Göttingen, 14th edn, 1971).

—*Christus und die Kirche im Epheserbrief* (BHT, 6; Tübingen, 1930).

Schmithals, W., 'The Heretics in Galatia', in *Paul and the Gnostics* (trans. J.E. Steely, Nashville, 1972), pp. 13-64.

Schnackenburg, R., *Der Brief an die Epheser* (EKKNT; Neukirchen-Vluyn, 1982).

Schweizer, E., *The Letter to the Colossians* (trans. A. Chester; London, 1982).

Scroggs, R., *The Last Adam: A Study in Pauline Anthropology* (Oxford, 1966).

—'The Sociological Interpretation of the New Testament. The Present State of Research', *NTS* 26 (1980), pp. 164-79.

Smith, G.A., *The Early Poetry of Israel* (London, 1912).

Snyman, A.H., 'On Studying the Figures (*schēmata*) in the New Testament', *Bib* 69 (1988), pp. 93-107.

—'Style and Meaning in Romans 8:31-39', *Neot* 18 (1984), pp. 94-103.

Spencer, A.B., *Paul's Literary Style: A Stylistic and Historical Comparison of IICorinthians 11.16–12.13; Romans 8.9-39 and Philippians 3.2–4.13* (Jackson, MS, 1984).

Standaert, B., 'La rhétorique ancienne dans saint Paul', in Vanhoye (ed.), *Paul*, pp. 78-92

Stock, A., 'Chiastic Awareness and Education in Antiquity', *BTB* 14 (1984), pp. 23-27.

Stott, J.R.W., *The Message of Ephesians: God's New Society* (BST; Leicester, 1979).

Strelan, J.G., 'Burden-Bearing and the Law of Christ : A Re-examination of Galatians 6:2', *JBL* 94 (1975), pp. 266-76.

Swee-Hwa Quek, 'Adam and Christ according to Paul', in Hagner and Harris (eds.), *Pauline Studies*, pp. 67-79.

Talbert, C.H., 'Artistry and Theology: An Analysis of the Architecture of Jn 1,19– 5,47', *CBQ* 32 (1970), pp. 341-66.

Taylor, V., *The Gospel according to Saint Mark* (London, 2nd edn, 1966).

Theissen, G., *The Social Setting of Pauline Christianity* (Edinburgh, 1982).

Thompson, M., *Clothed with Christ: The Example and Teaching of Jesus in Rom.12.1– 15.13* (JSNTSup, 59; Sheffield, 1991).

Thomson, I.H., 'Chiasmus in the Pauline Corpus' (unpublished PhD Thesis, Glasgow University, 1992).

Trench, R.C., 'The New Testament Synonyms' (Cambridge, 1863).

Tuckett, C., *Reading the New Testament: Methods of Interpretation* (London, 1987).

Turner, N., *Style*. Vol. 4, in J.H. Moulton, *A Grammar of New Testament Greek* (Edinburgh, 1976).

Vanhoye, A. (ed.), *L'apotre Paul: Personnalité, style et conception du ministère* (Leuven, 1986).

—*La structure littéraire de l'épitre aux Hébreux* (Paris, 1963).

Ward, M., Review of Bligh, *Galatians: Structure*, *ExpTim* 79 (1967), p. 15.

Watson, D.F., 'The New Testament and Greco-Roman Rhetoric: A Bibliography', *JETS* 31 (1988), pp. 465-72.

Watson, D.F. (ed.), *Persuasive Artistry: Studies in New Testament Rhetoric in Honor of George A. Kennedy* (JSNTSup, 50; Sheffield, 1991).

Watson, W.G.E., 'Chiasmus in Biblical Hebrew Poetry', in Welch (ed.), *Chiasmus*, pp. 118-68.

Wedderburn, A.J.M., *The Reasons for Romans* (Edinburgh, 1988).

Wegenast, K., *Das Verständnis der Tradition bei Paulus und in den Deuteropaulinen* (WMANT, 8; Neukirchen–Vluyn, 1962).

Weidinger, K., *Die Haustafeln* (Leipzig, 1928).

Weiss, J., *Beiträge zur paulinischen Rhetorik* (Göttingen, 1897).

—*Das Urchristentum* (Göttingen, 1917).

Welch, J.W. (ed.), *Chiasmus in Antiquity: Structures, Analyses, Exegesis* (Hildesheim, 1981).

Wengst, K., *Christologische Formeln und Lieder des Urchristentums* (Gütersloh, 1972).

Westcott, B.F., *St Paul's Epistle to the Ephesians* (London, 1906).

Whitman, C.H., *Homer and the Heroic Tradition* (Cambridge, MA, 1953).

Wilckens, U., *Der Brief an die Römer* (EKKNT; 2 vols.; Neukirchen–Vluyn, 1978).

Wright, N.T., *Colossians and Philemon* (TNTC; Leicester, 1986).

—'Poetry and Theology in Colossians 1.15-20', *NTS* 36 (1990), pp. 444-68.

Yates, R., 'Colossians 2.15: Christ Triumphant', *NTS* 37 (1991), pp. 573-91.

Zahn, D.T., *Der Brief des Paulus an die Römer* (Leipzig, 1910).

Zeller, D., *Der Brief an die Römer* (RNT; Regensburg, 1985).

Ziesler, J., *Paul's Letter to the Romans* (TPINTC; London, 1989).

INDEXES

INDEX OF BIBLICAL REFERENCES

OLD TESTAMENT

NEW TESTAMENT

JOURNAL FOR THE STUDY OF THE NEW TESTAMENT

Supplement Series